Lecture Notes in Computer Science 13272

More information about this series at https://link.springer.com/bookseries/558

David Eyers · Spyros Voulgaris (Eds.)

Distributed Applications and Interoperable Systems

22nd IFIP WG 6.1 International Conference, DAIS 2022
Held as Part of the 17th International Federated Conference
on Distributed Computing Techniques, DisCoTec 2022
Lucca, Italy, June 13–17, 2022
Proceedings

Springer

Editors
David Eyers ⓘ
University of Otago
Dunedin, New Zealand

Spyros Voulgaris ⓘ
Athens University of Economics
and Business
Athens, Greece

ISSN 0302-9743　　　　　ISSN 1611-3349 (electronic)
Lecture Notes in Computer Science
ISBN 978-3-031-16091-2　　ISBN 978-3-031-16092-9 (eBook)
https://doi.org/10.1007/978-3-031-16092-9

This Springer imprint is published by the registered company Springer Nature Switzerland AG
The registered company address is: Gewerbestrasse 11, 6330 Cham, Switzerland

Foreword

The 17th International Federated Conference on Distributed Computing Techniques (DisCoTec 2022) took place during June 13–17, 2022. It was organized by the IMT School for Advanced Studies Lucca, Italy. The DisCoTec series is one of the major events sponsored by the International Federation for Information Processing (IFIP) and the European Association for Programming Languages and Systems (EAPLS). This year's event comprised three conferences:

- COORDINATION, the IFIP WG 6.1 24th International Conference on Coordination Models and Languages;
- DAIS, the IFIP WG 6.1 22nd International Conference on Distributed Applications and Interoperable Systems; and
- FORTE, the IFIP WG 6.1 42nd International Conference on Formal Techniques for Distributed Objects, Components, and Systems.

Together, these conferences covered a broad spectrum of distributed computing subjects, ranging from theoretical foundations and formal description techniques to systems research issues. As is customary, the event also included several plenary sessions in addition to the individual sessions of each conference, which gathered attendants from the three conferences. These included joint invited speaker sessions and a joint session for the best papers from the respective three conferences.

Associated with the federated event, four workshops took place:

- DisCoTec Tools, a tutorial session promoting mature tools in the field of distributed computing;
- BlockTEE 2022, the First International Workshop on Blockchain Technologies and Trusted Execution Environments;
- CoMinDs 2022, the First International Workshop on Collaborative Mining for Distributed Systems;
- FOCODILE 2022, the 3rd International Workshop on the Foundations of Consensus and Distributed Ledgers; and
- ICE 2022, the 15th International Workshop on Interaction and Concurrency Experience.

Finally, in the context of the federated event, five tutorials were offered:

- An introduction to Spatial Logics and Spatial Model Checking;
- A Gentle Adventure Mechanising Message Passing Concurrency Systems;
- Smart contracts in Bitcoin and BitML;
- The ΔQ Systems Development Paradigm; and
- ChorChain: a Model-driven Approach for Trusted Execution of Multi-party Business Processes on Blockchain.

I would like to thank the Program Committee chairs of the different events for their help and cooperation during the preparation of the conference, and the Steering Committee and Advisory Boards of DisCoTec and its conferences for their guidance and support. The organization of DisCoTec 2022 was only possible thanks to the dedicated work of the Organizing Committee, including Letterio Galletta (chair of the local organizing committee), Marinella Petrocchi and Simone Soderi (members of the local organizing committee), Francesco Tiezzi (workshops and tutorials chair), Giorgio Audrito (publicity chair), and all the students and colleagues who volunteered their time to help. I would also like to thank the invited speakers for their excellent talks. Finally, I would like to thank IFIP WG 6.1 and EAPLS for sponsoring this event, Springer's Lecture Notes in Computer Science team for their support and sponsorship, EasyChair for providing the reviewing framework, and the IMT School for Advanced Studies Lucca for providing the support and infrastructure to host the event.

June 2022   Rocco De Nicola

Preface

This volume contains the papers presented at the 22nd IFIP International Conference on Distributed Applications and Interoperable Systems (DAIS 2022), sponsored by the International Federation for Information Processing (IFIP) and organized by IFIP WG 6.1. The DAIS conference series addresses all practical and conceptual aspects of distributed applications, including their design, modeling, implementation, and operation; the supporting middleware; appropriate software engineering methodologies and tools; and experimental studies and applications. DAIS 2022 was held during June 13–17, 2022, in Lucca, Italy, as part of DisCoTec 2022, the 17th International Federated Conference on Distributed Computing Techniques.

We offered three distinct paper tracks: full research papers, full practical experience reports, and work-in-progress papers. We received 19 initial abstract submissions, 16 of which were for research papers, one for a practical experience report, and two for work-in-progress papers. All submissions were reviewed by three to four Program Committee (PC) members. The review process included a post-review discussion phase, during which the merits of all papers were discussed by the PC. The committee decided to accept nine full research papers, one full practical experience report, two work-in-progress papers, and an invited paper.

The accepted papers cover a broad range of topics in distributed algorithms, scalability and availability, stream processing, privacy, distributed ledgers, and trusted hardware.

The conference was made possible by the hard work and cooperation of many people working in several different committees and organizations, all of which are listed in these proceedings. In particular, we are grateful to the PC members for their commitment and thorough reviews, and for their active participation in the discussion phase, and to all the external reviewers for their help in evaluating submissions. Finally, we also thank the DisCoTec general chair, Rocco De Nicola, and the DAIS Steering Committee chair, Luís Veiga, for their constant availability, support, and guidance.

June 2022

David Eyers
Spyros Voulgaris

Organization

General Chair

Rocco De Nicola   IMT School for Advanced Studies Lucca, Italy

Program Committee Chairs

David Eyers   University of Otago, New Zealand
Spyros Voulgaris   Athens University of Economics and Business, Greece

Steering Committee

Lydia Y. Chen   TU Delft, The Netherlands
Frank Eliassen   University of Oslo, Norway
Rüdiger Kapitza   Technical University of Braunschweig, Germany
Rui Oliveira   University of Minho and INESC TEC, Portugal
Hans P. Reiser   University of Passau, Germany
Laura Ricci   University of Pisa, Italy
Silvia Bonomi   Università degli Studi di Roma "La Sapienza", Italy
Etienne Riviére   Ecole Polytechnique de Louvain, Belgium
Jose Pereira   University of Minho and INESC TEC, Portugal
Luís Veiga (Chair)   INESC-ID and Universidade de Lisboa, Portugal

Program Committee

Eduardo Alchieri   Universidade de Brasília, Brazil
Pierre-Louis Aublin   Keio University, Japan
Silvia Bonomi   Università degli Studi di Roma "La Sapienza", Italy
Davide Frey   Inria, France
Vana Kalogeraki   Athens University of Economics and Business, Greece
Evangelia Kalyvianaki   University of Cambridge, UK
Fábio Kon   University of São Paulo, Brazil
João Leitão   Universidade Nova de Lisboa, Portugal
Daniel Lucani   Aarhus University, Denmark
Kostas Magoutis   University of Ioannina, Greece

Hein Meling	University of Stavanger, Norway
Claudio Antares Mezzina	University Urbino, Italy
Alberto Montresor	University of Trento, Italy
Daniel O'Keeffe	Royal Holloway, University of London, England
Emanuel Onica	Alexandru Ioan Cuza University of Iasi, Romania
Marta Patino	Universidad Politecnica de Madrid, Spain
José Orlando Pereira	Universidade do Minho and INESC TEC, Portugal
Hans P. Reiser	Reykjavík University, Iceland
Romain Rouvoy	University of Lille 1, France
Valerio Schiavoni	University of Neuchâtel, Switzerland
Pierre Sutra	Telecom SudParis, France

Local Organization

Rocco De Nicola
Letterio Galletta
Marinella Petrocchi
Simone Soderi
Francesco Tiezzi
Giorgio Audrito

Additional Reviewers

Christian Berger	University of Passau, Germany
Emile Cadorel	Inria, France
Johannes Köstler	University of Passau, Germany
Adrien Luxey	Inria, France
Antonis Papaioannou	FORTH, Greece
Olivier Ruas	Inria, France

Contents

Blockchains and Cryptocurrencies

An Evaluation of Blockchain Application Requirements and Their Satisfaction in Hyperledger Fabric

A Practical Experience Report

Sadok Ben Toumia[1]([✉]), Christian Berger[1], and Hans P. Reiser[2]

[1] University of Passau, Passau, Germany
bentou01@ads.uni-passau.de, cb@sec.uni-passau.de
[2] Reykjavík University, Reykjavík, Iceland
hansr@ru.is

Abstract. Blockchain applications may offer better fault-tolerance, integrity, traceability and transparency compared to centralized solutions. Despite these benefits, few businesses switch to blockchain-based applications. Industries worry that the current blockchain implementations do not meet their requirements, e.g., when it comes to scalability, throughput or latency. Hyperledger Fabric (HLF) is a permissioned blockchain infrastructure that aims to meet enterprise needs and provides a highly modular and well-conceived architecture. In this paper, we survey and analyse requirements of blockchain applications in respect to their underlying infrastructure by focusing mainly on performance and resilience characteristics. Subsequently, we discuss to what extent Fabric's current design allows it to meet these requirements. We further evaluate the performance of Hyperledger Fabric 2.2 simulating different use case scenarios by comparing single with multi-ordering service performance and conducting an evaluation with mixed workloads.

Keywords: Hyperledger Fabric · Distributed Ledger Technology · Application Requirements · Blockchain · Performance · Scalability · Benchmarking

1 Introduction

Since the invention of Bitcoin [24], many people are speculating about how blockchain can revolutionize our daily lives. Several sectors can profit from blockchain, whereas for many other areas it is considered an overkill [35]. Today, a number of industries still struggle with basic concerns like traceability, integrity protection, or privacy [8,16,17]. Competition is higher than ever, which makes certain parties secretive about their transactions. Such issues are often not being sufficiently handled by traditional applications.

© IFIP International Federation for Information Processing 2022
Published by Springer Nature Switzerland AG 2022
D. Eyers and S. Voulgaris (Eds.): DAIS 2022, LNCS 13272, pp. 3–20, 2022.
https://doi.org/10.1007/978-3-031-16092-9_1

This raises the demand of a platform that can handle these issues while meeting their standards in respect to resilience and performance [8,16]. Enterprises often need a permissioned blockchain that restricts participation to a consortium of members. Due to competitors being also on the blockchain network, these parties need privacy: not everyone should be able to see all their transactions – instead transactions must be on a need-to-know basis [7].

Hyperledger Fabric (HLF) [1] is an open-source, permissioned blockchain platform that intends to satisfy enterprise application requirements. It presents a modular architecture with pluggable consensus and can achieve high throughput. Previous studies have highlighted the issue of missing support for Byzantine fault tolerance (BFT) [31]. Starting from version 2.0, HLF switched from a Kafka-based ordering service to a Raft [25]-based ordering service. While Raft (like Kafka) does not assume BFT, it could be transformed to do so in future, and could essentially be a step towards implementing BFT in HLF.

We think that it is important to discuss and validate how far design decisions like these, which concern the infrastructure of a blockchain system, match up with the requirements concrete applications impose towards the underlying blockchain infrastructure.

Contribution and Outline. Our main contribution consists in investigating relevant requirements of blockchain applications and discussing how far these are addressed in HLF. In the remainder of this report, we refer to related work (Sect. 2), provide relevant background knowledge (Sect. 3), explain our methodology (Sect. 4) and conduct a requirements analysis for blockchain applications selected from different use-cases (Sect. 5). Further, we analyse design choices HLF makes to match these requirements (Sect. 6) and investigate on the question whether HLF can satisfy performance requirements by conducting experiments for different scenarios (Sect. 7). Finally, we draw our conclusions (Sect. 8).

2   Related Work

Li et al. [21] have recently published a survey paper highlighting Hyperledger Fabric and Hyperledger Composer's use-cases. The paper examined current theoretical and real-life HLF deployment while highlighting how HLF was used as a solution to solve existing enterprise problems. A recently published dissertation [8] has studied the requirements and unresolved issues of supply chains while also proposing architectures based on blockchains to address these issues, the main focus was however restricted to supply chain management.

Several papers have included benchmarks for Hyperledger Fabric [1,3,11,30, 33], mainly focusing on the v1.x versions of Fabric with FastFabric pushing an impressive 20,000 transactions per second (TPS) [11]. Androulaki et al. proposed the architecture, components and design choices behind HLF and experimentally validated the system performance [1] whereas Thakkar et al. studied how various parameters of the network impacted performance such as number of channels, number of endorsers and world-state database choice [33] - their proposals were incorporated in future Hyperledger Fabric versions.

Further, Guggenberger et al. [12] have recently published a detailed performance report for Hyperledger Fabric v2.0 combining several configurations and testing Fabric's fault-tolerance using DLPS [29]. Their report covers an in-depth benchmark analysis of HLF.

In our report, we focus on discussing *application requirements* of blockchain and how these requirements are met by HLF's design. Our report also includes a performance evaluation that conducts experiments on multi-ordering service performance and mixed workloads (e.g., read-heavy vs. write-heavy) which have yet not been sufficiently studied by previous works but are interesting from an application point of view.

3 Background

Blockchain. The term blockchain is not used consistently in academic literature. Our definition emphasizes that we are referring to a complete system rather than just a specific data structure:

A *blockchain* is a distributed system that manages an append-only and totally-ordered log of immutable transactions (also called the *ledger*) in a replicated fashion. Several nodes hold a consistent copy of the ledger, and several nodes are involved in validating transactions issued by clients. To order transactions, typically a *consensus* algorithm is employed. Further, transactions are usually grouped into *blocks*, which are chained by referencing the hash of the previous block in the block header.

The traceability and immutable history of transactions in a blockchain fundamentally increase the trustworthiness and transparency of the system. As long as a sufficiently large portion of nodes in the system (e.g., determined by quantity, resource allocation, or stake) behaves correctly, the overall system works as intended. There is no need to put trust into the correctness of any single node, thus eliminating single point of failure for blockchain applications. Immutability refers to the property that each block bears also the hash of the previous block, and a modification to a block modifies its hash, which results in the link being broken and thus invalidating subsequent blocks [31,37].

Hyperledger Fabric (HLF). HLF is a highly modular enterprise-grade distributed ledger platform. HLF has plug and play capabilities that allow it to be suitable for a wide range of use-cases. Further, HLF follows an *execute-order-validate* architecture, where transactions are first simulated (this means executed against the current state of the ledger) by endorsing peers, ordered by the ordering service, and then committed by committing peers.

The *transaction flow* consists of the following steps (also shown in Fig. 1) [1]: The *client* sends a transaction proposal to the peers specified in the endorsement policy and the *endorsing peers* simulate the transaction (①), which produces read sets and write sets, without changing the state of the ledger. After that, the client collects the responses of the endorsing peers (②), which contain the read and write sets, checks if the endorsement policy is satisfied, assembles them in an *envelope* and sends that to the *ordering service* (③). Subsequently, the ordering

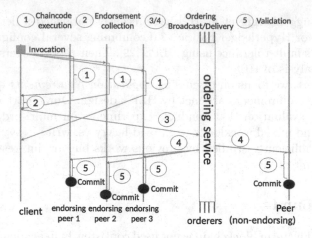

Fig. 1. Hyperledger fabric transaction flow [1].

service orders the transaction without knowing the contents of the envelope. Transactions are batched and once one of the conditions for cutting a block is met, the ordering service sends the block to the committing peers (④). Finally, committing peers validate or invalidate the transactions in the block and the block is eventually appended to the *ledger* (⑤).

4   Methodology

Our evaluation approach covers two dimensions: *performance* and *resilience*. Performance characteristics are quantitative (e.g., transaction throughput) and are used to assert that the blockchain can handle the application's workload. Resilience characteristics are often qualitative and describe if the blockchain can deliver a certain service quality (e.g., tolerating faults, providing confidentiality).

Aspects of Resilience. Resilience is a broad term that encompasses many aspects [5]. We employ the following aspects in our subsequent analysis:

Fault Tolerance Coverage (FTC). A measure of effectiveness for fault tolerance is *fault tolerance coverage* [2]: it encompasses the *error- and fault-handling coverage*, a measure to capture how many of the occurring faults are actually covered by the fault tolerance mechanism (development faults might restrict the intended fault-handling coverage) and the *fault assumption coverage*, which is a measure for reasoning about how closely assumptions of a fault model actually cover reality. In our analysis we employ assumption coverage to indicate which type of faults a blockchain can tolerate.

Fault Tolerance Proportion (FTP). Fault tolerance proportion is an assumed upper-bound that indicates the ratio of faulty nodes a blockchain can tolerate, to total nodes participating in the system (this property is also sometimes called resilience bound). Fault tolerance coverage and proportion are often coupled.

Table 1. Categorization of performance requirements.

	Low	Medium	High
Scalability	<100 nodes	100 to 1000 nodes	>1000 nodes
Throughput	<100 TPS	100 to 1000 TPS	>1000 TPS
Latency	<3 s	3 s to 10 s	>10 s

Membership (Node Authenticity). In permissioned blockchains a consortium of nodes is defined and a mechanism for managing membership is required. Providing membership information and node authenticity is an important feature for blockchains and blockchain applications might demand the blockchain system to be capable to changing (e.g., expanding) its consortium at run-time.

Confidentiality. There are different *types* of application requirements associated with confidentiality depending whether the content, sender, or other information of a transaction need to be confidential.

Integrity. Integrity is a main motivator towards blockchain adoption. Data integrity in blockchains is achieved by the immutability property of the ledger. Undetected tampering is almost infeasible, as hashes can be used to quickly validate for correctness. We argue that all blockchain applications share the need of this characteristic and will thus not use it in a comparison.

Aspects of Performance. We consider typical blockchain performance aspects that application might demand, in particular:

Scalability. Number of nodes that can participate in the blockchain system.

Throughput. Number of transactions per second (TPS) that can be processed by the blockchain system.

Latency. Time that elapses between a transaction being issued on the client side and being finalized within a block that is appended to the ledger.

For each aspect, we categorize performance requirements of blockchain applications into three categories: *low, medium* and *high* as shown in Table 1. This categorization is rough and aligns with performance magnitudes of blockchain systems. Achieving low latency is better and thus means a higher requirement towards the blockchain infrastructure. For the other aspects, higher is better.

5 Requirements Analysis

HLF is currently being used in a number of fields [23], some of them are already in production, but most of them are still in development or proof-of-concept status. These use-cases are high-risk environments with a lot at stake where some parties could be interested in gaining unauthorized access or tampering with the data for personal gain, thus requiring a highly resilient infrastructure.

In this section, we analyse use-cases and derive which of the characteristics (Sect. 4) are required by which application and present a summary in Table 2.

5.1   Electronic Voting (EVote)

EVote [27,28] is an open-source proof-of-concept application for holding an electronic election. The app leverages HLF to meet its needs for immutability and traceability, which in return reduce election fraud. Smart contracts are used to tally up votes, therefore reducing costs of manual work [28]. A voting network to hold an election is a highly adversarial environment that might encourage malicious behaviour of individuals. Therefore, we consider it valuable for such a system to be Byzantine fault-tolerant (and to tolerate up to 33% of participants becoming faulty). The system should be permissioned. It should further provide high confidentiality: When votes need to be checked for their validity (to prevent double voting) they should be untraceable to the voter to prevent any form of coercion. Subnetworks could help to enforce a need-to-know policy for different entities involved in the process.

From a performance standpoint, a high latency is tolerable in such a network, because voting is per user a one-time action. It should not exceed 30 s to maintain a pleasant user-experience. To maintain such latency, the system needs at least a medium throughput, as elections are usually held in a small time period where at peak times, many transactions are issued. In such a use-case, the scalability of the system has another goal other than being able to handle such a traffic and that is transparency and ensuring that not a single entity has more control over the voting process. An approach for this might be to have every election district host a peer node (or more in order to avoid a single point of failure) and as such a medium to high scalability becomes a requirement.

5.2   Supply Chains (IBM Food Trust and GoDirect Trade)

GoDirect Trade [16] is a practical use case for blockchain technology, offering an online marketplace for aerospace parts. The traceability feature of blockchain allows users to access the lifecycle of parts and any associated information required by the government. IBM Food Trust [17,20] is a project by Walmart, IBM, Nestle, and Unilever aimed at improving traceability of products and all their ingredients to the farms and also to access different data about the product to satisfy customer needs and guarantee the safety of foods [17]. IBM Foodtrust and GoDirect Trade both utilize the immutability and traceability aspects of blockchain, in that both are interested in the history and provenance of items recorded on the immutable ledger.

From a resilience perspective of view, IBM Foodtrust could go well with BFT (and have a resilience bound of 33%) whereas GoDirect Trade could benefit from using only CFT (and having a resilience bound of 50%). Contrary to IBM Foodtrust, where participants could bring up their own peers and deploy their own smart-contracts, GoDirect Trade's nodes are in-house [16]. Further, both applications need to be run on a permissioned blockchain, where participants are granted access based on their status on the market. Moreover, both systems require high confidentiality, as trade secrets are at stake here as in both networks competitors are present.

Table 2. Blockchain applications requirements towards the underlying blockchain infrastructure with very high (★), high (●), medium (◐) and low (○) demands. (Note that, lower latency is better, and is thus considered a higher demand towards the infrastructure, e.g., tolerating a higher latency as in EVote means a lower requirement.)

| Application | FTC | FTP | Resilience | | Performance | | |
			Membership	Confidentiality	Scalability	Throughput	Latency
EVote	BFT	33%	Yes	★ (sender, content)	◐	◐	○
IBM FoodTrust	BFT	33%	Yes	● (content)	◐	●	●
GoDirect Trade	CFT	50%	Yes	● (content)	○	◐	◐
Change Healthcare	CFT	50%	Yes	★ (sender, content)	○	◐	◐
Visa B2B Connect	BFT	33%	Yes	● (content)	◐	★	●

Contrary to EVote, where users are usually one-time users, supply chains, due to the globalisation of the markets, are usually comprised of a lot of actors and each one of them uses the network multiple times in a small time frame [8]. In terms of throughput and latency, GoDirect Trade requires only a medium throughput and a medium latency whereas IBM FoodTrust requires a high throughput and a low latency. This is due to the number of incoming transactions where supply chains in the context of food generate a lot more requests than supply chains in the context of aviation. In GoDirect Trade, network clients are not allowed to host their own nodes. As stated in [16] the system operates five validating nodes, which indicates that low scalability might suffice. In contrast, IBM FoodTrust subscribes are allowed to host their own nodes, install their own private smart-contracts on private channels to automate transactions, which indicates that it requires a higher scalability than GoDirect Trade and therefore needs a least medium scalability.

5.3 Healthcare (Change Healthcare)

Change Healthcare [15] is a company with the aim to modernize the American health system. Leveraging HLF the company is able to link providers and payers in a trustful environment to facilitate claims.

As an actor in the healthcare industry, Change Healthcare has to be very wary about how data on their network is handled. Providing access to unauthorized persons has serious legal consequences [26], which is why Change Healthcare needs very high confidentiality and private ledgers. Most importantly, transactions, such as financial or patient data, should be on a subnetwork with only participating entities granted access (need-to-know basis), for example a hospital at which a person was a patient in and the insurance company for claims processing. Similarly to GoDirect Trade, Change Healthcare's nodes are in-house and it can benefit from providing only CFT and having a fault tolerance proportion of up to $\epsilon < 50\%$.

The blockchain network has initially run on six nodes in the company's datacenter but now they are looking towards expanding to the cloud. As such, Change Healthcare only needs low scalability due to the nodes belonging to it like in

GoDirect Trade's case. Currently the system can process 550 transactions per second (TPS) but the company is aiming for a higher number in near future [15]. As such, the blockchain system needs at least medium throughput and works best with low to medium latency to maintain a satisfactory user-experience.

5.4   Banking (VISA B2B Connect)

VISA B2B Connect [34] is a project by VISA to facilitate cross-border and cross-currency payments. It leverages HLF to create a secure and trusted network of financial institutions where international transfers do not have to go through intermediate banks, thus drastically reducing both delays and costs.

The current standard for cross-border cross-currency payments and the main system VISA B2B Connect is challenging is SWIFT, which handles approximately 33.6 million transactions per day. VISA B2B circumvents the shortcoming of traditional banking applications by employing an one-to-many architecture, in which VISA B2B is directly linked to several financial institutions, therefore intermediaries can be bypassed. As a result of this centralization and the SWIFT system as a motivator, such a system requires medium scalability, and very high throughput to be capable of handling peak workloads. Typical other banking methods have varying throughput with PayPal having around 450 TPS [13] and credit-card companies such as VISA itself require 50,000 TPS [11].

This centralization also means VISA's nodes are in-house. However, unlike GoDiectTrade and other companies hosting their nodes in-house VISA should employ BFT along with a FTP of up to 33%. The nature of this system makes attacks highly rewarding and insider attacks are a legitimate concern, such as if a participant is compromised or participant himself being dishonest.

6   How HLF Meets Enterprise Requirements

In this section, we focus on the design considerations and features of Fabric that allow it to meet performance and resilience requirements of potential use-cases.

6.1   Resilience Requirements

In the following, we highlight Fabric's features, components and design choices while briefly explaining their role in increasing resilience.

Blockchain Features. Maintaining integrity of the data is a critical aspect of resilience and a priority for businesses. HLF, being an implementation of blockchain, comes with both immutability and traceability. Data is immutable once appended to the ledger, this way users can insure its integrity [1].

Permissions. Fabric is a permissioned blockchain, permissions are maintained by one or more membership service providers (MSP) which use cryptographic identities. Transactions are checked at every step to verify authenticity of requests. This in turn limits unwanted access and increases trust [1].

Channels. Unlike other blockchain implementations, HLF uses *channels*. A channel is a dedicated subnetwork with its own private ledger and a group of channel members that manage a copy of the ledger, thus ensuring that not every peer on the network has access to the ledger, therefore increasing confidentiality.

Endorsement Policy. Channel administrators define the endorsement policy, which specifies which peers (*endorsers*) have to approve a transaction before this is sent to the ordering service. If a client does not fulfill an endorsement policy he has to retry submitting the transaction again [1]. An endorsement policy consisting of multiple peers belonging to different organizations would increase transparency and trust in the system, as no single entity is in full control of endorsing transactions. A single point of failure can be avoided by defining a minimum number or percentage of endorsing peers.

Consensus. An appealing feature of HLF is pluggable consensus. Older versions of HLF use Kafka + ZooKeeper (ZK), while the current default consensus protocol is Raft. Both Raft and Kafka+ZK are crash fault-tolerant. Since consensus is pluggable, developers could opt for a BFT ordering service in future as a new BFT consensus library has been proposed for HLF recently [4]. Raft is embedded into HLF and thus enjoys the direct support of the HLF community whereas Kafka+ZK are supported by Apache. In terms of performance, a published benchmark [10] with v1.4.1 showed that Raft can be much more efficient.

Resilience of the Execute-Order-Validate Design. HLF employs an execute-order-validate architecture to separate these different concerns. A goal of this design is to help withstanding attacks that may target performance degradation or resource exhaustion. In particular, this design can help to circumvent bottleneck situations since it allows for transactions to be processed in parallel and by only a subset of nodes.

Peer Gossip. Peer gossip enables peers' ledgers stay in sync by distributing data to other peers on the channel. This aids resiliency in that peers that have gone offline for sometime are able to have synced ledgers and can endorse transactions again after they are back online.

Records of Invalid Transactions. All transactions in HLF, in contrast to other blockchain implementations, are recorded on the ledger whether they are valid or invalid. This allows dishonest or malicious users to be detected and black-listed from the network which results in a more secure platform [1].

Identity Mixer. HLF supports the use of *identity mixer* (Idemix) to enhance privacy by providing unlinkability and anonymity – this however, comes with limitations such as not being able to endorse transactions. An Idemix entity (issuer) certifies a user's attributes in form of a digital certificate, users are then able to generate a zero-knowledge proof of possession of a certificate while revealing only what they choose to reveal to a verifier.

Hardware Security Module. HLF supports the usage of hardware security modules (HSM) allowing cryptographic operations like signature generation to be offloaded to them. This has the advantage of letting the HSM manage private keys of peers or orderers, thus protecting the keys from unauthorized reading.

Transport Layer Security. Communication over a HLF network can be secured using TLS. This can be a one-way or a two-way authentication.

Private Data Collections. Channels support data privacy by having only organizations on the channel that are allowed to view these transactions. In cases where a subset of channel members need to conduct transactions between each other while not wanting other channel members to know the contents of these transactions, they could create a new channel. This is however associated with a higher administrative overhead. A solution for this would be the usage of *private data collections*[1]. Private data has a separate transaction flow compared to other data on the channel. Only authorized peers can see private data and it is communicated between them using gossip, all other nodes including ordering nodes only see hashes of this data, non-authorized nodes append the hashes of this private data in their ledgers, so they know a transaction has taken place privately between entities on the channel but they do not know its content. To comply with government regulations, some organizations might need to delete private data after a certain time, this is doable and will leave behind a hash in the peer's ledgers as evidence that some data was there [18].

Chaincode Lifecycle. Introduced in v2.0, the new Fabric chaincode lifecycle requires organizations participating in the endorsement process to approve a transaction. Previously, in v1.x one organization would define attributes of a chaincode and other organizations choose either to opt-in by installing the chaincode or opt-out and not be able to endorse transactions. The chaincode lifecycle provides equality on a channel by allowing the chaincode to be instantiated only after gathering enough approvals. Chaincode packages also do not need to be identical anymore, different organizations can install different chaincode packages and introduce organization-specific behaviour (for example perform different validations for their interests). This does not conflict with transaction approval as long as endorsement results match [19].

6.2   Performance Requirements

Further, some of Fabric's design choices were made to increase its performance.

The Advantage of Execute-Order-Validate. In HLF execution and ordering of transactions are separated. This allows for better scalability for both phases while increasing modularity and performance because of the decreased amount of work a node has to do [1]. Some blockchain implementations use an order-execute architecture, but this design has its limitations. HLF uses an execute-order-validate approach to allow for parallel execution and eliminate non-determinism of smart contracts (transactions can be processed by a subset of endorsers) therefore increasing throughput and decreasing latency [1].

---

[1] See https://hyperledger-fabric.readthedocs.io/en/release-2.2/private-data/private-data.html, last accessed 12-22-2020.

How Channels Help Performance. Dividing the network into channels where each channel is serving a purpose and linking a subset of the organizations on the network while having their own endorsers can increase performance due to the decreased workload. This is HLF's version of sharding (HLF can scale up horizontally using channels), which has frequently been proposed to increase performance in blockchains [9,10,36]. Generally, the idea of parallelizing transaction processing is an important scalability technique [6].

Peer Gossip. The optional peer gossip feature allows for better performance. The throughput of the ordering service is limited by the network capacity of its nodes, and adding more nodes can decrease throughput. This service elects a leader per organization that pulls blocks from the ordering service and distributes them to the rest [1]. This reduces the workload of the ordering service.

BatchSize and BatchTimeout. The ordering service in Fabric uses batching and forms blocks out of transactions. A new block is created if (1) the number of transactions in the block is equal to the maximum allowed, (2) the block's size in bytes has reached max, or (3) an amount of time has passed since the first transaction of a new block was received [1]. The parameters *BatchSize* and *BatchTimeout* are customizable, allowing adaptation to the use case. If, however, the wrong values are chosen Fabric's performance can be heavily affected [14].

Supporting Multiple Ordering Services. The ordering service is usually responsible for multiple channels. As the number of channels grows the load on the ordering service grows, scaling the ordering service leads to a performance decrease [1]. In cases where adding more channels would overwhelm the ordering service, a new ordering service instance can be brought up [10].

World-State Database Choice. Recent work [22] has investigated the difference in performance between the supported world-state databases in Fabric. Mostly with lower BatchSizes, LevelDB has shown better performance than CouchDB, but CouchDB offers better functionality through *rich queries*[2]. Applications should again make trade-offs here of whether they want more functionality in a database or a better performance. FastFabric has experimented with an in-memory hash table as a ledger [11] and achieved a large increase in throughput (from 3200 to 7500 TPS).

7 Performance Evaluation

In this section, we aim to examine HLF's performance under different conditions similar to real-world use-cases in terms of setup and transaction loads. For our purposes, we use Hyperledger Caliper[3], a state of the art tool for benchmarking different blockchain platforms such as Hyperledger Fabric and Ethereum.

---

[2] See https://hyperledger-fabric.readthedocs.io/en/release-2.2/couchdb_as_state_data base.html, last accessed 12-22-2020.
[3] See https://www.hyperledger.org/use/caliper.

In the first part of our evaluation, we focus on the ordering service by examining the benefits of operating a secondary ordering service whilst scaling the number of channels as well as the transaction load. In the second part of this evaluation, we investigate how HLF performs under different mixed application workloads in terms of read and write operations, thereby simulating real-world scenarios. To mimic a real application, we exemplary choose a *fabcar* chaincode deployment. The *fabcar* is a simple chaincode that allows users to add or change data (to be concrete: cars and their ownership) on the ledger using the Fabric contract API[4]. This way we can observe the effect of concurrent reads and writes, i.e., users browsing listings and at the same time users creating new listings.

For our purposes, we may employ setups (Fig. 2) with an increasing number of nodes. We are running each node on a 4 vCPU, 6 GB RAM Debian VM running in a private OpenNebula cloud in our university's virtualization farm.

7.1   Multi Ordering Services Performance

We examine the benefits of operating a secondary ordering service. The need for a secondary ordering service could arise when the first ordering service is already operating at a high load and servicing a high number of channels or to include only a certain subset of organizations in the ordering phase for certain channels.

Setup. We experiment with 8, 16 and 28 two-peer channels where each peer is a member of 2, 4 or 7 channels respectively (Fig. 2). For the load generation, we used a suitable number of workers for each workload, since employing too many workers can result in inaccuracies in terms of maintained transaction load, while too few workers may not be able to maintain the desired load.

Method. In this experiment we scale up the number of channels while experimentally controlling the transaction loads with Hyperledger Caliper. Note that, for a multi-ordering service setup, each orderer manages half the channels and processes and as such half the transaction load. Further, we use Caliper for the load generation and performance measurement, where each invocation of the

```
Channels: [variable]
Organizations: 8
Peers per Organization: 1
Peers per Channel: 2
Nodes per Ordering Service: 3
MaxMessageCount: 10
BatchTimeOut: 0.5
Endorsement: 50%
Chaincode: fabcar
```

```
Channels: 1
Organizations: 8
Peers per Organization: 1
Peers per Channel: 8
Ordering Service Nodes: 5
MaxMessageCount: 100
BatchTimeOut: 0.4
Endorsement: 50%
Chaincode: fabcar
```

(a) Multi channels setup.   (b) Mixed workload setup.

Fig. 2. Setups used for the evaluation.

---

[4] See https://github.com/hyperledger/fabric-samples/tree/master/chaincode/fabcar.

submitTransaction() method generates a new transaction per channel thus guaranteeing a fair load distribution among channels and ordering services.

Caliper provides rate controllers to conduct different types of experiments. For our purposes, we decided on the *fixed-load* controller which we slightly modified because it was too inaccurate in terms of maintaining a constant (or minimally oscillating) load. For this, we have overestimated the perceived network throughput in the controller which minimized the delta between the specified *transactionLoad* and the actual load at any time during the experiment.

Observations. We make the following observations:

Observation 1: Figure 3a shows that throughput is continuously increasing as the transaction load increases and converges to approximately 600 TPS for 28 and 16 channel deployments and to 425 TPS for 8 channel deployments. Increasing the number of channels increases throughput, a 100 Requests per Second (RPS) transaction load per channel achieves approximately 425 TPS for 8 channel deployments and 600 TPS for 16 channel and 28 channel multi-ordering service deployments. The same holds for a network level load, a 800 RPS network load (50 RPS per channel for a 16 channel deployment and 100 RPS per channel for an 8 channel deployment) achieves approximately 550 TPS at 16 channels compared to 425 TPS at 8 channels.

Takeaway 1: Increasing the number of channels increases throughput. The difference in throughput between a 28 channel and 16 channel setup is insignificant with both setups reaching a peak of approximately 600 TPS whereas for an 8 channel setup the peak is reached at approximately 425 TPS. Increasing transaction load also increases throughput however the throughput converges after a certain point.

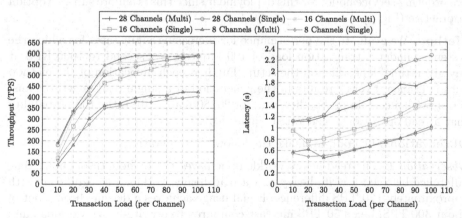

(a) Throughput comparison of multi ordering services and single ordering service.

(b) Latency comparison of multi ordering services and single ordering service.

Fig. 3. Ordering services setups in HLF with variable number of channels.

Observation 2: Figure 3b shows that increasing the number of channels leads to an increase in latency. For 28 channel setups the latency difference between a single ordering service setup and a multi-ordering service setup is somewhat significant with approximately 2.4 s and 1.8 s, respectively.

Takeaway 2: Increasing the number of channels increases latency. This increase is more noticeable in single ordering service setups. Latency has increased by more than 100% between 28 channel and 8 channel setups.

Observation 3: Having a secondary ordering service results in a small throughput increase (¡20 TPS) and a slight latency improvement.

Takeaway 3: A multi-ordering service setup does not seem to lead to a significant performance increase, at least when the ordering phase is not the bottleneck. Several papers have highlighted the validation phase being the bottleneck in HLF [3,11]. In light of this, using a secondary ordering-service solely to improve performance is not beneficial. However, a secondary ordering service makes sense when it comes to separating concerns, i.e., a party that is operating an OSN in the first ordering service and is not involved in channels belonging to the second ordering service, can be excluded from ordering for privacy or security reasons.

7.2   Mixed Workloads

In this experiment we investigate how HLF performs with mixed application workloads. For this reason, we measure performance for different read-to-write ratios, in particular *mostly write* (20/80 read/write), then *mostly read* (80/20 read/write), and also *equal usage* (50/50 read/write).

Setup. Our mixed workloads deployment, is similar to our multi-ordering-service deployment in terms of number of organizations and endorsement. We are using five ordering-service nodes for this deployment since this is a more suitable option in practice (Fig. 4).

Method. We evaluate the performance for increasing input rates for which the system is under a transaction load of 100 requests per second to 1000 RPS at any given time depending on the setup. Further, each invocation of the method `submitTransaction()` results in the generation of a single read or write transaction with a certain probability, e.g., for 20/80 read-write ratio, the probability that a read operation is generated equals 20%.

Observations. Overall, we make the following observations:

Observation 1: The read-heavy workload achieves the highest throughput. The difference between a write-heavy and a read-heavy workload is significant with approximately 120 TPS difference. Equal usage achieves a decent throughput of about 300 TPS, i.e., a 50 TPS increase compared to a write-heavy workload and a 70 TPS decrease compared to a read-heavy workload at 1000 RPS.

Takeaway 1: The read-heavy workload results in a noticeable throughput increase when compared to a write-heavy workload with 376 TPS and 248 TPS respectively at 1000 RPS.

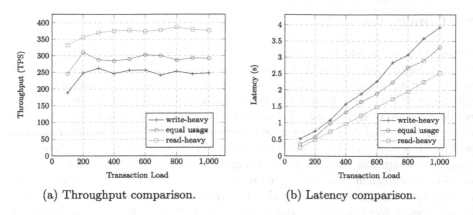

(a) Throughput comparison. (b) Latency comparison.

Fig. 4. Employing different mixed read/write application workloads in HLF.

Observation 2: Latency increases with an increased transaction load. The mostly write workload achieves the worst latency with approximately 4 s at 1000 RPS. Note that the difference between the latencies of the individual workloads is more noticeable at higher transaction loads.

Takeaway 2: An increased read-to-write ratio results in a latency decrease with approximately 4 s at a write-heavy workload compared to approximately 2.5 s at a read-heavy workload.

7.3 Discussion

The obtained results indicate that HLF achieves performance of several hundreds of transactions per second even on commodity hardware. It is performance-wise superior to some other blockchain platforms, e.g., Ethereum (as of time of writing). Applying our results to the aforementioned applications, it seems that HLF meets their requirements to a certain extent. For GoDirect Trade and Change Healthcare, HLF proves to be a perfect fit as a platform. For other applications such as Visa B2B Connect and EVote, Fabric lacks BFT support, which is vital in adversarial environments. However, HLF's modularity allows to opt for a BFT ordering service to meet the resiliency requirements of these applications. Such a setup was demonstrated using BFT-SMaRt [31] and SmartBFT-Go [4], respectively. There are also plans for the Mir-BFT library [32] to be eventually integrated into HLF as its ordering service, thus replacing Raft. Further, for VISA B2B Connect and payment settlement in general, HLF could be a bit slow due to the massive workload (in particular of peak loads) such applications bear. Summarizing, HLF, compared to other solutions, already meets most business requirements performance and security-wise with some trade-offs, and future releases could potentially narrow the gap between enterprise requirements and HLF, especially the planned introduction of BFT.

8   Conclusion

Enterprises previously had minimal interest in blockchains due to the scalability and performance issues. This is however continuously changing in the recent years. The use cases discussed in this paper, as shown in Sect. 5, all have different needs which make the modularity, customizability, privacy features and the coinless nature of Hyperledger Fabric attractive. HLF, on its part, tries to meet these needs by mainly diverting from traditional architectures like order-execute and by increasing privacy through the usage of channels and private data collections. Its design also allows it to be integrated easily, in the way, that potential users can setup their own certificate authority or employ their own version of an ordering service. Previous work and our own experiences with HLF show that it is progressing towards being more decentralized while setting new performance and security standards for other blockchain platforms.

Acknowledgements. This work has been funded by the Deutsche Forschungsgemeinschaft (DFG, German Research Foundation) grant number 446811880 (BFT2Chain).

References

1. Androulaki, E., et al.: Hyperledger fabric: a distributed operating system for permissioned blockchains. In: 13th EuroSys Conference, pp. 1–15. ACM (2018)
2. Avizienis, A., Laprie, J.C., Randell, B., Landwehr, C.: Basic concepts and taxonomy of dependable and secure computing. Trans. Dep. Sec. Comp. **1**(1), 11–33 (2004)
3. Baliga, A., Solanki, N., Verekar, S., Pednekar, A., Kamat, P., Chatterjee, S.: Performance characterization of hyperledger fabric. In: Crypto Valley Conference on Blockchain Technology (CVCBT), pp. 65–74. IEEE (2018)
4. Barger, A., Manevich, Y., Meir, H., Tock, Y.: A Byzantine fault-tolerant consensus library for hyperledger fabric. In: International Conference on Blockchain and Cryptocurrency (ICBC), pp. 1–9. IEEE (2021)
5. Berger, C., Eichhammer, P., Reiser, H.P., Domaschka, J., Hauck, F.J., Habiger, G.: A survey on resilience in the IoT: taxonomy, classification, and discussion of resilience mechanisms. ACM Comput. Surv. (CSUR) **54**(7), 1–39 (2021)
6. Berger, C., Reiser, H.P.: Scaling byzantine consensus: a broad analysis. In: 2nd Workshop on Scalable and Resilient Infrastructures for Distributed Ledgers, pp. 13–18 (2018)
7. Cocco, S., Singh, G.: Top 6 technical advantages of hyperledger fabric for blockchain networks (2018). https://developer.ibm.com/technologies/blockchain/articles/top-technical-advantages-of-hyperledger-fabric-for-blockchain-networks/. Accessed 22 Dec 2020
8. Costa, P.M.L.: Supply chain management with blockchain technologies (2018). https://repositorio-aberto.up.pt/bitstream/10216/114335/2/278462.pdf. Accessed 22 Dec 2020
9. Dang, H., Dinh, T.T.A., Loghin, D., Chang, E.C., Lin, Q., Ooi, B.C.: Towards scaling blockchain systems via sharding. In: International Conference on Management of Data, SIGMOD 2019, pp. 123–140. Association for Computing Machinery, New York (2019). https://doi.org/10.1145/3299869.3319889. Accessed 22 Dec 2020

10. Ferris, C.: Does hyperledger fabric perform at scale? (2019). https://www.ibm.com/blogs/blockchain/2019/04/does-hyperledger-fabric-perform-at-scale/. Accessed 22 Dec 2020
11. Gorenflo, C., Lee, S., Golab, L., Keshav, S.: FastFabric: scaling hyperledger fabric to 20 000 transactions per second. Int. J. Netw. Manage. **30**(5), e2099 (2020)
12. Guggenberger, T., Sedlmeir, J., Fridgen, G., Luckow, A.: An in-depth investigation of performance characteristics of hyperledger fabric. CoRR abs/2102.07731 (2021). https://arxiv.org/abs/2102.07731
13. Hartnett, S.: When it comes to throughput transactions per second is the wrong blockchain metric (2018). https://energyweb.org/2018/05/10/when-it-comes-to-throughput-transactions-per-second-is-the-wrong-blockchain-metric/. Accessed 22 Dec 2020
14. Hua, S., Zhang, S., Pi, B., Sun, J., Yamashita, K., Nomura, Y.: Reasonableness discussion and analysis for hyperledger fabric configuration. In: International Conference on Blockchain and Cryptocurrency (ICBC), pp. 1–3. IEEE (2020)
15. Hyperledger.org: Case study: change healthcare using hyperledger fabric to improve claims lifecycle throughput and transparency (2019). https://www.hyperledger.org/wp-content/uploads/2019/06/Hyperledger_CaseStudy_ChangeHealthcare_Printable_6.19.pdf. Accessed 22 Dec 2020
16. Hyperledger.org: Case study: honeywell aerospace creates online parts marketplace with hyperledger fabric (2019). https://www.hyperledger.org/wp-content/uploads/2019/12/Hyperledger_CaseStudy_Honeywell_Printable_12.12.19.pdf. Accessed 22 Dec 2020
17. Hyperledger.org: How Walmart brought unprecedented transparency to the food supply chain with hyperledger fabric (2019). https://www.hyperledger.org/wp-content/uploads/2019/02/Hyperledger_CaseStudy_Walmart_Printable_V4.pdf
18. Hyperledger.org: Private data (2020). https://hyperledger-fabric.readthedocs.io/en/release-2.2/private-data/private-data.html. Accessed 7 Oct 2021
19. Hyperledger.org: What's new in hyperledger fabric v2.x (2020). https://hyperledger-fabric.readthedocs.io/en/release-2.2/whatsnew.html. Accessed 22 Dec 2020
20. IBM.com: IBM food trust (2019). https://www.ibm.com/downloads/cas/8QABQBDR. Accessed 22 Dec 2020
21. Li, D., Wong, W.E., Guo, J.: A survey on blockchain for enterprise using hyperledger fabric and composer. In: 2019 6th International Conference on Dependable Systems and Their Applications (DSA), pp. 71–80 (2020). https://doi.org/10.1109/DSA.2019.00017
22. Lincoln, N.: Hyperledger fabric 1.4.0 performance information report. https://hyperledger.github.io/caliper-benchmarks/fabric/resources/pdf/Fabric_1.4.0_javascript_node.pdf. Accessed 22 Dec 2020
23. Muscara, B.: Hyperledger fabric use-cases (2020). https://wiki.hyperledger.org/display/LMDWG/Use+Cases. Accessed 22 Dec 2020
24. Nakamoto, S.: Bitcoin: a peer-to-peer electronic cash system (2009). http://bitcoin.org/bitcoin.pdf. Accessed 22 Dec 2020
25. Ongaro, D., Ousterhout, J.: In search of an understandable consensus algorithm. In: USENIX Annual Technical Conference (Usenix ATC 2014), pp. 305–319 (2014)
26. Peterson, K.J., Deeduvanu, R., Kanjamala, P., Mayo, K.: A blockchain-based approach to health information exchange networks (2016). https://www.healthit.gov/sites/default/files/12-55-blockchain-based-approach-final.pdf. Accessed 22 Dec 2020

27. Porutiu, H.: Evote (2019). https://github.com/IBM/evote. Accessed 22 Dec 2020
28. Porutiu, H., Bablini, D., Zhang, G., Ryan Bouchard, K.W., Hernandez-Lu, E., Ramamurthy, S.G.: Build a secure e-voting app (2019). https://developer.ibm.com/technologies/blockchain/patterns/how-to-create-a-secure-e-voting-application-on-hyperledger-fabric/. Accessed 22 Dec 2020
29. Sedlmeir, J., Ross, P., Luckow, A., Lockl, J., Miehle, D., Fridgen, G.: The DLPS: a new framework for benchmarking blockchains. In: 54th Hawaii International Conference on System Sciences, p. 10 (2021)
30. Shalaby, S., Abdellatif, A.A., Al-Ali, A., Mohamed, A., Erbad, A., Guizani, M.: Performance evaluation of hyperledger fabric. In: International Conference on Informatics, IoT, and Enabling Technologies (ICIoT), pp. 608–613. IEEE (2020)
31. Sousa, J., Bessani, A., Vukolic, M.: A Byzantine fault-tolerant ordering service for the hyperledger fabric blockchain platform. In: 48th annual IEEE/IFIP International Conference on Dependable Systems and Networks (DSN), pp. 51–58. IEEE (2018)
32. Stathakopoulou, C., David, T., Vukolić, M.: Mir-BFT: high-throughput BFT for blockchains. arXiv:1906.05552 (2019)
33. Thakkar, P., Nathan, S., Viswanathan, B.: Performance benchmarking and optimizing hyperledger fabric blockchain platform. In: 26th International Symposium on Modeling, Analysis, and Simulation of Computer and Telecommunication Systems (MASCOTS), pp. 264–276. IEEE (2018)
34. VISA.com: Visa B2B connect a network solution for global large-value payments (2019). https://usa.review.visa.com/dam/VCOM/global/partner-with-us/documents/visa-b2b-connect-white-paper.pdf. Accessed 22 Dec 2020
35. Wüst, K., Gervais, A.: Do you need a blockchain? In: 2018 Crypto Valley Conference on Blockchain Technology (CVCBT), pp. 45–54 (2018). Accessed 22 Dec 2020
36. Zamani, M., Movahedi, M., Raykova, M.: RapidChain: scaling blockchain via full sharding. In: SIGSAC Conference on Computer and Communications Security, pp. 931–948. ACM (2018)
37. Zheng, Z., Xie, S., Dai, H., Chen, X., Wang, H.: An overview of blockchain technology: architecture, consensus, and future trends. In: International Congress on Big Data (BigData Congress), pp. 557–564. IEEE (2017). Accessed 22 Dec 2020

Using SGX for Meta-Transactions Support in Ethereum DApps

Emanuel Onica[1,2]([⊠]) and Ciprian Amariei[1]

[1] Alexandru Ioan Cuza University of Iaşi, Iaşi, Romania
eonica@info.uaic.ro
[2] Eman Tech SRL, Iaşi, Romania

Abstract. Decentralized applications (DApps) gained traction in the context of the blockchain technology. Ethereum is currently the public blockchain that backs the largest amount of the existing DApps. Onboarding new users to Ethereum DApps is a notoriously hard issue to solve. This is mainly caused by lack of cryptocurrency ownership, needed for transaction fees. Several meta-transaction patterns emerged for decoupling users from paying these fees. However, such solutions are mostly offered via off-chain, often paid relayer services and do not fully address the security issues present in the meta-transaction path. In this paper, we introduce a new meta-transaction architecture that makes use of the Intel Software Guard Extensions (SGX). Unlike other solutions, our approach would offer the possibility to deploy a fee-free Ethereum DApp on a web server that can directly relay meta-transactions to the Ethereum network while having essential security guarantees integrated by design.

Keywords: DApps · Blockchain · Ethereum · Meta-Transactions · SGX

1 Introduction

Blockchain networks created the context for developing new applications that leverage decentralized trust. The role of nodes in a blockchain network is to maintain a replicated data structure, the main part of it being commonly referred as the ledger. Nodes validate transactions sent by clients that change the replicated data. Blocks of multiple transactions are formed and mutually agreed in a decentralized manner. Finally, confirmed blocks are appended to the ledger.

Newer blockchains provide support for smart contracts, small programs executed on the blockchain nodes. Transactions can trigger functions operating over a contract state stored as part of the blockchain replicated data. This significantly expanded the range of blockchain applications, from the fintech area to games and others, coined under the generic name of *DApps*. Ethereum [24] was the first platform to support smart contracts, and is still dominating the DApps

© IFIP International Federation for Information Processing 2022
Published by Springer Nature Switzerland AG 2022
D. Eyers and S. Voulgaris (Eds.): DAIS 2022, LNCS 13272, pp. 21–28, 2022.
https://doi.org/10.1007/978-3-031-16092-9_2

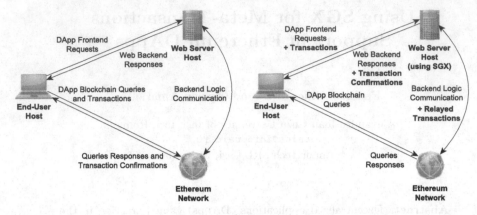

Fig. 1. Typical flow for Ethereum DApp interaction.

Fig. 2. Interaction flow when relaying using SGX meta-transactions. (Simple queries not changing the smart contract state are considered free in Ethereum, otherwise these should follow the same path as transactions.)

market [5,19]. An Ethereum DApp is most often implemented as a web application deployed on a web server having part of its backend using smart contracts on the blockchain. The frontend can query the blockchain for information. Also, actions performed by end-users can trigger transactions to smart contracts. A simplified view of the DApp interaction flow is depicted in Fig. 1.

Users onboarding is a known major issue in Ethereum DApps development [3,13,22]. This stems from the requirements a user must fulfill for enabling DApp interaction with the blockchain backend. Ethereum transactions charge a fee. This fee is required to regulate the transaction processing load and as incentive for the network nodes, and must be paid by the transaction initiator. This implies Ethereum cryptocurrency ownership by the user of the application. Unfortunately this prevents DApps to target many users that might not even be familiar with the notion of cryptocurrency or simply are not willing to pay.

Meta-transactions [9,17] emerged as a solution for users onboarding. In essence, this implies wrapping end-user transaction data in transactions paid by a different entity, which can be either the DApp owner or another sponsor. Although the concept seems simple, the implementation and deployment are not. Some important issues arise when integrating meta-transaction relaying with a DApp. The funds paying for transactions must be secured, as well as the integrity of the end-user transaction data. The few maintained solutions are typically offered as third party relayer services [2,6,11]. These address transaction integrity but disregard the protection of funds allocated for paying transactions. Some also charge a relayer fee or require consistent changes in the DApp architecture. This complicates the task of a developer in finding a suitable DApp design.

In this paper we introduce the *SGX meta-transaction* architecture, intended to facilitate secure meta-transaction relaying integration for DApp developers. Our purpose is to permit meta-transaction wrapping to be handled securely by the DApp host, which will act as transaction relayer. For this, we use a trusted execution environment (TEE), namely the Intel Software Guard Extensions (SGX) [4]. This changes the transaction path as depicted in Fig. 2.

Our paper is structured as follows. In Sect. 2 we present some background on Ethereum DApps and the context of meta-transactions. In Sect. 3 we introduce our architecture and an initial proof-of-concept implementation. We discuss some extensions in Sect. 4. Finally, we conclude in Sect. 5.

2   Background

Users interacting with Ethereum DApps can trigger transactions, such as cryptocurrency transfers or calling functions in smart contracts that change the blockchain data. The latter is the more general case and our focus. Transactions come at a cost quantified in *gas* units. This cost increases with the complexity of operations executed in the smart contract. The user must pay a transaction fee equal to the cost in gas multiplied with a price per gas unit set in the Ethereum cryptocurrency. This price per gas unit is composed of a variable base network fee to which a priority fee can be added to speed up transaction processing.

Two types of accounts are defined in Ethereum: externally owned accounts (EOAs) and contract accounts. Both types are identified by an address and have a balance in the Ethereum currency. Transactions can be submitted by EOAs, essentially user accounts controlled by private keys used to sign the transactions. The fees of verified transactions are deducted from the EOA balance. The main part included in a transaction message is either or both of a data payload encoding a smart contract function call and a currency value to be transferred. Other transaction fields include an incremental nonce bound to the EOA, a gas limit, the maximum gas price, the recipient address and the EOA's signature.

We consider DApps where the interaction does not imply a payment and users can have a zero balance in Ethereum currency. In such cases, a *meta-transaction* would wrap the original end-user's transaction data, and must be signed and paid by an EOA address capable of covering the transaction fees. The DApp developer is faced with the challenge of implementing a signature delegation pattern to such an EOA address, providing appropriate trust guarantees.

Deployed solutions typically require DApps to use off-chain relayer services [2, 6,11]. Integrating a third party service into the transaction path comes with an inherent risk to the transaction integrity. Therefore, these solutions focus on ensuring that the service itself cannot tamper the original data when wrapping it into a meta-transaction. Provided APIs require the user's EOA signature to be present in their sent data and to adapt the smart contracts backend of the DApp to verify that. However, this does not protect the private key used for signing the meta-transaction itself. The relayer service must be provided with funds for paying the meta-transaction. This makes critical storing securely the relayer's signing key. If an attacker gains access to this key it can drain the relayer funds, by simply signing transactions transferring the relayer's balance to the attacker.

In a normal transaction scenario, keeping the signing key safe is solely the responsibility of the end-user who operates with her own funds. In the relayed meta-transaction scenario this guarantee should be provided by the relayer. Unfortunately, none of the relayer implementations we are aware of offers details on how it secures the meta-transaction signing key. Some relayer providers do not even specify whether they host their service on their private infrastructure or on a public cloud, case proven vulnerable to sensitive data leaks [16,20,25].

We propose a meta-transaction architecture that does not depend on an external relayer and overcomes the security issues above. This simplifies integrating meta-transaction support in a DApp and saves fees charged by external relayers.

3   Basic Solution Design

The purpose of our design is to provide easy integration for safe meta-transaction support with the DApp backend implementation and to use the DApp host as a secure relayer. Eliminating a third party relayer service from the transaction path automatically eliminates the concern of this party tampering with the transactions. However, we consider the web server host where the DApp is deployed untrusted with respect to preserving the confidentiality of sensitive information. The main threat we tackle is an attack trying to leak private credentials from this host, such as the key used in signing the meta-transactions.

To prevent private key leakage we employ the use of Intel SGX, a widely available TEE solution. Its core abstraction is an *enclave*, which isolates sensitive code execution within an encrypted memory region. An enclave implementation can provide a set of functions - *ECalls*, to be called from untrusted code outside the enclave for executing code in secure isolation within the enclave. Another set of functions, the *OCalls* are used when the code inside the enclave initiates calls to untrusted code. The definition of ECalls and OCalls forms the interface of the enclave. An enclave can be remotely attested in order to verify the integrity of the enclave code and if this is executed on a genuine SGX capable processor. The remote attestation can also be used to establish a shared secret base for encrypted communication between the enclave and the party requesting the attestation.

We use an SGX enclave integrated with the DApp for the sensitive operations in the transaction flow. Once the DApp is deployed, the DApp owner must execute an enclave initialization protocol. This protocol establishes a set of *master credentials*, namely an Ethereum account address and the corresponding signing key, to be used within the enclave. These credentials are randomly generated in the enclave and can be sent to the DApp owner via a secure channel established as part of the attestation. The DApp owner will use the master account address to transfer funds for covering the meta-transaction fees. The master signing key must be safely stored by the DApp owner and is not used in normal operation outside enclave space. This key is required to be sent to the DApp owner only to maintain control over the funds in case of enclave failure.

After this initialization the enclave is ready to operate on transaction data sent by a user. We define a *SGX meta-transaction* as a meta-transaction prepared and signed within the secure enclave space. A simplified overview of the enclave integration within the transaction flow is presented in Fig. 3. The transaction data contains the serialized encoding of the smart contract function call and the contract address. This is received at the DApp web backend and passed via an ECall to the enclave. Additional information necessary to form an Ethereum transaction such as gas related parameters can be passed with the transaction data or established in the enclave space. The SGX meta-transaction is prepared within the enclave using an encoding required by Ethereum, wrapping the data and the rest of fields including a sequentially increasing nonce. This nonce is associated to the enclave's master Ethereum address and is required for trans- action ordering. Finally, the enclave code signs the SGX meta-transaction using the master signing key and passes it to the web backend through an OCall.

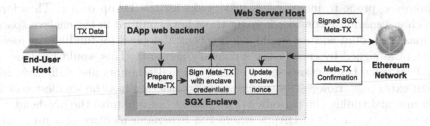

Fig. 3. High level overview of the SGX meta-transaction flow.

Following the above steps, the web backend code of the DApp can relay the signed SGX meta-transaction to the Ethereum blockchain. The enclave main- tains a trusted keystore, secured using the sealing key - a hardware key unique per CPU accessible only in the enclave. The keystore is loaded in the enclave memory when needed and can be stored encrypted on disk. The structure of this keystore can be adapted to fit the needs of the DApp. In its simplest form it holds the set of master credentials. Once the web backend receives the transac- tion confirmation an ECall will trigger the nonce increment in the keystore.

We have implemented a proof-of-concept of the above design wrapping the SGX enclave within a native Node.js module [14]. This module allows the DApp backend to trigger the necessary meta-transaction flow operations within the enclave. Most Ethereum DApp implementations use JavaScript libraries [7, 21] for interacting with the blockchain network. Therefore, providing our solution as a Node.js module makes seamless the integration with most DApps. We per- formed a functionality test of our transaction flow on a mockup DApp where the user can change a value in a smart contract deployed on the Ethereum Rop- sten test network. Our SGX meta-transaction constructed within the enclave was successfully validated by the network.[1] We tested the implementation on a SGX capable machine equipped with an Intel i7-7700 CPU running Ubuntu 18.04.5 LTS. The measured time overhead for preparing the signed SGX meta-transaction was in the range of 3ms including logging, orders of magnitude smaller than the average confirmation time of an Ethereum transactions block at almost 14s.

4   Discussion and Open Directions

The description in the previous section is limited to the bare necessities in the transaction flow. In the following we examine some of the extensions we consider.

A more complex structure of the keystore could include multiple Ethereum credentials generated for signing meta-transactions. This scenario could fit allocating separate funds for different users or attempts to scale the transaction flow. Exporting multiple addresses and safely storing their private keys would be, however, prone to increased security risks for the DApp owner. Therefore, for such a scenario we consider keeping these keys confined in the enclave space. The master account address would act as a central deposit for funding the meta-transactions signed by each of the secondary accounts. This would be done by periodical value transactions sent to these internal accounts and will obviously add an extra cost. However, a simple value transaction has the smallest cost in Ethereum and tuning the periodicity of funding can minimize the overhead.

A particular case is of DApps where the Ethereum identity of a user must be preserved in the transactions: DApps using tokens, either fungible, essentially virtual coins built over Ethereum, or NFTs. The approach in other solutions [6,9–11] is to include a signature using user's own Ethereum credentials in the meta-transaction and adapt the smart contract logic to verify it. Our design in Sect. 3 can easily accommodate such changes in the carried transaction data.

EIP-2771 [18] proposes a contract level protocol for validating data signed with user's Ethereum credentials in meta-transactions. This architecture can be integrated with our solution. However, we note that its main scope is to guarantee integrity against a relayer controlled by an untrusted third party. In our design the DApp owner controls the relayer. Nevertheless, we could consider a possible integrity attack escalation over the web server. This can be mitigated by a TLS channel terminated within the enclave over which the end-user will send the transaction data. This guarantees the integrity up to the enclave on the relaying host. Further, the SGX meta-transaction is securely signed in the enclave, therefore it cannot be altered until verified in the blockchain network. We have considered various TLS implementations in conjunction with SGX for future extension [1,8,12,23]. Some provide performance advantages, while others seem to be easier to integrate with our web oriented architecture. For brevity we leave further technical details for a future extended report of our work.

---

[1] The record of the first SGX meta-transaction relayed via our implementation is available at the following address: https://ropsten.etherscan.io/tx/0xdcb13cdaaf847ddce26307988ac4938c9037e03b747276f46b222df2a42d302b.

Finally, an aspect to consider is the solution deployment. An attractive option would be to deploy the DApp over a public cloud platform. Currently the support for SGX offered in virtualized environments comes with a performance impact as discussed in [15]. Further analysis is required, but we believe the transaction confirmation time plus the network latency would still overshadow the additional penalties inflicted by the virtualization.

5   Conclusion

We introduced in this paper a new architecture for relaying Ethereum meta-transactions. Unlike external, sometimes paid services, our solution takes a different approach aiming for a secure integration of meta-transaction relaying support directly within the DApp. Our design introduces the SGX meta-transaction prepared and signed within a secure enclave space. This provides independence to a DApp developer, it relaxes integrity concerns by not needing to trust an extra third party and offers solid guarantees on preventing leaks that could lead to losing funds allocated for paying the meta-transaction fees.

We emphasize that our proposed architecture is a work-in-progress. We briefly discussed multiple extensions we consider. We believe that our proof-of-concept integrating SGX meta-transactions via a Node.js module already shows the practicality of our design and promising potential for use within DApps.

References

1. Aublin, P.L., et al.: TaLoS: secure and transparent TLS termination inside SGX Enclaves (2017). https://github.com/lsds/TaLoS. Accessed 27 Jan 2022
2. Biconomy (2021).https://docs.biconomy.io/. Accessed 27 Jan 2022
3. Chandra, S., Aggarwal, S.: Web3: onboarding the next billion users - the road ahead (2022). https://cointelegraph.com/news/web3-onboarding-the-next-billion-users-the-road-ahead. Accessed 31 Mar 2022
4. Costan, V., Devadas, S.: Intel SGX explained. cryptology ePrint Archive, Report 2016/086 (2016). https://eprint.iacr.org/2016/086. Accessed 27 Jan 2022
5. DappRadar - The World's Dapp Store (2021). https://dappradar.com/. Accessed 27 Jan 2022
6. Ethereum Gas Station Network (GSN) (2021). https://docs.opengsn.org/. Accessed 27 Jan 2022
7. Ethers.js (2022). https://docs.ethers.io/v5/. Accessed 27 Jan 2022
8. Gramine (2022). https://gramine.readthedocs.io/en/latest/. Accessed 17 Feb 2022
9. Griffith, A.T.: Ethereum meta transactions - lowering barriers to drive mass ethereum adoption (2018). https://medium.com/@austin_48503/ethereum-meta-transactions-90ccf0859e84. Accessed 27 Jan 2022
10. Griffith, A.T.: Native meta transactions (2018). https://medium.com/gitcoin/native-meta-transactions-e509d91a8482. Accessed 31 Mar 2022
11. Infura transactions (ITX) (2022). https://docs.infura.io/infura/features/transactions. Accessed 17 Feb 2022
12. Intel software guard extensions SSL (2022). https://github.com/intel/intel-sgx-ssl. Accessed 27 Jan 2022

13. Khatri, Y.: Ethereum onboarding solution provider UniLogin is shutting down due to high gas fees (2020). https://www.theblockcrypto.com/post/78358/ethereum-onboarding-unilogin-shutting-down-high-gas-fees. Accessed 31 Mar 2022
14. Native abstractions for Node.js (2022). https://nodejs.org/api/addons.html. Accessed 31 Mar 2022
15. Ngoc, T.D., et al.: Everything you should know about intel SGX performance on virtualized systems. In: Proceedings of the ACM on Measurement and Analysis of Computing Systems, vol. 3, no. 1, pp. 5:1–5:21 (2019)
16. Ristenpart, T., Tromer, E., Shacham, H., Savage, S.: Hey, you, get off of my cloud: exploring information leakage in third-party compute clouds. In: Proceedings of the 16th ACM Conference on Computer and Communications Security, CCS 2009, pp. 199–212 (2009)
17. Rush, N.: Making uPort smart contracts smarter, part 3: fixing user experience with meta transactions (2017). https://medium.com/uport/making-uport-smart-contracts-smarter-part-3-fixing-user-experience-with-meta-transactions-105209ed43e0. Accessed 31 Mar 2022
18. Sandford, R., et al.: EIP-2771: secure protocol for native meta transactions (2020). https://eips.ethereum.org/EIPS/eip-2771. Accessed 27 Jan 2022
19. State of the DApps - explore decentralized applications (2022). https://www.stateofthedapps.com/. Accessed 27 Jan 2022
20. Varadarajan, V., Zhang, Y., Ristenpart, T., Swift, M.: A placement vulnerability study in multi-tenant public clouds. In: Proceedings of the 24th USENIX Conference on Security Symposium, SEC 2015, pp. 913–928 (2015)
21. Web3.js - ethereum JavaScript API (2020). https://web3js.readthedocs.io/en/v1.7.0/. Accessed 17 Feb 2022
22. Whinfrey, C.: Gas spectrum transactions (2019). https://medium.com/authereum/gas-spectrum-transactions-bd34b65107b. Accessed 31 Mar 2022
23. WolfSSL with Intel SGX (2017). https://www.wolfssl.com/wolfssl-with-intel-sgx/. Accessed 27 Jan 2022
24. Wood, G.: Ethereum: a secure decentralised generalised transaction ledger - yellow paper (2021). https://ethereum.github.io/yellowpaper. Accessed 27 Jan 2022
25. Zhang, Y., Juels, A., Reiter, M.K., Ristenpart, T.: Cross-tenant side-channel attacks in PaaS clouds. In: Proceedings of the 2014 ACM SIGSAC Conference on Computer and Communications Security, CCS 2014, pp. 990–1003 (2014)

Understanding Cryptocoins Trends Correlations

Pasquale De Rosa[✉] and Valerio Schiavoni

University of Neuchâtel, Neuchâtel, Switzerland
{pasquale.rosa,valerio.schiavoni}@unine.ch

Abstract. Crypto-coins (also known as cryptocurrencies) are tradable digital assets. Notable examples include Bitcoin, Ether and Litecoin. Ownerships of cryptocoins are registered on distributed ledgers (*i.e.*,, blockchains). Secure encryption techniques guarantee the security of the transactions (transfers of coins across owners), registered into the ledger. Cryptocoins are exchanged for specific trading prices. While history has shown the extreme volatility of such trading prices across all different sets of crypto-assets, it remains unclear what and if there are tight relations between the trading prices of different cryptocoins. Major coin exchanges (*i.e.*,, Coinbase) provide trend correlation indicators to coin owners, suggesting possible acquisitions or sells. However, these correlations remain largely unvalidated.

In this paper, we shed lights on the trend correlations across a large variety of cryptocoins, by investigating their coin-price correlation trends over a period of two years. Our experimental results suggest strong correlation patterns between main coins (Ethereum, Bitcoin) and alt-coins. We believe our study can support forecasting techniques for time-series modeling in the context of crypto-coins. We release our dataset and code to reproduce our analysis to the research community.

Keywords: cryptocoins · correlations · work-in-progress

1 Introduction

Cryptocurrencies, also known as crypto-coins, are tradable digital assets, backed by secure encryption techniques to ensure the security of transactions (typically, the transfer of coins across wallets). Notable examples include Bitcoin [14], Ether (the native cryptocurrency of the Ethereum blockchain [8]) or Litecoin (used in a fork of the original Bitcoin network). Nowadays there exists thousands of cryptocurrencies (CoinMarketCap [3] lists 10039 coins as of April 2022). Cryptocoins are designed to be traded as a form of digital money: the first useful Bitcoin transaction was used by a peer-to-peer payment between Satoshi Nakamoto (Bitcoin's founder) and one of its early adopters, and dates back to 2009.[1] Cryptocoins are nowadays traded over online (centralized or decentralized) *exchanges*, including

---

[1] https://www.blockchain.com/btc/block/170.

© IFIP International Federation for Information Processing 2022
Published by Springer Nature Switzerland AG 2022
D. Eyers and S. Voulgaris (Eds.): DAIS 2022, LNCS 13272, pp. 29–36, 2022.
https://doi.org/10.1007/978-3-031-16092-9_3

Coinbase [2], Kraken [5], Binance [1], Uniswap [6], *etc.* With a current estimated worldwide market-cap of 1.71 Trillion dollars, the cryptocoins economy roughly match the GDP of South Korean in 2021 [4].

Fig. 1. Normalized (min-max) average prices of the top-5 cryptocoins since January 2020.

The ownership of cryptocoins is registered on distributed ledgers (*i.e.,*, blockchains), together with the corresponding transactions (transfers of coins across wallets). Cryptocoins are exchanged (*i.e.,*, sold, bought) for specific trading prices. While it is beyond the scope of this work to understand the exact nature of those prices, history has shown the extreme volatility of such trading prices across all different sets of crypto-assets. For instance, Fig. 1 shows the normalized average daily prices of 5 popular cryptocoins (*i.e.,*, BTC, ETH, BNB, XRP, ADA) since January 2020.

It remains unclear what and if there are tight relations between the trading prices of different cryptocoins. Major cryptocoin exchanges, in particular given the enormous popularity that such digital assets have grown into the large public, and further facilitated by the easy access to these markets via mobile apps, started to provide *trend correlation* indicators to coin/wallet owners. Such correlation indicators can possibly drive end-users towards acquisitions or sells. Coinbase, among the most popular cryptocoin exchanges, indicates the price correlation as *the tendency of other asset prices to change at the same time as the asset shown on the page*. In their case, correlation is computed leveraging the Pearson correlation with USD order books over the last 90 d.

However, the nature of such correlations, their intensity as well as the evolution of the correlations through time, remain largely unvalidated.

The **contributions** of this work-in-progress paper are twofold. First, we extract the trading prices, as well as other exchange metadata (*e.g.,*, open and closing price, market cap, volume), for the top-100 cryptocoins since the last two years from a popular cryptocoin monitoring web-site. Second, we leverage this dataset to carry out our preliminary study of the trend correlations between and across crypto-coins. Specifically, we investigate daily, weekly and monthly correlation patterns exhibited by two principal cryptocoins, *i.e.,*BTC and ETH, against the remaining set of *alt-coins* in our dataset. Our analysis show strong correlations between the observed trends. We will leverage these observations in our future work, where we plan to exploit the observed correlations to forecast the future trading trends and by considering the problem of time-series forecasting applied to the crypto-coin market.

We follow an *open science* approach: our datasets will be released and made available to the research and open-source community.

Roadmap. This paper is organized as follows. Section 2 provides background materials on Bitcoin, Ethereum, as well as general notions of correlation analysis. Section 3 describes our dataset, as well as our work-in-progress analysis. We briefly cover related work in Sect. 4, before concluding and presenting our future work in Sect. 5.

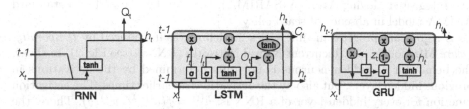

Fig. 2. ML-based time series forecasting approaches: RNN, LSTM and GRU.

2   Background

Cryptocoins in a Nutshell. Cryptocoins are digitally encrypted assets. They were typically designed to replace fiat currencies and used mostly in peer-to-peer networks. Depending on the incentive natures of the underlying blockchain, cryptocoins (or token) are rewarded to nodes in the network. We differentiate between three main types of cryptocoins: *(i)* Bitcoin, *(ii)* alt-coins, and *(iii)* stable coins.[2] Alt-coins are *alternative* coins to Bitcoin. Notable examples include Ether (ETH), Cardano (ADA), Litecoin (LTC), or Ripple (XRP). A stablecoin is a class of cryptocurrencies that attempt to offer price stability and are backed by a reserve asset, *e.g.,*gold or the value of the American dollar. Examples include USDT (Tether) and USDC.

Time Series Analysis. A time series is an n-tuple of observations collected sequentially over time. Common examples of time series include trends of interest rates and stock prices, daily high and low temperatures, the electrical activity of the heart, *etc.* The purpose of time series analysis is generally twofold: *(i)* to understand the mechanisms and the inner dynamics of an observed series, and *(ii)* forecast the future values of the series based on the historical ones. To analyze

---

[2] Some characterizations define stable coins as sub-classes of alt-coins, together with secure tokens, utility tokens, and more. We leave as future work to study in-depth the correlations between such sub-types of alt-coins.

time series as sequences of random variables (*i.e.*,stochastic processes), it is common to assume their stationarity: a time series is *stationary* if the probability laws that govern its behavior do not change, and its mean μ is constant over time. The Autoregressive Moving Average is a state-of-the-art stationary time series modeling approach, which combines an Autoregressive (AR) process of order p and of a Moving Average (MA) process of order q.

Real applications do not expose stationary trends. The Autoregressive Integrated Moving Average model (ARIMA) differentiates a nonstationary process a number d of times, until it becomes stationary. It is common to observe the presence of a seasonality in the trend of a time series, especially in applications where cyclical tendencies are very common (like business or economics). To handle periodical components, a common model is the Seasonal Autoregressive Integrated Moving Average (SARIMA), that can be mapped to a standard ARIMA model in absence of seasonality [10].

A significant progress in time series modeling was introduced by *temporally-aware* ML models, *i.e.*,Recurrent Neural Networks (RNNs) (see Fig. 2). In those, the behaviour of hidden neurons is not only determined by the activations in previous hidden layers, but also by the activations at earlier times. The activation function for every hidden layer of a RNN is: $h^{(t)} = f(h^{(t-1)}, x^{(t)}, \theta)$. There, the hidden layer at the time t, $h^{(t)}$, is a function of the previous status, $h^{(t-1)}$, of the current input $x^{(t)}$ and of the activation function adopted, θ.

The training process of RNNs is usually complex, due to the *unstable gradient problem*: the gradient of the adopted cost function tends to get smaller or bigger as it is propagated back through layers, resulting in a final vanishing or exploding effect, respectively. RNNs are unable to model *long term dependencies*, lacking predictive ability when dealing with long sequences of data. To solve this problem, more effective sequence models are adopted in practical applications, such as Long Short-Term Memory (LSTM) and networks based on the Gated Recurrent Unit (GRU). Such *gated RNN* architectures allow the network to accumulate information over a long time period, learning to decide how to forget the old states once that information has been used and processed [11].

Table 1. Mean/standard deviation for the top-5 cryptocoins since January 2020 (Open, High, Low and Close expressed in 1K US dollars, volume and market Cap in 1B US dollars).

Coin	Open	High	Low	Close	Volume	Market Cap
BTC	29.39/19.55	30.18/20.07	28.50/18.92	29.42/19.53	39.63/20.41	550.41/368.54
ETH	1.57/1.44	1.63/1.49	1.51/1.39	1.57/1.44	20.48/11.05	184.19/170.90
BNB	0.20/0.21	0.21/0.22	0.19/0.20	0.20/0.21	1.63/1.91	33.18/35.39
XRP	5.64e-4/3.94e-4	5.90e-4/4.17e-4	5.36e-4/3.68e-4	5.64e-4/3.94e-4	4.59/4.91	25.70/17.96
ADA	7.97e-4/8.21e-4	8.33e-4/8.55e-4	7.60e-4/7.84e-4	7.99e-4/8.21e-4	2.29/2.77	25.67/26.77

3   Preliminary Evaluation

We describe here our experimental evaluation of the correlations between cryptocoins. First we describe our dataset, and then we show several correlation patterns.

Dataset. We collected our dataset from CoinMarketCap [3], a leading aggregator of cryptocurrency market data. It contains records (High, Low, Open, Close, Volume and Market Capitalization) for 68 coins registered during a time frame of 25 months, namely from 24.12.2019 to 24.01.2022. "High" and "Low" are the highest and lowest prices reached by the asset during the considered time frame; "Open" and "Close" the opening and closing market prices; "Volume" the measure of how much it was traded in the last period. Finally, "Market Capitalization" indicates the total market value of its circulating supply. The dataset includes a total of 51884 observations. The resulting time series for each coin trend includes 763 steps. Table 1 reports mean and standard deviation for the gathered records and across the top-5 cryptocoins in our dataset.

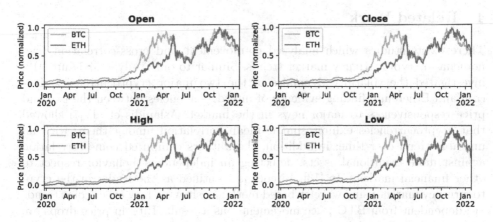

Fig. 3. Trend of Bitcoin and Ethereum prices during the last 2 years.

The two major coins in terms of Volume and Market Capitalization are Bitcoin (BTC) and Ethereum (ETH), that we selected as the benchmarks for our subsequent study. The price trend of those cryptocoins over the past two years (shown in Fig. 3) showed on average a high positive correlation (with a Pearson coefficient ≈0.9).

Correlation Patterns. The aim of the present study is to identify and analyze the presence of cross-correlation patterns in cryptocurrency trends. To do so, we analyze the correlations of 66 alt-coins present in our dataset against BTC and ETH, and for three different time frames: daily, weekly and monthly. For weekly and monthly correlations we define the sequence segments adopting a sliding window approach, where observations are grouped within a window that slides across the data stream. The daily observations for each coin are averaged over sliding partitions of 7 and 30 d respectively, and then the correlations with other coins are computed on the resulting aggregated values. Note that we postpone the study of *thumbing* windows, where there is no overlapping of data clusters, to future work. We represent those correlations, averaged among all the studied variables (*i.e.,*, High, Low, Open, Close, Volume and Market Cap), as a series of "cross-correlograms" of coins (Fig. 4). The radius of each circle represents the strength of the relation (in terms of Pearson coefficient) between each of the considered alt-coin and BTC (Figs. 4a/c/e) or ETH (Figs. 4b/d/f). The color identifies the sign of the correlation (green if positive, red otherwise). The analysis of the cross-correlogram clearly shows how the vast majority of considered alt-coins are strongly correlated with and follows the same trend of the two market leaders. Their average values of the Pearson coefficient very close to 1. Not surprisingly, the only visible exceptions are represented by the stablecoins available in our dataset (*i.e.,*, USDP, TUSD, DAI, BUSD, USDC, USDT), that are pegged to the US dollar and follow standalone trends with total independence from the rest of the coins in the market.

4   Related Work

There exists studies which analyzed co-movement and cross-correlation phenomena in cryptocurrency market trends. Similar to our study, Katsiampa [12] investigated the volatility dynamics of the two major cryptocurrencies, Bitcoin and Ethereum, finding evidence of interdependencies between the two and price responsiveness to major news in the market. Aslanidis et al. [7] showed that cryptocurrencies exhibit similar mean correlation among them, with an unstable trend over time; in addition, the authors computed coins correlation against more traditional assets, detecting an independent behavior respect to other financial markets. In [13], Bitcoin is identified as the leader in the cryptocurrency market using wavelet-based methods, showing how other coins trends are dependent from BTC price movements: as a result, Bitcoin price drops are immediately reflected in other cryptocurrency prices. Finally, [9] studied the collective behaviour for the cryptocurrency market discovering distinct and not time-persistent community structures characterized by cross-correlation.

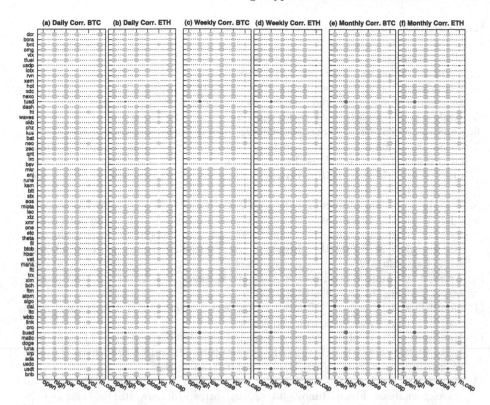

Fig. 4. Daily, weekly and monthly cross-correlations between the alt-coins and BTC/ETH.

5 Conclusion and Future Work

Cryptocoins present very volatile trends on public exchanges. In this work-in-progress paper, we presented our preliminary evaluation of the correlations between BTC, Ether and 66 other alt-coins. Our analysis shows strong correlations, suggesting alt-coins follow closely the trends of the two main ones. Following this initial study, we will further investigate the cross-correlation between the two market leaders and the alt-coins, in the perspective to forecast their price trends by using the time-series techniques from Sect. 2. We believe that our work could represent a significant starting point for further analyses in co-movement behaviors within the cryptocoin markets and in modeling and forecasting trends of the asset prices.

Metadata, analysis data, tools and code for reproducibility are available to the research community at https://github.com/quapsale/cryptoanalytics/.

References

1. Binance exchange. https://www.binance.com
2. Coinbase exchange. https://www.coinbase.com
3. CoinMarketCap web service. https://coinmarketcap.com/
4. International monetary fund. https://www.imf.org/en/Publications/WEO
5. Kraken exchange. https://www.kraken.com
6. UniSwap decentralized exchange. https://uniswap.org/
7. Aslanidis, N., Bariviera, A.F., Martínez-Ibañez, O.: An analysis of cryptocurrencies conditional cross correlations. Finan. Res. Lett. **31**, 130–137 (2019). https://doi.org/10.1016/j.frl.2019.04.019, https://www.sciencedirect.com/science/article/pii/S1544612319302168
8. Buterin, V., et al.: Ethereum white paper. GitHub Repository **1**, 22–23 (2013)
9. Chaudhari, H., Crane, M.: Cross-correlation dynamics and community structures of cryptocurrencies. J. Comput. Sci. **44**, 101–130 (2020). https://doi.org/10.1016/j.jocs.2020.101130, https://www.sciencedirect.com/science/article/pii/S1877750320304312
10. Cryer, J., Chan, K.S.: Time Series Analysis. Springer, New York, NY, USA (2008). https://doi.org/10.1007/978-0-387-75959-3
11. Goodfellow, I., Bengio, Y., Courville, A.: Deep Learning. MIT Press, Cambridge (2016). http://www.deeplearningbook.org
12. Katsiampa, P.: Volatility co-movement between bitcoin and ether. Finan. Res. Lett. **30**, 221–227 (2019). https://doi.org/10.1016/j.frl.2018.10.005, https://www.sciencedirect.com/science/article/pii/S1544612318305580
13. Kumar, A., Ajaz, T.: Co-movement in crypto-currency markets: evidences from wavelet analysis. Finan. Innov. **33** (2019). https://doi.org/10.1186/s40854-019-0143-3, https://jfin-swufe.springeropen.com/articles/10.1186/s40854-019-0143-3
14. Nakamoto, S.: Bitcoin: A peer-to-peer electronic cash system. Decentralized Bus. Rev. 212–260 (2008)

Rebop: Reputation-Based Incentives in Committee-Based Blockchains

Arian Baloochestani[(✉)], Leander Jehl, and Hein Meling

Department of Electrical Engineering and Computer Science, University of Stavanger,
Stavanger, Norway
{arian.masoudbaloochestani,leander.jehl,hein.meling}@uis.no

Abstract. Blockchains based on proof-of-work suffer from serious drawbacks, such as high computational overhead, long confirmation time, and forks. Committee-based blockchains provide an alternative that tackles these problems. These blockchains use a committee to approve a block at each height. However, rewarding the committee for their work is challenging. The reward mechanism must be fair and robust to attacks.

In this paper, we study leader-based reward mechanisms in committee-based blockchains in the presence of rational, colluding, and Byzantine committee members. First, we study the incentives of committee members to deviate and show that an existing reward mechanism is susceptible to attacks from both colluding and Byzantine members.

We then propose a reputation-based leader selection mechanism that provides sufficient incentives to coerce rational members to abide by the protocol, and significantly limits the possible gains of collusion. Additionally, our approach reduces the ability of Byzantine members to perform targeted attacks.

Keywords: Committee-based blockchains · Reward mechanisms · Incentives · Reputation-based rewarding · Fairness

1 Introduction

The blockchain was first introduced in 2008 as an infrastructure for the Bitcoin cryptocurrency [27] and has since become an appealing technology for various applications. A *blockchain* is a secure database where users share their data in a distributed and trusted environment [34]. The unknown and untrusted participants that maintain a blockchain do not rely on a trusted third party [15].

The foundation of a blockchain is its underlying consensus protocol. Processes acting on behalf of users produce blocks of transactions, and consensus protocols

This work is partially funded by the BBChain and Credence projects under grants 274451 and 288126 from the Research Council of Norway.

D. Eyers and S. Voulgaris (Eds.): DAIS 2022, LNCS 13272, pp. 37–54, 2022.
https://doi.org/10.1007/978-3-031-16092-9_4

determine how *participating processes* agree on which block to append next to the blockchain [5]. This allows processes to securely and consistently update shared states following the state machine approach [33].

There are various kinds of consensus protocols with different configurations and characteristics. In Proof-of-Work (PoW) [27] and Proof-of-Stake (PoS) [32], a single participating process is selected to propose a new block and successively rewarded if the block was valid. The probability of selecting a process is proportional to the energy and computational resources spent in PoW, or the amount of digital currency the process has invested in PoS. While PoS avoids the tremendous amounts of resources used by PoW blockchains, the mechanism suffers from various security problems such as the *nothing at stake* and the *long-range attacks* [21]. Therefore, some blockchains use a combination of PoS and a committee to overcome these drawbacks.

In committee-based blockchains, a group of processes is responsible for updating the blockchain. Numerous committee-based blockchains exists, such as Tendermint [17], LibraBFT/HotStuff [6,37], Algorand [8], and HyperLedger Fabric [4]. In these blockchains, one process is selected as the leader to propose a new block. The other committee members (aka validators) vote for this block. If a majority of validators vote for the block, it will be added to the blockchain.

Shifting the responsibility for block creation from a single process to a committee requires adjusting the reward mechanism. A fair reward mechanism should reward participating committee members and prevent free-riding processes from gaining rewards [3,25]. Designing such mechanisms involves multiple tradeoffs. The key challenges include tolerating message loss and transient outages of individual processes. Repeated retransmissions and reconfiguration can address these challenges but requires complex protocol adaptations [20]. Leader-based mechanisms are more efficient but suffer from false detections, which both benign and malicious leaders may trigger.

This paper analyzes leader-based reward mechanisms and their robustness against different attacks. Unlike previous work, we consider misbehavior from rational, colluding, and Byzantine committee members. Rational and colluding attackers try to increase their share of rewards and can be dissuaded by proper incentives. Byzantine members, however, may perform attacks regardless of the offered incentives, e.g., motivated by factors outside the system. Further, such attacks may target individual members instead of the system as a whole.

We propose Reputation-based Reward Opportunity (Rebop), which relies on reputation-based leader election to give well-behaved processes opportunities to earn a bonus for serving as leaders. Taking longer behaviour into account, Rebop is able to distinguish between a constant and one-time misbehaviour and thus significantly reduce the profitability of attacks. Different from pure monetary mechanisms, reputation-based leader election can also reduce the capabilities of Byzantine attackers, that may not care about lost rewards.

We devise a normal form game-theoretic framework for incentive schemes to determine their robustness against attacks from rational and colluding committee members. We model Rebop and Cosmos' incentive scheme [18] in this

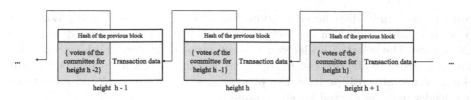

Fig. 1. Blockchain structure. Each block contains data, the previous block's hash, and proof of commit. The proof contains votes from the committee for the previous block.

framework. Our analysis shows that Rebop and Cosmos require similar bonuses to thwart attacks up to a given coalition size. However, for larger coalitions, profitable misbehavior is significantly restricted in Rebop compared to Cosmos. Further, Cosmos provides no countermeasures to restrict Byzantine behaviors.

We use simulations to verify our analytical results and evaluate our reputation-based method in more complex scenarios, including multiple concurrent attacks and message loss.

2   Committee-Based Blockchains

A blockchain is stored as a cryptographically secured append-only log that is shared among several processes. Each block or entry in the log contains data; for example, in cryptocurrencies like Bitcoin, this data is a set of new transactions in which money is transferred from one user to another. Additionally, every block contains a cryptographic hash of its predecessor, as shown in Fig. 1. These hashes ensure the integrity of the stored data. Users of the system are identified by a public key and authorized through digital signatures [22]. To ensure a consistent system state, i.e., account balances, processes need to agree on the order in which blocks are appended to the blockchain and transactions are executed. This is achieved through a consensus algorithm. The number of blocks between the genesis block and a particular block is called the *block height*.

In some consensus algorithms, such as PoW, processes compete to find and issue a new block; thus, different processes may produce more than one valid block at a particular height. This leads to different paths in the blockchain called forks, and consequently, processes will be confused about which fork to follow. To prevent forks, some blockchains use a committee to confirm the new block proposed by a leader [6,8,9,13,17]. In these blockchains, at every height, a leader is elected, responsible for proposing a new block. Then, other committee members vote for the proposed block if it is valid. The block is committed if a sufficiently large fraction of the members vote for the block in one or more rounds. The fraction and the number of rounds depend on the algorithm.

Different committee-based blockchains employ public or private leader election procedures. In private leader election, processes can secretly determine if they are the leader and publish proof of such leadership. Some blockchains, such as Algorand [8] and Snow White [9], use verifiable random functions [24] to

produce uniformly distributed random values with non-interactive proofs. All
processes run the function privately at every height, and its output determines
the leader. The selected leader can present proof of leadership along with the
proposed block to any process. In Algorand, committee members and leaders are
chosen randomly with probabilities proportional to their stakes, and more than
one leader may get elected for each round.

In a public leader election, all processes can infer who will be the next leader.
Typically, the next leader depends on randomness derived from the previous
round. In Dfinity [13], this randomness is the input of a pseudo-random per-
mutation. The original Tendermint [17] protocol uses round-robin for electing
the leader in each round. However, in current Tendermint, referred to as Cosmos [18], the probability of becoming a leader is proportional to the processes'
stake.

3   System and Protocol Model

In this section, we discuss the system model and the related assumptions. In
addition, we give a high-level model for a committee-based blockchains that
suits multiple protocols.

We assume a set $\Pi = \{p_1, p_2, ..., p_n\}$ of processes which are all functioning as
committee members. This assumption fits well for consortium-based or permissioned blockchains. However, PoS-based blockchains may also exhibit a relatively
stable committee. For example, in Cosmos, 125 processes with the most stake
are selected in the committee, and they remain until replaced by other processes with more stake. We note that it is common to pose restrictions on how
quickly deposited stake may be withdrawn [28]. Moreover, while our methods
focus on the leader, they could also be applied to systems that randomly select
the committee from a larger set of processes. We assume that the network is
synchronous, but it may lose messages.

We assume that every process p_i has a voting power $m_i \in (0, 1)$, such that
$\sum_{p_i \in \Pi} m_i = 1$. Typically, voting power will be evenly distributed among processes. To model coalitions, we also allow a process to control a larger fraction
of the total voting power than its fair share.

In our *blockchain model* progress is measured through a parameter height h,
which represents the current length of the blockchain. A block is added to the
chain at each height, following the process in Fig. 2. The details of individual
consensus algorithms are abstracted.

Several rounds might be needed for a block to be approved at some height h.
At each round t, a leader $L_t \in \Pi$ is selected to propose a new block. We assume
that leader selection is randomized and write $P[L_t = p_i]$ for the probability that
p_i becomes the leader at round t. We further assume that $P[L_t = p_i]$ may depend
on the voting power m_i and the history of the blockchain up to height $h - 1$.

To publish a new block at height h, the leader needs to collect votes for the
previous block, proposed at height $h - 1$. As shown in Fig. 1, these votes need
to be included in the new block. We use a parameter f to specify, the amount
of voting power for which votes may be missing:

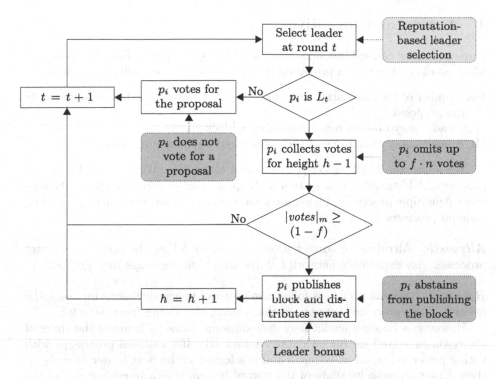

Fig. 2. Overview of the system model. At every height, a leader collects votes for the preceding block and publishes a new block. The figure also shows possible attacks (red) and countermeasures (blue) discussed in Sects. 4 and 5. (Color figure online)

$$|votes|_m = \sum_{p_i \in voted} m_i \geq 1 - f, \quad \text{where } f \text{ is typically } \frac{1}{3},$$

If the leader cannot collect enough votes the system progresses to the next round. The parameter f typically also specifies the amount of voting power (processes) that can be faulty, and may vary depending on the protocol. Committee members sign their votes with their private keys; hence, the identity of each vote is known to all processes. We assume that digital signatures cannot be forged. Processes broadcast their votes for the next potential leader to collect.

A reward R is paid out to motivate the processes to follow the protocol at height h. The reward is distributed, according to their voting power, among the processes whose votes are included at height $h + 1$. This ensures that processes that did not participate do not receive a reward. We assume that R is constant and is not related to the contents of the block. R may be fixed in a cryptocurrency due to economic concerns such as inflation and money circulation.

As shown in Fig. 2, a faulty leader may omit some votes. Next, we discuss how and why this might happen and how it affects the utility of the processes.

4   Attacks and Incentives

Some processes can exhibit malicious behavior by deviating from the protocol. More precisely, the model presented in Sect. 3 allows three different attacks:

I A member of the committee may not vote for a proposal or fail to disseminate the proposal.
II A leader may abstain from publishing a block.
III A leader may omit some of the votes when publishing a block.

We follow the BAR model [1], assuming altruistic, rational, and Byzantine processes. Additionally, in a system with open membership, a single entity may control multiple processes. Therefore, we also consider the possibility of colluding rational processes [35].

Altruistic. Altruistic or correct processes strictly follow the protocol. Correct processes may experience network failures, and their messages may get lost.

Rational. Rational processes follow the protocol unless deviating increases the reward. These processes vote to get the reward, abstaining from Attack I.

However, a rational leader may exclude some votes to increase the share of the reward received for his own vote (Attack III). If a rational process p_r with voting power m_r voted at height h and is selected as the next leader $p_r = L_{h+1}$, then it may increase its share of the reward by omitting a fraction $e < f$ of the votes. Thus, instead of the honest share $share[honest] = m_r R$, p_r will receive $share[omit_e] = \frac{m_r R}{(1-e)}$. We can see that p_r has a solid motivation to deviate from the protocol to maximize its share of the reward. Authors in [17] claim that this problem will not occur due to the tit-for-tat strategy taken by the validators; however, due to the probability of message loss in the network, no one can prove that it is excluded from the reward intentionally. Thus, a process that is subject to message loss would suffer unfairly from such retaliation.

Finally, resource constraint rational processes may also try to avoid the additional steps performed by a leader, leading to Attack II.

Colluding. While a rational process p_r deviates from the protocol if that leads to more profit, a coalition works together to increase the group's total profit. We model colluding processes as a single process with a larger voting share. Similar to rational processes, colluding processes also have the same motivation to perform Attack III.

Byzantine. Byzantine processes arbitrarily deviate from the protocol. Unlike rational processes, Byzantine attackers do not care about their outcome; because they have an external motivation unknown to anyone else. They may, for example, try to harm the system or specific other processes. Committee based protocols remain functional despite a certain fraction (f) of Byzantine processes. We therefore ignore attacks on the protocol in this work and focus on the rewarding mechanism, especially on targeted attacks, where Byzantine processes try to reduce the reward of targeted committee members. In such a targeted attack, a Byzantine process may selectively distribute its vote (Attack I) or, if selected as the leader, ignore the votes of some processes in the committee (Attack III). Note that incentives cannot discourage Byzantine behavior because Byzantine processes are motivated by external goals. Instead of monetary punishment, we need to reduce Byzantine processes' ability to conduct attacks.

In the next section we present our reputation-based incentive scheme.

5   Rebop: Reputation-Based Reward Opportunity

In a committee-based scheme, the leader role carries a special responsibility and must perform additional tasks. Therefore, the leader should be rewarded more than other committee members. Additionally, this reward should discourage rational or colluding processes from omitting votes. We note that benign leaders may also lose votes due to message loss. In our incentive scheme, Rebop, we reward correct leaders with the possibility of additional earnings rather than punishing misbehavior.

As the flowchart in Fig. 2 indicates, Rebop combines two mechanisms. We use reputation-based leader election to select leaders in each round. In addition, we propose to give a fixed fraction of the block reward as a bonus to the leader to enforce long-term benefits for rational and colluding processes. The bonus encourages leaders to actually propose a block, preventing Attack II.

If we penalize deviating processes for Attack III by selecting them less often as the leader in the subsequent blocks, we reduce the ability of Byzantine attackers. Additionally, deviating processes are punished by losing bonus now given to other leaders. This can motivate rational processes against Attack III. Rebop computes *reputation* based on the average number of votes a process p_i has included as the leader during the last T blocks. Let $leader(i, h)$ determine whether p_i was a leader at height h:

$$leader(i, h) = \begin{cases} 1 & \text{if } p_i \text{ is } L_h \\ 0 & \text{otherwise} \end{cases}$$

Then, the reputation $r_{i,h} \in [0, 1]$ of p_i at height h is calculated as:

$$r_{i,h} = \begin{cases} 1 & \text{if } \sum_{t=h-T}^{h} leader(i, t) = 0 \\ \dfrac{\sum_{t=h-T}^{h} leader(i,t) \cdot \left(\frac{f - e_t}{f}\right)^\alpha}{\sum_{t=h-T}^{h} leader(i,t)} & \text{otherwise} \end{cases} \tag{1}$$

where $e_t \in [0, f]$ is the number of votes missing from the block at height t, and $\alpha \geq 1$ is a parameter of the protocol. T should be selected in a way to allow each process to become the leader at least once during the next T rounds. For $\alpha > 1$ repeated omission of even a few votes results in a lower reputation than a one time omission of many votes. This helps to reduce the ability of Byzantine attackers to omit individual players. Thus, larger α gives better protection from Byzantine attackers, but may open to additional attacks from colluding processes as we show below. A large α may also result in punishments for correct processes that suffer from message loss.

We write r_i for the reputation of p_i at the current height The chances of the process p_i to be selected as the leader is proportional to r_i and m_i. The more the reputation of p_i, the more chances for it to be the leader, and consequently, the more bonus it gets.

$$P[p_i = L_h] = \frac{r_i m_i}{\sum_{i \le n} r_i m_i} \tag{2}$$

Rational players may not produce a block if they lose too many votes to prevent their reputation from being slashed (Attack II). However, because reputation is an average of the number of votes gathered in the last T blocks, a small value for reputation in one round cannot affect the total reputation much.

In addressing Attack III, we note that reputation-based leader election can make Attack I more attractive for rational and colluding players. By omitting votes and reducing the reputation of other processes, rational processes may try to gain a larger share of the rewards. However, our analysis in the next section shows that the reward lost to this attack is often higher than the earned bonuses.

6   Incentive Analysis

We use game theory to analyze the different strategies of committee members. Specifically, we use a normal form game $G = \langle N, S, U \rangle$, where N is the player set, S is the strategy set, and U is the utility function.

Player Set. We consider players in the game as the processes in the committee who contribute to maintaining the blockchain ($N = \Pi$). We model colluding processes as one player p_i with voting-power $m_i \in [0, f]$.

Strategy Set. To simplify our analysis, we only consider constant strategies, i.e. strategies where players follow conduct a certain attack with constant probability every round. We analyze some additional strategies through simulation. The strategy $S(\rho, e, e_a)$ of a player is parameterized by $\rho \in [0, 1]$, $e \in [0, f]$, and $e_a \in [0, m_i]$. If a process p_i is a follower, it votes with only $m_i - e_a$ fraction of its power for a proposed block. If it is the leader, it votes with its full power. Additionally, a leader publishing a block will omit e votes with probability ρ. With probability $1 - \rho$ it will include all votes it received. Therefore, having $e > 0$ and $\rho > 0$ indicate Attack III, while Attack I is demonstrated by having $e_a > 0$.

The strategy profile $S(0, 0, 0)$ in which the players always follow the protocol is used by Altruistic processes, and is denoted by S_{honest}.

Utility Function. We define the utility function of each player as its expected payoff during a round, excluding the first T. This payoff includes both the voting reward and leader bonus. We note that due to our restriction to constant strategies, the expected payoff is constant for all rounds after the first T.

6.1   Baseline Analysis

As a baseline, we analyze the incentive mechanism introduced in Cosmos [18]. In this mechanism, the leader L_{h+1} receives an extra reward $b \times R$ as a bonus if it does include votes from all committee members. If votes from a fraction $e \leq f$ of the committee members are missing, the bonus is reduced to $b \times \frac{f-e}{f}$. We refer to this incentive scheme as the **variational bonus**. In this scheme, the expected payoff of players only depends on their behaviour in the current round. We, therefore, ignore the parameters ρ in the strategy profile and concentrate on e. In rounds, where p_i is the leader, its payoff for strategies S_{honest} and $S(1, e, 0)$ is calculated as:

$$share[\text{honest}] = m_i \cdot R + b \cdot R \quad share[\text{S(1,e,0)}] = \frac{m_i \cdot R}{1-e} + \frac{f-e}{f} \cdot b \cdot R \quad (3)$$

In order to prevent rational processes from excluding each other, the bonus must ensure that $share[\text{honest}] > share[\text{S(1,e,0)}]$. Thus, Inequality (4) must hold:

$$b > \frac{f \cdot m_i}{1-e} \quad (4)$$

Example. *If we consider $f = 1/3$, then b must be greater than $1/(2 \cdot n)$ to stop a rational process. For instance, the size of the committee in Cosmos is between 100 and 300. A block needs at least 2/3 of the votes to be considered as approved. Therefore, according to Eq. 4, a bonus of $b = 0.005$ would be sufficient to prevent misbehaviour in individual rational nodes. The bonus of 5% employed in Cosmos is sufficient to thwart off coalitions of size up to 10%.*

Theorem 1. *If and only if Eq. 4 holds, for all m_i, the strategy profile S_{honest} is a Nash equilibrium.*

Proof. If Eq. 4 holds, $share[\text{S(1,e,0)}]$ is smaller than $share[\text{honest}]$, meaning the payoff of staying correct is more than omitting other processes for p_i with power m_i. Therefore, if all other players follow S_{honest}, player p_i cannot increase its payoff by changing e and omitting votes, when it is the leader.

Lemma 1. *The right side of Eq. 4 reaches its maximum for $e = f$ fraction of the committee.*

6.2   Collusion Resistance of Rebop

Attack III. To analyze the resistance of Rebop against Attack III, we focus on strategies deviating from S_{honest} through $\rho > 0$ and $e > 0$.

Lemma 2. *Any strategy $S(\rho, e, e_a)$ is dominated by a strategy $S' = S(\rho', f, e_a)$.*

We omit the detailed proof due to space constraints. The idea is to choose ρ', such that for $\alpha = 1$ both strategies give the same reputation. For $\alpha > 1$, S' will even give a larger reputation. Since according to Lemma 1, omitting a larger fraction is more profitable, S' gives a bigger reward.

Assume now, that all players but p_i follow S_{honest}. Further, we assume that p_i follows a strategy $S' = S(\rho', f, 0)$. If $\rho' = 0$ (i.e. $S' = S_{honest}$), the expected payoff received by p_i is:

$$payoff_i[S_{honest}] = P_{honest}[L_h = p_i] \cdot b \cdot R + m_i \cdot R \tag{5}$$

where $P_{honest}[L_h = p_i] = m_i$, since all players have reputation 1. If p_i follows S', as a payoff, it receives $\frac{m_i R}{1-f}$ reward in the rounds it is the leader and decides to omit f votes (with probability ρ).

$$payoff_i[\text{omit}] = P_{S'}[L_h = p_i]\left(\rho\frac{m_i R}{1-f} + (1-\rho)m_i R + bR\right) + P_{S'}[L_h \neq p_i]m_i R \tag{6}$$

Following S', $r_i = (1 - \rho)$. This gives the following equation:

$$P_{S'}[L_h = p_i] = \frac{m_i(1-\rho)}{1 - m_i + m_i(1-\rho)} \tag{7}$$

By comparing the Eqs. 5 and 6, the bonus threshold for preventing the colluding behaviour is derived as follows:

$$b > \frac{m_i \cdot f \cdot (1-\rho)}{(1-f)(1-m_i)} \tag{8}$$

Lemma 3. *For $\rho \in [0,1]$ the right hand side of Inequation 8 reaches its maximum when ρ is 0.*

Theorem 2. *If Inequation 8 holds, and all players but p_i follow S_{honest}, then p_i will receive a worse payoff following S' than following S_{honest}.*

Example. *Considering $f = 1/3$, in Rebop, a bonus of 0.005 is sufficient to motivate rational players not to omit votes in a system with more than 100 players with equal power. A bonus of 5% allows Rebop to thwart off coalitions of size up to 9%.*

Attack I. In Rebop, a process p_i may also try to reduce others reputation by not voting for their proposed blocks with part of its power $e_a < m_i$. We note that this attack becomes less effective if p_i itself also omits votes. We therefore analyze the payoff of strategies $S_a = S(0, 0, e_a)$. By reducing others' reputations, a process itself receives a bonus more often. However, it loses the m_a part of its reward by not voting to the approved blocks. This attack is unprofitable if the lost reward is bigger than the expected increase in bonus.

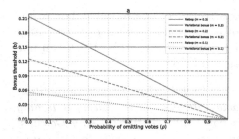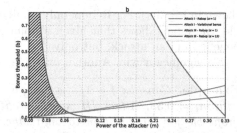

Fig. 3. a) A comparison between variational bonus (red lines) and reputation-based leader election with a fixed bonus (blue lines). The plot illustrates the minimal bonus to make omitting votes with probability ρ unprofitable for 3 different values of m_i. b) Bonus threshold for preventing Attack III for reputation-based leader election and variational bonus, and Attack I for $\alpha = [1, 15]$ and $e_a = m_i$. The blue and hatched areas show the bonuses that can tolerate both attacks together. In both plots $f = \frac{1}{3}$. (Color figure online)

$$\left(e_a - \left(\frac{m_i - e_a}{1 - e_a}\right) e_a\right) P_{S_a}[L_h = p_i] > P_{S_a}[L_h = p_i]b - P_{S_{honest}}[L_h = p_i]b \quad (9)$$

Under strategy S_a the reputation of p_i is 1, while the reputation of all correct players is $r_{c,a} = \left(\frac{f - e_a}{f}\right)^{\alpha}$. Thus

$$P_{S_a}[L_h = p_i] = \frac{m_i}{r_{c,a} \cdot (1 - m_i) + m_i} \quad (10)$$

Simplifying Inequation 9, the bonus threshold for stopping Attack I is calculated as follows:

$$b < \frac{e_a \cdot r_{c,a}}{m_i(1 - e_a)(1 - r_{c,a})} \quad (11)$$

The next theorem follows from the above analysis and Theorem 2.

Theorem 3. *If Inequation 11 and 8 hold, for all m_i, the strategy profile S_{honest} is a Nash equilibrium.*

Discussion. Figure 3 b) correlates the bonus size with the maximum attacker power tolerated. We see that a small bonus tolerates a similar coalition size for both analyzed methods. Nevertheless, a larger bonus is needed for Rebop to tolerate larger coalitions. Additionally, the analysis on Attack I shows that for Rebop, there exists a maximum bonus for keeping a given coalition correct. Different from the lower bound on the bonus, this upper bound depends on the value α.

Interestingly, Lemma 3 suggests that for processes with power above the threshold, the two methods differ in which attacks become profitable. This is shown in Fig. 3 a). For Rebop, only small omissions become profitable. For example, the figure shows that given a bonus of 5% a coalition with $m_i = 0.1$ may benefit from an attack, but only if $\rho \leq 0.1$. While effective, this attack will not give a significant win. Another example is given below:

Example. *Consider $f = 1/3$, a bonus $b = 0.1$. Under Rebop, even for a coalition with $m_i = 0.33$, Attack III is only profitable with $\rho < 0.6$, meaning it is only profitable for the coalition to omit others votes 60% of time. Using Cosmos' variational bonus however, all attacks with $e > 0$ are profitable for the same coalition, meaning it is profitable to omit others in every round.*

6.3   Preventing Byzantine Attacks

None of the above schemes prevent Byzantine attackers from excluding targeted processes when they are the leader. In Cosmos, for example, Byzantine processes lose reward by attacking other processes, but it does not stop them from misbehaviour. However, different from the Cosmos' variational bonus, Rebop reduces the abilities of Byzantine attackers by prioritizing correct processes as the leaders. Assume a Byzantine process p_b with voting-power m_b in the system. Assume p_b is targeting a victim p_v with power m_v. In the schemes that use a random or round-robin leader election (Cosmos), the probability of p_b to be selected as the next round leader is always constant and proportional to its power m_b. In Rebop the probability for p_b to be the leader is reduced with its reputation r_b:

$$P[L_h = p_b] = \frac{m_b \cdot r_b}{m_b \cdot r_b + (1 - m_b)} = \frac{m_b (f - m_v)^\alpha}{m_b (f - m_v)^\alpha + f^\alpha (1 - m_b)} \quad (12)$$

According to Eq. 12 Byzantine attacks also on small victims (e.g. $m_v = 1\%$) can be significantly reduced by choosing a large enough α. Note that while Rebop reduces the ability of attacker to do Attack III, it gives the power to attacker for Attack I. The effect of attacks is further analyzed in Sect. 7.2.

7   Simulation Results

We conduct simulations to verify our analysis and evaluate additional situations, including Byzantine attacks. Since the committee's composition has little effect on our proposed methods, we use a constant committee in all simulations. For simplicity, we assume that all processes have an equal voting power which does not change during the experiments. We use $f = 1/3$, $|\Pi| = n = 100$, and $T = 10\,000$ in all simulations, and run for $60\,000$ rounds. This ensures that even with a small reputation of 0.05 a node is likely the leader at least once during T rounds.

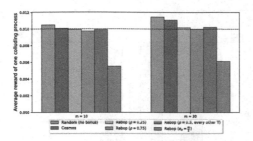

Fig. 4. Final share of one colluding process with two different coalition sizes for different attacks. In a fair environment, the share of each process is 0.01 of the total reward.

7.1   Resistance Against Colluding Processes

To show the impact of Rebop on colluding processes, we simulate Attack III by coalitions with 10% and 30% of the committee members. There is no message loss in this simulation, and the leaders receive all the votes. Bonus is set to 5% of the block reward. We evaluate Cosmos' variational bonus and the basic protocol without bonus with $e = f$ and $\rho = 1$.

We also simulated Rebop with 4 different strategies for the colluding processes: 1) $e = f$ and $\rho = 0.25$. 2) $e = f$ and $\rho = 0.75$. 3) attack every other T with $e = f$ and $\rho = 0.5$. 4) $e_a = \frac{m}{2}$.

The results of this simulation are shown in Fig. 4. It is evident that under random leader election with no bonus, even a 10% coalition can benefit from attacking the system. Variational bonus (Cosmos) makes things better, but forming a coalition in large sizes leads to a significant outcome; colluding processes can gain more than their fair share from the system by excluding any process other than themselves. However, Rebop is effective against such behavior. Even the large coalition of 30% benefits more from fewer omissions ($\rho = 0.25$). Thus, the 5% bonus is sufficient to limit attacks. In addition, because the bonus is small, Attack I is not effective. Note that attacking every other T with $\rho = 0.5$ leads to almost the same reward as attacking every round with $\rho = 0.25$.

7.2   Byzantine Resistance

We simulate the effect of Rebop in the presence of message loss and Byzantine attacks with $\alpha = 1$ and $\alpha = 15$. We also used the variational bonus (Cosmos) as our baseline. Figure 5 shows how much the resulting shares are reduced and increase through message loss and attacks. We use a bonus of $b = 5\%$. Processes exhibit different message loss and attack behavior, as summarized in Table 1. We assume that a leader with message loss loses every message with the constant probability given in the table.

Comparing shares of under attack processes, we see that Cosmos allows Byzantine processes to inflict significant harm. Consistent with our results on coalition resistance, the attackers (G7-G10) gain less than the correct G1. Rebop reduces the harm done by Attack III. G6, which has voting power 5%, loses 9%

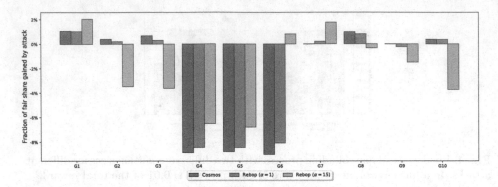

Fig. 5. The difference between final share and fair share (0.01) under message loss and attack for processes in three different configurations: random leader selection with variational bonus (Cosmos), Rebop with $\alpha = 1$, and Rebop with $\alpha = 15$. Processes are categorized into 10 groups based on Table 1.

Table 1. Summary of message loss and Byzantine attacks in the Byzantine resistance experiment.

Group	Type	Group size	Message loss	Target	Attack
G1	Correct	42	-	-	-
G2	Correct	10	5%	-	-
G3	Correct	1	-	-	-
G4	Correct	1	-	-	-
G5	Correct	1	-	-	-
G6	Correct	5	-	-	-
G7	Byzantine	10	-	G3	Attack I
G8	Byzantine	10	-	G4	Attack III
G9	Byzantine	10	-	G5	Attack I and Attack III
G10	Byzantine	10	-	G6	Attack III

of its fair share with Cosmos, 8% in Rebop with $\alpha = 1$ and gains 0.8% if α is increased to 15. For victims with smaller voting power (G5, G6), Rebop is less effective but still outperforms Cosmos. Our method still leaves some ability for attacks. That is because our model cannot distinguish between votes omitted by attackers and those omitted through message loss. We also note from G3's share that a large α opens the possibility of Attack I. To this end, the α should be carefully selected. However, even under this attack, the attacker G7 earns less than the correct G1.

8   Related Works

Fair rewarding mechanisms for blockchains have been studied for different consensus types and perspectives [11,12,30,31]. In the following, we restrict exposition to committee-based blockchains.

Lagaillardie et al. [19] studied the fairness of Tendermint in the presence of rational processes. They proposed delayed rewarding, which allows votes for a block at height h to be included and rewarded up to the height $h+\Delta$. Amoussou-Guenou et al. [2] analyzed the fairness of the rewarding mechanism used in Tendermint. They proved that the current rewarding mechanism used by Tendermint is not fair under message loss. They also proved that if a system is eventually synchronous and Byzantine behavior is detectable, an eventual fair rewarding mechanism exists for it. This differs from our assumptions, where Byzantine behavior is indistinguishable from message loss. They further extended their work in [3] to study fairness in all committee-based blockchains. They analyzed the fairness of two critical elements of committee-based blockchains: rewarding mechanisms and selection mechanisms. Liu et al. [23] proposed a fair selection mechanism for permissionless committee based blockchains, which has two main components: the mining process and the confirmation of the new nodes list. Motepalli et al. [25] designed a framework for analyzing different reward mechanisms in PoS-based blockchains using evolutionary game theory.

All of the above works either do not consider Byzantine behavior or assume that such behavior, especially denial to receive a message, can be detected. On the other hand, FairLedger [20] proposes a detection mechanism that includes both echoing messages in case of message loss and explicit reconfiguration in case of detection.

Using reputations for different areas such as blockchain is not new. Many approaches assign a score to each user that represents the probability of that user to behave honestly [7,14,16,26]. De Oliveira et al. [29] proposed a reputation-based consensus mechanism to overcome the problem of high energy consumption. In their model, each node needs to have a higher reputation than a threshold to append a new block to the blockchain. Do et al. [10] presented an improvement for delegated PoS by replacing coin-staking with a reputation-based ranking system. Wang et al. [36] proposed a reputation-based incentive module that can be added to most consensus algorithms and help them to achieve a better consensus state. In most of the current approaches, reputations deter the reward of each process. This is different from our proposed method in which only a small part of the reward is given based on the reputation, and its main purpose is to take the ability to misbehave away from the processes.

9   Conclusion

We have analyzed different attacks on leader-based reward mechanisms in committee-based blockchains. We showed that rational processes might gain more than their fair share by building a coalition, and Byzantine processes can reduce others' share of rewards. Then, we proposed Rebop, which uses a leader bonus and reputation-based leader election to overcome these attacks. Our analysis proves the ability of the proposed method to tackle these problems. We show that Rebop reduces the effect of Byzantine attacks, which the bonus and incentives alone do not achieve.

References

1. Aiyer, A.S., Alvisi, L., Clement, A., Dahlin, M., Martin, J.P., Porth, C.: Bar fault tolerance for cooperative services. In: Proceedings of the Twentieth ACM Symposium on Operating Systems Principles, pp. 45–58 (2005)
2. Amoussou-Guenou, Y., Del Pozzo, A., Potop-Butucaru, M., Tucci-Piergiovanni, S.: Correctness and fairness of tendermint-core blockchains. arXiv preprint arXiv:1805.08429 (2018)
3. Amoussou-Guenou, Y., del Pozzo, A., Potop-Butucaru, M., Tucci-Piergiovanni, S.: On fairness in committee-based blockchains. In: 2nd International Conference on Blockchain Economics, Security and Protocols (Tokenomics 2020) (2020)
4. Androulaki, E., et al.: Hyperledger fabric: a distributed operating system for permissioned blockchains. In: Proceedings of the Thirteenth EuroSys Conference, pp. 1–15 (2018)
5. Bano, S., et al.: Consensus in the age of blockchains. arXiv preprint arXiv:1711.03936 (2017)
6. Baudet, M., et al.: State machine replication in the libra blockchain. The Libra Association, Technical report (2019)
7. Cai, W., Jiang, W., Xie, K., Zhu, Y., Liu, Y., Shen, T.: Dynamic reputation-based consensus mechanism: real-time transactions for energy blockchain. Int. J. Distrib. Sens. Netw. **16**(3), 1550147720907335 (2020)
8. Chen, J., Micali, S.: Algorand: a secure and efficient distributed ledger. Theoret. Comput. Sci. **777**, 155–183 (2019)
9. Daian, P., Pass, R., Shi, E.: Snow White: robustly reconfigurable consensus and applications to provably secure proof of stake. In: Goldberg, I., Moore, T. (eds.) FC 2019. LNCS, vol. 11598, pp. 23–41. Springer, Cham (2019). https://doi.org/10.1007/978-3-030-32101-7_2
10. Do, T., Nguyen, T., Pham, H.: Delegated proof of reputation: a novel blockchain consensus. In: Proceedings of the 2019 International Electronics Communication Conference, pp. 90–98 (2019)
11. Fanti, G., Kogan, L., Oh, S., Ruan, K., Viswanath, P., Wang, G.: Compounding of wealth in proof-of-stake cryptocurrencies. In: Goldberg, I., Moore, T. (eds.) FC 2019. LNCS, vol. 11598, pp. 42–61. Springer, Cham (2019). https://doi.org/10.1007/978-3-030-32101-7_3
12. Garay, J., Kiayias, A., Leonardos, N.: The bitcoin backbone protocol: analysis and applications. In: Oswald, E., Fischlin, M. (eds.) EUROCRYPT 2015. LNCS, vol. 9057, pp. 281–310. Springer, Heidelberg (2015). https://doi.org/10.1007/978-3-662-46803-6_10
13. Hanke, T., Movahedi, M., Williams, D.: DFINITY technology overview series, consensus system. arXiv preprint arXiv:1805.04548 (2018)
14. He, Q., Wu, D., Khosla, P.: SORI: a secure and objective reputation-based incentive scheme for ad-hoc networks. In: 2004 IEEE Wireless Communications and Networking Conference, pp. 825–830. IEEE (2004)

15. Herlihy, M., Moir, M.: Enhancing accountability and trust in distributed ledgers. arXiv preprint arXiv:1606.07490 (2016)
16. Kantarci, B., Glasser, P.M., Foschini, L.: Crowdsensing with social network-aided collaborative trust scores. In: 2015 IEEE Global Communications Conference (GLOBECOM), pp. 1–6. IEEE (2015)
17. Kwon, J.: Tendermint: consensus without mining. Draft v. 0.6, fall 1(11) (2014)
18. Kwon, J., Buchman, E.: Cosmos: a network of distributed ledgers (2016). https://cosmos.network/whitepaper
19. Lagaillardie, N., Djari, M.A., Gürcan, Ö.: A computational study on fairness of the tendermint blockchain protocol. Information 10(12), 378 (2019)
20. Lev-Ari, K., Spiegelman, A., Keidar, I., Malkhi, D.: FairLedger: a fair blockchain protocol for financial institutions. In: 23rd International Conference on Principles of Distributed Systems (OPODIS 2019) (2020)
21. Li, W., Andreina, S., Bohli, J.-M., Karame, G.: Securing proof-of-stake blockchain protocols. In: Garcia-Alfaro, J., Navarro-Arribas, G., Hartenstein, H., Herrera-Joancomartí, J. (eds.) ESORICS/DPM/CBT -2017. LNCS, vol. 10436, pp. 297–315. Springer, Cham (2017). https://doi.org/10.1007/978-3-319-67816-0_17
22. Liu, J., Li, W., Karame, G.O., Asokan, N.: Toward fairness of cryptocurrency payments. IEEE Secur. Priv. 16(3), 81–89 (2018)
23. Liu, Y., Liu, J., Zhang, Z., Yu, H.: A fair selection protocol for committee-based permissionless blockchains. Comput. Secur. 91, 101718 (2020)
24. Micali, S., Rabin, M., Vadhan, S.: Verifiable random functions. In: 40th Annual Symposium on Foundations of Computer Science, pp. 120–130. IEEE (1999)
25. Motepalli, S., Jacobsen, H.A.: Reward mechanism for blockchains using evolutionary game theory. arXiv preprint arXiv:2104.05849 (2021)
26. Mousa, H., Mokhtar, S.B., Hasan, O., Younes, O., Hadhoud, M., Brunie, L.: Trust management and reputation systems in mobile participatory sensing applications: a survey. Comput. Netw. 90, 49–73 (2015)
27. Nakamoto, S.: Bitcoin: a peer-to-peer electronic cash system. Technical report (2008)
28. Nguyen, C.T., Hoang, D.T., Nguyen, D.N., Niyato, D., Nguyen, H.T., Dutkiewicz, E.: Proof-of-stake consensus mechanisms for future blockchain networks: fundamentals, applications and opportunities. IEEE Access 7, 85727–85745 (2019)
29. de Oliveira, M.T., Reis, L.H., Medeiros, D.S., Carrano, R.C., Olabarriaga, S.D., Mattos, D.M.: Blockchain reputation-based consensus: a scalable and resilient mechanism for distributed mistrusting applications. Comput. Netw. 179, 107367 (2020)
30. Pass, R., Shi, E.: FruitChains: a fair blockchain. In: Proceedings of the ACM Symposium on Principles of Distributed Computing, pp. 315–324 (2017)
31. Pass, R., Shi, E.: The sleepy model of consensus. In: Takagi, T., Peyrin, T. (eds.) ASIACRYPT 2017. LNCS, vol. 10625, pp. 380–409. Springer, Cham (2017). https://doi.org/10.1007/978-3-319-70697-9_14
32. Saleh, F.: Blockchain without waste: proof-of-stake. Rev. Financ. Stud. 34, 1156–1190 (2018)
33. Schneider, F.B.: Implementing fault-tolerant services using the state machine approach: a tutorial. ACM Comput. Surv. (CSUR) 22(4), 299–319 (1990)
34. Sukhwani, H., Martínez, J.M., Chang, X., Trivedi, K.S., Rindos, A.: Performance modeling of PBFT consensus process for permissioned blockchain network (hyperledger fabric). In: 2017 IEEE 36th Symposium on Reliable Distributed Systems (SRDS), pp. 253–255. IEEE (2017)

35. Vilaça, X., Denysyuk, O., Rodrigues, L.: Asynchrony and collusion in the N-party BAR transfer problem. In: Even, G., Halldórsson, M.M. (eds.) SIROCCO 2012. LNCS, vol. 7355, pp. 183–194. Springer, Heidelberg (2012). https://doi.org/10.1007/978-3-642-31104-8_16
36. Wang, E.K., Liang, Z., Chen, C.M., Kumari, S., Khan, M.K.: PORX: a reputation incentive scheme for blockchain consensus of IIoT. Futur. Gener. Comput. Syst. **102**, 140–151 (2020)
37. Yin, M., Malkhi, D., Reiter, M.K., Gueta, G.G., Abraham, I.: HotStuff: BFT consensus with linearity and responsiveness. In: Proceedings of the 2019 ACM Symposium on Principles of Distributed Computing, pp. 347–356 (2019)

Fault Tolerance

Lesser Evil: Embracing Failure to Protect Overall System Availability

Viktória Fördős[1,2]([⊠]) [iD] and Alexandre Jorge Barbosa Rodrigues[1] [iD]

[1] Cisco Systems, Stockholm, Sweden
{vfordos,albarbos}@cisco.com
[2] Faculty of Informatics, ELTE, Eötvös Loránd University, Budapest, Hungary

Abstract. Low memory conditions degrade system performance, challenge programs to fulfil their SLA and can lead to out-of-memory errors causing a major system outage. Running low on memory is an especially dangerous situation in case of mission critical, embedded Erlang systems with high availability requirements. In such systems, total system outage must be avoided at all costs. Nonetheless, no solution exists today that can be added to an Erlang system without code modification and would treat memory pressure out of the box.

We propose an approach, called Lesser Evil, that can treat low memory pressure in any fault-tolerant Erlang system without the need of any code modification. Our experiments suggest that, with the help of Lesser Evil, an embedded Erlang system can survive low memory conditions and avoid a major outage.

Keywords: Embedded systems · Memory management · Fault tolerance · Erlang

1 Introduction

In our digitalised world we depend on mission critical, embedded systems. These systems need to be always available regardless of the current load on the system. Parallelism is a key enabler to accommodate a system to variable workload. However, what stays constant in a system is the total memory installed (per a single host). If a system runs low on available memory, it will not perform as expected. Since it is struggling to allocate memory enough to execute requests, it will not satisfy its QoS metrics, neither SLA requirements. Considering best case scenarios, its performance will degrade while in the worst case the program will stop with an out-of-memory error causing the system to reboot. Taking into account that embedded systems have strongly constrained resources and slow processing capabilities, the reboot can take significant amount of time while the system stays offline. Hence, running low on memory is a critical event in case of mission critical, embedded systems that should not be ignored as it can compromise the availability of the system.

© IFIP International Federation for Information Processing 2022
Published by Springer Nature Switzerland AG 2022
D. Eyers and S. Voulgaris (Eds.): DAIS 2022, LNCS 13272, pp. 57–73, 2022.
https://doi.org/10.1007/978-3-031-16092-9_5

The presented problem is especially relevant in case of embedded systems that are written in Erlang. The Erlang programming language was designed in the Ericsson software technology lab for systems that will never stop or fail. Early use cases of Erlang at Ericsson include a multi-service switch, AXD 301 [12], where the control system was implemented in Erlang. Since then, Erlang has become well-known and used in the telecommunication segment, multiple companies have decided to adapt Erlang to implement mission critical, embedded systems. An illustrative example of the significance of Erlang in this sector is that Cisco ships about 2 million devices per year with Erlang in them and that 90% of all internet traffic goes through Erlang controlled nodes [4].

Motivation. Running low on memory is an especially dangerous situation in case of mission critical, real-time embedded systems with high availability requirements. In such systems, total system outage must be avoided at all cost, even by allowing temporary, partial failures. Nonetheless, no solution exists today that can be added to an Erlang system without code modification and would treat memory pressure out of the box. Having such a solution would enable existing Erlang systems to perform better under low memory conditions. It would help any Erlang system to deal with unexpectedly large workload but *would be very beneficial for embedded systems* where virtual memory is disabled and physical memory is very limited and constrained.

Our Contributions. In this paper, we propose an approach, called Lesser Evil, that can treat memory pressure in any Erlang system without the need of any code modification. Lesser Evil is ready to use and is applicable to any fault-tolerant Erlang systems. We discuss why our approach is viable, how it identifies low memory conditions, what strategy it employs and how it treats memory pressure.

Summary of Results. Our evaluation shows that an Erlang system can survive and keep functioning under low memory conditions with the help of our approach. We have confirmed that Lesser Evil's strategy is correct: it is able to identify and execute compensating actions on the components most responsible for the situation without damaging the other components or the overall system.

2   Problem Statement

Let us take an imaginary, fault-tolerant, embedded Erlang system as a motivating example. The Erlang system is designed to run on and control an embedded device with limited memory and slow processing capability. The Erlang system and the device are expected to be always available. The Erlang system receives administrative requests that it processes, and as a result of processing, it executes commands on the embedded device. The Erlang system usually receives a few, small requests that never fills up the device memory, but sometimes a large request arrives that may require all the available memory of the device to process. If part of the device memory is used to process other small requests, the available memory is not enough to process the large requests: the device runs out of memory, becomes unresponsive or it even reboots.

To protect the availability of the device, the only available solution to use today is a generic solution for Linux systems, called the Out of Memory Manager (OOM manager) [23]. However, the OOM manager is not an option in our example, as the OOM manager would terminate the whole Erlang system that controls the device; making the device unavailable. A more fine grained solution would be more appreciated that would not cause the termination of the whole Erlang system. Instead, it would free up enough memory to resume the normal operation of the Erlang system, for example, by terminating the large request.

The motivating example illustrates that we need a solution that treats memory pressure differently. The primary goal is to free up enough memory to resume the normal operation of the Erlang system. When releasing memory we accept local failures but we cannot tolerate abnormal termination of the whole Erlang system neither the risk of introducing permanent data inconsistencies. Under local failures we mean failures that may effect some end-user but not all users and also failures that may result in interruption of some requests but not all requests. Our goal is to prevent a major outage, but we accept temporary, partial system degradations.

To achieve our goals, a tool is needed that is able to monitor, assess and interact with the running Erlang system. The tool needs to monitor the running Erlang system to identify low memory conditions. If low memory conditions are identified the tool needs to select some entities to execute compensating actions. The tool needs to have a strategy to select entities and the strategy should consider multiple criteria when making the selection. The strategy should be based on metrics of the entities gathered from the runtime, and characterise the *badness* of the entity. Compensating actions need to be defined on entity level, ensuring that the impact of the action is limited; will not have a negative impact on the overall Erlang system.

3   Erlang

In this section we discuss the Erlang ecosystem and highlight its key features that our approach uses to treat memory pressure.

Erlang [9] is a dynamically typed functional programming language that has built-in support for concurrency and distribution. Erlang systems are well known about their high availability, thanks to their failure handling and hot code loading capabilities.

An Erlang system can be considered as an actor based system, built up of interacting Erlang processes. Erlang processes [14] are light-weight processes with small memory overhead, fast to create and terminate, and the scheduling overhead is low. The Erlang processes communicate with each other via asynchronous message passings [19]. They share nothing with the outside world, they exclusively own their data (excl. large binaries that are reference counted and stored in a shared heap). If data is shared between two processes (via message passing), the data is copied to the another process's heap. Processes, while scheduled, are executing code, which is measured in *reductions*. The scheduler [20] de-schedules a process after a certain amount of reductions or when the process enters into a waiting state (e.g. waiting for messages or IO). The fact that processes share nothing and that they can yield to be de-scheduled enables Erlang's garbage collector [15] to work on a single process at a time without interfering with other running processes. Moreover, when an Erlang process terminates all its allocated memory can be freed as there are no other users to those memory blocks.

Fault tolerance is built into the language [13], processes are allowed to fail. Hence, interacting processes can never assume that their peer is alive. To detect the termination of their peer, processes can monitor other processes. If the monitored process terminates, the process will be notified by a message. If the interacting processes depend on each other they can use another language construct, called the process link. A process link is a bidirectional link forwarding events of termination, called error signals, between the linked processes. The forwarded error signal may terminate the receiving process as well, depending whether the process trapping exits. Using links and monitors, more complex and robust architectures can be built that define restart strategies for the important processes. An example is the supervisor process [18] that is responsible for starting, terminating and restarting its children. A common practice is to build supervisor trees that allow managing processes in a structured way and handling runtime errors where it is convenient.

From the system architecture point of view, an Erlang system is built up from a single or a set of Erlang nodes organised into a full mesh cluster. An Erlang node, which is an OS process, is built up from the Erlang Runtime System (ERTS) and the Erlang release. An Erlang release [17] consists of a set of Erlang applications. The Erlang applications [16] are the reusable units of the Erlang ecosystem, can be bundled into multiple releases and be part of different deployments. (Readers experienced in the Java programming language can consider Erlang applications as Java packages.) An Erlang application is the implementation of a functionality and can cooperate with other Erlang applications to implement more complex functionality. An Erlang application defines and includes its Erlang processes. When an application starts the runtime starts an application_master process as the main responsible process for the application. The application_master in turn starts a process called 'x' that is responsible for the IO and to start the main supervisor for the application. The main supervisor is the first processes implemented by the user, the root of the supervisor tree for the application. The ERTS enables interaction with the running Erlang node. Processes can be created and terminated, and existing processes can be inspected at runtime: various process metrics can be retrieved. Applications can be started, stopped and upgraded without stopping the Erlang node.

4   Lesser Evil

In this section we describe our approach for Erlang systems, called Lesser Evil [22]. First, we outline the approach and then we discuss the details: what entities are considered, how badness is characterised, how the strategy is evaluated and what compensating actions are employed. We show the architecture and discuss the different ways the approach can be added to an Erlang system.

Our approach aims at treating memory pressure of an Erlang system without the need of code modification. It proposes to monitor the running program and upon low memory conditions select some entities with the greatest badness values and execute compensating actions on the selected entities. Mapping the approach to Erlang systems, the approach monitors an Erlang node and collect its memory consumption. As Erlang processes are owning their data, they hold memory in the system, thus the Erlang processes are the entities. The goal is to characterise the badness of processes with the help of process level metrics. As the runtime provides interaction possibilities with the running system, the approach employs two compensating actions: triggering garbage collection on a selected process, and terminating the process.

4.1 Entities

Lesser Evil considers Erlang processes as entities. However, it does not consider all processes, as there are critical processes in an Erlang node. As examples, consider the various system processes started by the runtime and the processes belonging to critical user applications. Automatically identifying and excluding the system processes is possible, however, distinguishing between critical and non-critical user processes is not. Lesser Evil takes the approach of letting the user decide, and requires a list of Erlang applications that are non-critical for the system (e.g. the implementation of an HTTP API). Processes belonging to the listed applications are considered only. However, this is still not enough. As discussed in Sect. 3, each application includes 3 critical processes (application_master, process 'x' and the main supervisor of the application) that must be excluded. If they terminate, the whole application terminates, which must be prevented.

4.2 Badness

Determining the badness of processes is the heart of the strategy: the compensating actions executed on the selected processes should help the Erlang node to survive low memory conditions, and their negative impact on the rest of the processes should be minimal. In this section we discuss how such a metric can be constructed.

To treat memory pressure effectively, the badness assigns greater values to processes that (1) have high memory usage; (2) have several pending tasks, therefore, they have a bad future outlook.

To minimise the negative impact of the compensating actions on the rest of the processes, the badness assigns lower values to processes that (1) are long-lived and, therefore, have proven their good behaviour; (2) are important to the user; (3) play a central role in the system in the sense of several processes depend on them.

In conclusion, the goal is to select isolated, relatively new processes with high memory usage and a bad future outlook. Therefore, the *badness* is a composite metric that assigns a real value to a process based on the following process level metrics.

- *Memory*. Number of bytes the process uses.
- *MessageQLength*. Number of messages delivered to but not yet processed by the process. The metric expresses how much more tasks a process has pending.
- *Reds*. Reduction count shows the amount of work the process has done. As for long lived processes this value can be several order of magnitudes large, the logarithm with base 10 is applied to the reduction count in the badness formula.
- *Age*. Number of checks the process has stayed alive.
- *Links*. The number of processes linking to the process. The metric expresses how central the process is.
- *Mons*. The number of processes monitoring the process. The metric expresses how central the process is.
- *Prio*. Erlang processes can have different priorities. The higher the process priority is, the more important the process to the user is. This is what the metric expresses by selecting a value from $\{1, 10, 100\}$.

The *badness* metric that assigns a real value to a process can be formalised as shown by

$$badness \equiv \frac{Memory * (MessageQLength + 1)}{log_{10}(Reds) * (Links + 1) * (Mons + 1) * Age * Prio}$$

4.3   Strategy

In this section we define the strategy and how it is evaluated. The strategy works with an Erlang node, and takes the memory limit, further denoted as *MemLimit*, the Erlang node can occupy as a configuration parameter.

The strategy maintains a state to store historical data about the processes (i.e. age) and about the compensating actions executed in the past. Data about the past actions is necessary to prevent cascading failures that would be caused by too frequent compensating actions. Thus, the strategy ensures a cool down interval is respected between two compensating actions.

The strategy is invoked when new system and process level metrics arrive. The strategy decides whether compensating actions are required, executes actions if required and updates its state. To decide whether compensating actions are required, it first checks if it is not in cool down interval (*NotInCoolDownInterval*) by testing that a certain amount of seconds (currently, it is 5 seconds) has elapsed since the last action was executed. We have chosen to use 5 seconds as cool down interval to minimise the risk of cascading process failures. Then, it looks at the system level metrics, namely, memory used by the Erlang node (*Mem*) to check whether the current memory allocations are close to the maximum. To summarise, the strategy triggers as follows.

$$trigger \equiv Mem > 0.8 * MemLimit \ \wedge \ NotInCoolDownInterval$$

When compensating actions are required the strategy selects a compensating action as follows.

$$select\_action \equiv \begin{cases} trigger\_gc & \text{if } Mem < MemLimit \\ terminate\_proc & \text{otherwise} \end{cases}$$

After that, the strategy orders the processes by their badness score that is calculated using the received process level metrics and historical data stored in its state. Now the goal is to counterbalance the low memory conditions by freeing up memory. Thus, it takes as many processes from the beginning of the process list as it needs to have the memory condition settled. The resulting set contains processes with the highest badness score.

4.4 Compensating Actions

The strategy has selected a compensating action and a list of processes to execute the compensating action on. We defined two compensating actions *trigger_gc* and *terminate_proc*. The *trigger_gc* action is to trigger garbage collection on the selected processes, while the *terminate_proc* action is to terminate the selected processes. The *trigger_gc* action is based on calling `erlang:garbage_collect/1` function in order to trigger a full sweep garbage collection of the process. The *terminate_proc* action is non-trivial, we discuss its details now. The action first sends a trappable exit signal to the process. The exit signal will terminate the process if it is not trapping exits, however, if the process is trapping exits, the exit signal is delivered as a message in its mailbox and it is up to the process to decide whether to terminate. Hence, the action waits a few milliseconds and checks if the process is still alive. If it is alive, the action sends a non-trappable exit signal that will terminate the process immediately. In order to avoid cascading process failures, the action waits 3 seconds between the termination of two processes.

4.5 Architecture

In this section we put things together: we show the main components of Lesser Evil and discuss how it can be applied to Erlang systems with different requirements.

Lesser Evil is organised into two Erlang applications: `lesser_evil` and `lesser_evil_agent`. The main responsibility of the `lesser_evil` application is to monitor the Erlang node(s) and to evaluate the strategy based on the metrics it receives from the agent(s). The application was designed in a way that it supports supervising multiple Erlang nodes. The `lesser_evil_agent` application is responsible for collecting and forwarding system and process level metrics to the `lesser_evil` application and executing actions it receives from the `lesser_evil` application.

In the rest of the section, we provide guidance on how to use Lesser Evil: how to deploy, configure and install Lesser Evil for Erlang systems with different requirements.

In case of deployments where the network is not reliable or not secure, the two applications should be included into the monitored Erlang node. Otherwise, the agent should be included in the monitored Erlang node but the `lesser_evil` application should be deployed as a standalone Erlang node. If the deployment has multiple nodes and the network is stable, secure and the bandwidth is not constrained, a central `lesser_evil` node handling all the nodes seems to be a better choice.

As the next discussion point we provide guidance on how Lesser Evil can be configured and added to an Erlang system. First of all, programmers need to choose the Erlang applications to be monitored by the agent code. The selected applications should be fault-tolerant applications that are non-critical from the system point of view. Adding the core parts of the persistence layer is advised against, while adding the northbound API, the cache layers, data consumers are encouraged. After selecting the entities Lesser Evil will work with, one need to decide on the memory limit that will be enforced by Lesser Evil. One should work with historical data, and aim to choose a memory limit that does not activate Lesser Evil during normal load and trigger garbage collection only for a bit more intense load scenarios. We recommend to perform load tests to choose the memory limit best fitting the Erlang system, and also to ensure that the applications Lesser Evil interacts with are prepared for failures.

4.6 Discussion

In this section we discuss the design decisions we have made and the implications Lesser Evil can have on the monitored node.

Badness. We start the discussion with the badness metric (Sect. 4.2), that is the heart of the strategy that Lesser Evil employs.

One observation to make is that the messages are handled uniformly, nonetheless, they are not and they can have different implication on the process in real-life. Processing one message may take only a few reductions while handling another message can lead to thousands of reductions. Nevertheless, we choose to consider all messages uniform as processes usually have a quasi-empty mailbox in Erlang systems. Moreover, processes with large message queues are considered a performance bottleneck in an Erlang system, hence we believe it is justified to prioritise selecting them.

Another observation one may make is that due to the age factor older processes are more protected, that can lead to the starvation of new processes. However, we argue that this is not a problem. First of all, when Lesser Evil is triggered the system is already at risk, there is no point in initiating more work. Second, long lived processes are long lived for a reason: they are central parts of the system with possibly lot of dependent processes and important responsibilities. Therefore, their protection is necessary to avoid cascading failures and to limit the impact of system degradations.

Compensating Actions. Another discussion point is the compensating actions (Sect. 4.4) that are triggering garbage collection on process level or terminating a selected process.

Triggering immediate garbage collection can have side-effect on the process, as the process must not be executing code while the garbage collection occurs. Therefore, *if* the process is scheduled when the garbage collection is triggered, the process is going to be de-scheduled while the garbage collection takes place, resulting in longer execution times.

Terminating a process is a more serious event in the system. As an example, what happens with files opened by the terminated process? In Erlang, files are opened through an auxiliary process that is linked to the process that opened the file, implying that upon the termination of the process, the auxiliary process gets notified and will close the file. The same holds for other shared resources.

Another point to consider is the question of cascading failures. When a process terminates all processes that have monitors on or are linked to the terminated process get notified and may decide to terminate themselves, leading to cascading failures. Cascading failures further reduce the memory and increase the impact of the compensating action, which is meant to be kept minimal. To avoid cascading failures the badness metric down-prioritises processes that are central.

Furthermore, if the process was supervised, the supervisor is notified and decides on whether to restart the process. Too frequent restarts make the supervisor to give up: it terminates all its supervised processes and itself. The 5 seconds of cool down interval and the waiting time of 3 seconds between two process terminations are there to avoid such scenarios. The constants were determined based on reviewing popular, open-source Erlang applications, however, the authors believe that there can be cases where the constants need to be changed, hence they will become configuration parameters of Lesser Evil.

4.7 Note on Applicability

In 2011, the Elixir language [32] was introduced that runs on the same virtual machine, called the BEAM, as Erlang. Elixir has become a success, it is in the 48th place on the TIOBE index [33] published in May 2021 [1]. Elixir has managed to attract even more companies, thus the BEAM has become more widespread. Processes started in Elixir have the same capabilities and properties as Erlang processes, thus Lesser Evil is able to monitor Elixir processes as well. Furthermore, as Erlang system level API functions used by Lesser Evil are available in Elixir systems and Erlang applications can be part of Elixir releases, Lesser Evil works not only with Erlang systems but with Elixir systems as well. This fact greatly increases the applicability of our approach.

5   Evaluation

In this section we present the evaluation of Lesser Evil. The primary use case of Lesser Evil is embedded systems, thus we built a test system using popular, open-source Erlang applications to evaluate Lesser Evil. We show the test subject, present the experiments, assess the results and discuss the limitations.

5.1   Test Subject

In this section we show the representative Erlang system we built for evaluation purposes: an embedded device controller. We use the system to evaluate Lesser Evil. During the experiments we do not use representative load or scale, our goal is to push the system to its limit, because we want to confirm that Lesser Evil helps the Erlang node avoid a major outage.

The system under test (SUT) is an embedded device controller. The device controller is reachable via an HTTP API. Requests sent to the controller are being processed in memory, and confirmations are returned as response. The processing time and the memory required to process the request grow with the size of the request. Table 1 shows the processing time and the allocated memory per request size.

Table 1. Impact of an Incoming Request on the SUT

Size	Request Size	Used Memory	Processing Time
XS	1 KB	16 KB	1 ms
S	10 KB	160 KB	24 000 ms
M	100 KB	1 600 KB	48 000 ms
L	1 000 KB	16 000 KB	96 000 ms

The SUT is a one-node Erlang system built up from one application, the http_api, implementing the HTTP handlers. To implement the HTTP handlers we used the cowboy [27] and the jsone [30] applications as applications dependencies of the http_api application. The cowboy application depends on the ranch application [28] that is a socket acceptor pool for TCP protocols.

5.2   Configuration

All experiments ran on a machine that has 16 GB of memory and is equipped with a 2,6 GHz 6-Core Intel Core i7 processor. The SUT was running in a Docker container. To measure the memory consumption of the SUT we periodically queried the memory allocations of the Erlang VM using the erlang:memory/1 function provided by the Erlang VM. To generate load for the SUT, we used Basho Bench [2].

The lesser_evil application was deployed as a standalone Erlang node and configured to allow 90 MB memory for the SUT. The SUT packaged together with lesser_evil_agent was deployed as another Erlang node inside of a Docker container. The lesser_evil_agent application was configured to monitor and report metrics about the ranch application in every second. Note that the ranch application is not written by the authors. The Docker container running the SUT was configured to limit both real and virtual memory to 120 MB.

To generate load for the SUT, we used the following load configurations. All tests were run for 10 min, maintaining 5 concurrent connections. The generated requests were random binaries, belonging to one of the request types (see Table 1). The mix of load was 20% of XS-sized requests, 40% of S-sized requests, 20% of M-sized requests, and 20% of L-sized requests. The mix of load characterises normal operation (80% of the requests are small requests) where unusually large requests (20% of the requests) occur. The only variable part in the load generation was the number of requests per second generated by each connection, that were one of the followings: {5, 10}. Observe the followings.

- The memory usage of the SUT correlates with the number and the size of requests being processed.
- The SUT can exceed the available memory when unusually large requests (L-sized requests) arrive.
- L-sized requests are the ones mainly responsible for increased memory consumption of the SUT.

5.3 Experiments

The goal of the experiments is to test the following hypotheses.

Hypothesis #1: Lesser Evil can control the memory usage of an Erlang node, therefore, it helps an Erlang node survive low memory conditions. For this purpose, we first establish a baseline: we start a test run without Lesser Evil and record the memory consumption of the SUT. Then, we start another test run with Lesser Evil and record the memory consumption. We expect to see that with Lesser Evil the memory consumption of the SUT is constrained by the given memory limit.

Hypothesis #2: Lesser Evil can prevent major outages. For this purpose, the test runs need to employ a load configuration that stresses the SUT enough to require more memory than what is available in the system. Without Lesser Evil we expect to see that the SUT will be terminated by the Linux OOM manager causing a major outage, while with Lesser Evil we expect to see that the SUT keeps operating. We accept temporary, partial system degradations.

Hypothesis #3: Lesser Evil selects and executes actions on those processes that are mainly responsible for the memory usage and does not interfere with the rest of the processes. Considering the embedded device controller, we know that the processes handling L-sized requests are the ones mainly responsible for holding memory. We expect to see that if the SUT is about to exceed the memory limit only these HTTP requests will fail. Moreover, we also expect to see that the system will continue to operate and processes executing the inexpensive HTTP requests (XS- and S-sized requests) will continue to succeed.

Hypothesis #4: Lesser Evil's agent is non-intrusive to the Erlang node, its memory usage is low. For this purpose, we first establish a baseline: we start the SUT without Lesser Evil and record its memory consumption. Then, we start the SUT packaged together with Lesser Evil and record the memory consumption. No load is generated in both cases. We expect to see that with Lesser Evil the increase in memory consumption is low.

Table 2. Experiments Conducted on the Embedded Device Controller. Note that the number of requests (# Req.s) is only shown if the experiment was successfully completed.

L.E active	Req/sec per Con.	Got OOM-ed	Max Mem.	# Req.s	# Error	# GC	# Kill
No	5	After 13 s	67 MB	n/a	n/a	n/a	n/a
Yes	5	No	161 MB	41	9	54	22
No	10	After 9 s	126 MB	n/a	n/a	n/a	n/a
Yes	10	No	117 MB	54	8	34	22

5.4 Results

The experiments were run multiple times, the test results were consistent. Table 2 summarises the experiments conducted on the test subject. It shows whether Lesser Evil was used, the maximum number of requests each connection sent per second, whether the SUT got killed by the Linux OOM manager, the maximum amount of used memory, the total number of requests the SUT received, the number of requests the SUT did not serve because of an error, the number of times Lesser Evil initiated garbage collection on a process and the number of times Lesser Evil terminated a process.

We can observe that the SUT without Lesser Evil never managed to complete any experiments; all experiments ended prematurely as the SUT ran out of memory and the Linux's OOM manager terminated the whole Erlang node. As the SUT never got OOM-ed while Lesser Evil was active and the memory usage of the SUT was 93% of the time below the configured maximum, the experiments confirm Hypothesis #1 and partially Hypothesis #2. The results suggest that Lesser Evil can control the memory usage of an Erlang node.

Figure 1 shows the memory usage of the SUT recorded during the experiment where Lesser Evil was active and each connection was configured to send 10 requests per second. Observe how effectively Lesser Evil reacts: once the memory limit (90 MB) is exceeded, Lesser Evil executes a compensating action that fixes the problem.

Based on the logs written by Lesser Evil, there were several actions executed. Both the *trigger_gc* and the *terminate_proc* actions were invoked by Lesser Evil. Actions were triggered frequently but the cool down period was always respected. As there were processes terminated by Lesser Evil, we need to confirm that the right processes were selected for termination. As only L-sized requests failed in both experiments (9 and 8 errors), we conclude that Lesser Evil chose the right processes to terminate, did not interfere with the rest of the processes, and effectively controlled the memory usage of the SUT, confirming Hypothesis #3. Due to the failed requests there was a temporary, partial system degradation that effected only the requesters of L-sized requests. However, a temporary, partial system degradation is still a better choice compared to the test runs where the SUT got terminated by the Linux OOM manager and, therefore, a major outage occurred. The experiments confirm Hypothesis #2.

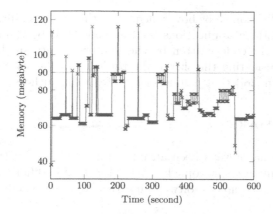

Fig. 1. Memory usage over time of the embedded device controller with Lesser Evil.

Overhead. We started the SUT with and without Lesser Evil and recorded the rss size [29] for a minute. Then, we calculated the difference point by point of the recorded values; the difference we got is the memory used by the Lesser Evil agent code. The minimum, median and maximum values of memory used by the agent code are: 848 KB, 1 000 KB, 1 148 KB, which we consider low enough. The experiment confirms Hypothesis #4.

5.5   Conclusion and Limitations

The experiments confirm all 4 hypotheses. Lesser Evil can control the memory usage of an Erlang node and avoid major outage. Its negative impact on the overall system is minimal. Considering the embedded device controller use case, which is the primary use case of Lesser Evil, that includes an Erlang system with high availability but with very limited memory and slow processing capabilities, Lesser Evil can help in scenarios where a few unusually large requests arrive that take long to process and fill up the available memory.

We have experimented with other use cases. We have found that if the memory pressure is due to a continuously arriving, vast amount of short lived (ca 2 milliseconds) processes with high memory consumption, Lesser Evil cannot effectively control the memory usage of the Erlang node. To fix memory pressure, Lesser Evil would need to execute the *terminate_proc* action without respecting the cool down internal: risking to cause the termination of the Erlang node.

5.6   Threats to Validity

Our evaluation is subject to threats to validity. The results were obtained from an Erlang system, and hence, they cannot necessarily be generalized to all Erlang systems. We minimised this threat in three ways. First, by reviewing the most widespread use cases of Erlang to build a representative test system that characterises well the given use case of Erlang. Second, by building the test subject using Erlang applications (cowboy, ranch, etc.) that are widespread and heavily used in real-life Erlang applications, and are not built by the authors. Third, by ensuring that the code written by the authors is very small (202 lines out of 267K lines) considering the size of the project, and Lesser Evil monitors an application (`ranch` [28]) that is independent from the authors.

6   Related Work

Memory pressure has always been an important challenge of the research and practitioner community. The topic has been discussed in different contexts ranging from operating systems to software libraries targeting specific software applications.

Considering operating system level, there is a generic solution for Linux systems, called the OOM manager [23]. The OOM manager is tasked to monitor the host and, under low memory conditions, select and terminate an OS process to treat memory pressure. Its goal is to protect the availability of the overall host. It employs a strategy to select new, non-user preferred processes that have high memory usage. Considering Erlang systems, our experience and the evaluation presented in this paper show that OOM is not a help, we have never seen a case when killing the Erlang node solved the underlying problem. Instead, it damaged the Erlang systems. Lesser Evil and the OOM Manager work on different abstraction level, however, both protect the overall system availability, employ a strategy and treat memory pressure by killing processes.

Virtualisation techniques have become significant to better utilise available resources and to isolate applications. An example is Apache Mesos [11,24] that sits between the application layer and the operating system and makes it easier to deploy and manage applications in large-scale clustered environments more efficiently. Apache Mesos supports oversubscription [31] for better resource utilisation with the promise of keeping QoS metrics. Their approach is to monitor the entire host and if CPU pressure occurs the QoS controller kills revocable tasks. To further improve killing tasks when oversubscription occurs, the authors of [10] propose a user-assisted OOM killer in kernel space for agile task killing. Lesser Evil and the Mesos's QoS controller have different focus (memory versus CPU), however, both select and terminate entities that are non-critical to the system.

As there is no general solution for programming language and runtime level, researchers have proposed various solutions to better manage specific use cases [5,7,8,21]. Browsing through the articles, one can notice that there has been a targeted interest in Java programs. ITask proposed in [21] is a promising choice for Java workflow applications that requires code modification, however, promises protection of tasks and performance improvements in high load scenarios. This is a considerable benefit compared to Lesser Evil, however, on the other hand rewriting applications is not required by Lesser Evil. Besides, as Erlang applications often employs restart strategies for important worker processes offering the restoration of interrupted tasks, it is not a necessity. The authors of [6] proposed a more general solution for handling out of memory errors in Java applications. The idea is to overallocate memory that is not used and release the non-used memory when out of memory errors occur. The authors of [35] looks at the problem from another perspective, taming the garbage collection, and proposes a system that enables garbage-collected applications to predict an appropriate heap size, allowing the system to maintain high performance while adjusting dynamically to changing memory pressure.

When embedded systems are targeted, memory management becomes more critical as memory is more limited and virtual memory is often disabled. Researchers have proposed several low level memory management techniques that focus on memory allocation strategies and minimises memory fragmentation [26,34]. The authors of [3] observed that application performance is impacted by the employed memory allocation strategy in embedded systems. They propose to manage memory per task and introduce a runtime scheduler for memory management policy switching and kernel overlapping. Their evaluation suggests that their approach can treat memory pressure and improve response time. Virtualisation ensures isolation of applications that is necessary in smart consumer electronics. However, with a virtualised embedded device, flexible memory management is required to run multiple VMs efficiently on resource-constrained hardware. The authors of [25] tackle the challenge by introducing an in-memory compressed swap device (CSW) that prioritises the memory reservations of the critical applications running on the embedded device by swapping out only the memory of third-party applications in response to memory pressure. Lesser Evil and CSW employ different compensating actions but both activate when low memory conditions occur and distinguish between critical and non-critical entities.

7   Conclusion

In this paper we have proposed and implemented an approach, called Lesser Evil, that can treat low memory pressure in Erlang systems without the need of any code modification. Lesser Evil embraces failures to protect overall system availability. It monitors the running program and upon low memory conditions selects some non-critical entities based on the badness metric and execute compensating actions on the selected entities to help the system avoid a major outage. Lesser Evil is ready to use and is applicable to any Erlang systems. The prototype implementation is available on GitHub [22].

The evaluation shows that Lesser Evil can control the memory usage of an Erlang node and an embedded Erlang system can avoid a major outage and keep functioning under low memory conditions with the help of our approach. We have confirmed that Lesser Evil's negative impact on the overall system is minimal, and Lesser Evil's strategy is correct: it is able to identify and execute compensating actions on the components most responsible for the situation without damaging the other components or the overall system.

References

1. Statistics and data: the most popular programming languages - 1965/2021 - new update. https://statisticsanddata.org/data/the-most-popular-programming-languages-1965-2021/
2. Basho: basho bench. https://github.com/alexandrejbr/basho_bench
3. Bateni, S., Wang, Z., Zhu, Y., Hu, Y., Liu, C.: Co-optimizing performance and memory footprint via integrated CPU/GPU memory management, an implementation on autonomous driving platform. In: 2020 IEEE Real-Time and Embedded Technology and Applications Symposium (RTAS), pp. 310–323 (2020). https://doi.org/10.1109/RTAS48715.2020.00007
4. Bevemyr, J.: How Cisco is using Erlang for intent-based networking. Talk at Code BEAM STO 2018, Stockholm, Sweden, 31 May 2018. https://youtu.be/077-XJv6PLQ?t=109
5. Borkar, V., Carey, M., Grover, R., Onose, N., Vernica, R.: Hyracks: A flexible and extensible foundation for data-intensive computing. In: 2011 IEEE 27th International Conference on Data Engineering, pp. 1151–1162 (2011). https://doi.org/10.1109/ICDE.2011.5767921
6. Boyland, J.T.: Handling out of memory errors. In: ECOOP 2005 Workshop on Exception Handling in Object-Oriented Systems, vol. 2005 (2005)
7. Bu, Y., Borkar, V., Jia, J., Carey, M.J., Condie, T.: Pregelix: big(GER) graph analytics on a dataflow engine. Proc. VLDB Endow. **8**(2), 161–172 (2014). https://doi.org/10.14778/2735471.2735477
8. Bu, Y., Borkar, V., Xu, G., Carey, M.J.: A bloat-aware design for big data applications. In: Proceedings of the 2013 International Symposium on Memory Management, ISMM 2013, pp. 119–130. Association for Computing Machinery, New York (2013). https://doi.org/10.1145/2464157.2466485
9. Cesarini, F., Thompson, S.: ERLANG programming. O'Reilly Media Inc, 1st edn, Sebastopol (2009)
10. Chen, W., Pi, A., Wang, S., Zhou, X.: OS-augmented oversubscription of opportunistic memory with a user-assisted OOM killer. In: Proceedings of the 20th International Middleware Conference, Middleware 2019, pp. 28–40. Association for Computing Machinery, New York (2019). https://doi.org/10.1145/3361525.3361534
11. Choudhury, D.G., Perrett, T.: Designing cluster schedulers for internet-scale services: Embracing failures for improving availability. Queue **16**(1), 98–119 (2018). https://doi.org/10.1145/3194653.3199609
12. Cronqvist, M.: Troubleshooting a large erlang system. In: Proceedings of the 2004 ACM SIGPLAN Workshop on Erlang, ERLANG 2004, pp. 11–15. Association for Computing Machinery, New York (2004). https://doi.org/10.1145/1022471.1022474
13. Ericsson AB: erlang reference manual: errors and error handling. https://erlang.org/doc/reference_manual/errors.html
14. Ericsson AB: erlang reference manual: processes. http://erlang.org/doc/reference_manual/processes.html
15. Ericsson AB: erlang run-time system application, internal documentation: erlang garbage collector. https://erlang.org/doc/apps/erts/GarbageCollection.html
16. Ericsson AB: OTP design principles: applications. https://erlang.org/doc/design_principles/applications.html

17. Ericsson AB: OTP design principles: releases. https://erlang.org/doc/design_principles/release_structure.html
18. Ericsson AB: OTP design principles: supervisor behaviour. https://erlang.org/doc/design_principles/sup_princ.html
19. Stenman, E.: The BEAM book: mailboxes and message passing. https://blog.stenmans.org/theBeamBook/#_mailboxes_and_message_passing
20. Stenman, E.: The BEAM book: scheduling: non-preemptive, reduction counting. https://blog.stenmans.org/theBeamBook/#_scheduling_non_preemptive_reduction_counting
21. Fang, L., Nguyen, K., Xu, G., Demsky, B., Lu, S.: Interruptible tasks: treating memory pressure as interrupts for highly scalable data-parallel programs. In: Proceedings of the 25th Symposium on Operating Systems Principles, SOSP 2015, pp. 394–409. Association for Computing Machinery, New York (2015). https://doi.org/10.1145/2815400.2815407
22. Fördős, V., Rodrigues, B., Jorge, A.: Lesser evil prototype. https://github.com/viktoriafordos/lesser-evil
23. Gorman, M.: Understanding the Linux Virtual Memory Manager. Prentice Hall PTR, USA (2004)
24. Hindman, B., et al.: Mesos: a platform for fine-grained resource sharing in the data center. In: Proceedings of the 8th USENIX Conference on Networked Systems Design and Implementation, NSDI 2011, pp. 295–308. USENIX Association, USA (2011)
25. Hwang, J., Jeong, J., Kim, H., Choi, J., Lee, J.: Compressed memory swap for QoS of virtualized embedded systems. IEEE Trans. Consum. Electron. $58(3)$, 834–840 (2012). https://doi.org/10.1109/TCE.2012.6311325
26. Liu, D., Wang, T., Wang, Y., Qin, Z., Shao, Z.: A block-level flash memory management scheme for reducing write activities in PCM-based embedded systems. In: Proceedings of the Conference on Design, Automation and Test in Europe, DATE 2012, pp. 1447–1450. EDA Consortium, San Jose, CA, USA (2012)
27. Hoguin, L.: Cowboy. https://github.com/ninenines/cowboy
28. Hoguin, L.: Ranch. https://github.com/ninenines/ranch
29. Kerrisk, M.: Linux manual page: ps(1). https://man7.org/linux/man-pages/man1/ps.1.html
30. Ohta, T.: Jsone. https://github.com/sile/jsone/
31. The apache software foundation: apache mesos documentation: oversubscription. http://mesos.apache.org/documentation/latest/oversubscription/
32. Thomas, D.: Programming elixir: functional, Concurrent, Pragmatic, Fun. 1st edn., Pragmatic Bookshelf, Eau Claire (2014)
33. TIOBE software BV: TIOBE index. https://www.tiobe.com/tiobe-index/
34. Venkataramani, V., Chan, M.C., Mitra, T.: Scratchpad-memory management for multi-threaded applications on many-core architectures. ACM Trans. Embed. Comput. Syst. $18(1)$ (2019). https://doi.org/10.1145/3301308
35. Yang, T., Berger, E.D., Kaplan, S.F., Moss, J.E.B.: CRAMM: virtual memory support for garbage-collected applications. In: Proceedings of the 7th Symposium on Operating Systems Design and Implementation, pp. 103–116 (2006)

Failure Root Cause Analysis
for Microservices, Explained

Jacopo Soldani(✉), Stefano Forti, and Antonio Brogi

University of Pisa, Pisa, Italy
{jacopo.soldani,stefano.forti,antonio.brogi}@unipi.it

Abstract. Determining the root causes of observed failures is a main issue in microservice-based applications. Unfortunately, available root cause analysis techniques do not focus on explaining how root failures actually caused the observed failure. On the other hand, the availability of such explanations would greatly help to pick adequate counter-measures, e.g., by introducing circuit breakers or bulkheads. We hence present a declarative root cause analysis technique, which can determine the cascading failures that possibly caused an observed failure, identifying also (or starting from) a root cause. We also introduce a prototype implementation of our technique, and we use it to assess our technique by means of controlled experiments.

1 Introduction

Microservices gained momentum in the software industry. For instance, Netflix and Spotify are already delivered as microservice-based applications [33]. This is because microservice-based applications are *cloud-native*, meaning that they are composed by loosely coupled services, which can be independently deployed and scaled to fully exploit the potentials of cloud computing [9].

Microservice-based applications are often composed by hundreds of services, which are typically replicated by instantiating multiple instances of each service. The multiple instances of the various different services in an application interact to deliver the end users' requests, possibly resulting in thousands of interactions happening at the same time. Service instances can fail, e.g., by returning error responses to their invokers, or not even answering since they suddenly crashed.

Whilst failing service instances can be promptly detected at runtime, understanding the possible root causes for a failing service instance is an offline task, which is inherently complex [28]. Did the service instance fail on its own? Did it instead fail in cascade, since it interacted with another failing service instance? Did the latter fail on its own or in cascade to some other service instance? Answering such questions is not easy, when you have possibly thousands of interactions among different service instances happening in parallel [33]. At the

© IFIP International Federation for Information Processing 2022
Published by Springer Nature Switzerland AG 2022
D. Eyers and S. Voulgaris (Eds.): DAIS 2022, LNCS 13272, pp. 74–91, 2022.
https://doi.org/10.1007/978-3-031-16092-9_6

same time, answering the above questions is crucial to enact countermeasures and avoid the same failure cascade to happen again [28].

Existing root cause analysis techniques can help determining the service instances that may have failed first [28]. This is typically done by correlating the performance of the different service instances or the events they log, so as to determine the set of possible root causes. Identified root causes are also sometimes ranked by returning first those having higher chances to have caused the observed failure. However, there is no explanation of whether/how root causing failures propagated to other service instances, up to causing the failure observed on a service instance. Explanations —given as the possible failure cascades originating from an identified root causing failure— would enable intervening not only on the service that first failed, but also on those that failed in cascade [28]. They would enable, e.g., to equip intermediate services with circuit breakers enhancing the failure resilience of their instances [24], or to introduce bulkheads limiting failure propagations to only certain parts of an application [20].

We propose here a novel explainable root cause analysis technique, together with its prototype implementation and experimentation. Our technique automatically determines both the possible root causes for a failure observed on a service instance, and the failure cascades due to which the root causing failure possibly propagated up to that observed. It can also be used by restricting the possible root causes to a given set, hence enabling to explain the possible root causes identified with other existing techniques. In both cases, the explainable root cause analysis starts from the distributed logs of an application's service instances. Such logs are processed by means of declarative rules, which enable eliciting the interactions occurring among service instances, and determining whether a service instance failed on its own or in cascade, e.g., because it interacted with another failing service instance.

We also present yRCA, an open source prototype implementation of our explainable root cause analysis technique. We show how we used yRCA to run controlled experiments assessing our technique, based on an existing chaos testbed. The results of our experiment show that our technique can effectively determine the possible root causes and their explanations in 99.74% of the cases, whilst also keeping the number of returned explanations low enough to be counted on one hand. Our experiments also show that yRCA already achieves good time performances, with a processing time that is low on average, especially if we consider that root cause analysis is a batch process to be enacted offline [28].

The paper is organised as follows. Section 2 motivates our work. Sections 3 and 4 introduce our explainable root cause analysis technique and its prototype implementation, respectively. Section 5 presents some controlled experiments assessing our technique. Finally, Sects. 6 and 7 discuss related work and draw some concluding remarks, respectively.

2   Motivating Scenario

Consider *Sock Shop* [34], an open source application simulating an e-commerce website selling socks. The microservice-based architecture of *Sock Shop* is dis-

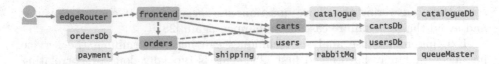

Fig. 1. *Sock Shop*'s microservice-based architecture. Darker nodes and dashed arcs highlight the portion of *Sock Shop* discussed in our motivating example.

played in Fig. 1. Clients connect to *Sock Shop* through an edgeRouter, which redirects clients' requests to the possibly multiple instances of the application's frontend. The latter displays a graphical user interface for e-shopping socks, backed by the microservices managing the catalogue of socks, the application users, and the users' carts and orders. Each of such microservices interacts with its own database to persist data, viz., catalogueDb, usersDb, cartsDb, and ordersDb. orders also interact with carts and payment to allow placing orders by simulating the online payment of the socks in a cart, and with shipping to simulate the actual shipping of an order. This is done with the microservice shipping placing to-be-shipped orders in a message queue (viz., rabbitMq), which is consumed by queueMaster to simulate their actual shipping.

Consider a running deployment of *Sock Shop*, with two replicated instances of each microservice, and focus on the highlighted portion of *Sock Shop* in Fig. 1. Suppose that an instance of carts fails (e.g., because of an internal error) and starts returning error responses to its clients. Suppose also that frontend's instances can tolerate the failure of carts' instances, e.g., by caching carts. Suppose instead that orders' instances fail when carts replies with error responses, becoming unable to process the requests from frontend's instances. When this happens, we have cascading failures in frontend as well, due to which *Sock Shop*'s end users cannot place orders.

For *Sock Shop* to get back fully working, application operators must identify the internal failure of an instance of carts as the root cause of the failures in frontend's instances, as well as that such root causing failure propagated to frontend through orders. This would enable first recovering the failing instance of carts, e.g., by restarting it, which would then result in the instances of orders and frontend getting back fully working as well. Also, by identifying the failure cascades that made frontend's instances unable to place orders, application operators could operate *only* on such cascades to avoid this to happen again. For instance, they could introduce a circuit breaker enabling orders to tolerate the failure of carts' instances, whilst not intervening on frontend, which can already tolerate the failure of carts.

There exist techniques for identifying the possible root causes of functional failures in microservice-based applications, e.g., [8,12,13,18,21,22,26,31]. However, they only identify the root causing microservice without stating how its failure propagated to other microservices. Understanding failure propagation still requires to manually inspect the distributed logs of an application, or its distributed traces, if the application is instrumented to feature distributed tracing.

Due to the number of microservices in an application, their complex interactions, and considering that microservices can be replicated over multiple instances, the resulting process is cumbersome, error-prone, and time consuming [28].

To this end, we provide a novel technique for identifying the failure cascades that can have possibly caused a failure in a microservice instance. Our technique inputs the distributed application logs, and it can automatically identify the possible root causing failures and how they propagated to a failing microservice instance. Our technique can also be used to complement the existing root cause analysis techniques, if any is in place, by identifying the possible cascades explaining how the identified root causing failure propagated and caused that observed on a failing microservice instance.

3 Declarative Failure Root Cause Analysis

In this section, we describe the declarative Prolog[1] methodology that enables determining explanations for failure root causes, through interaction-based analyses, which rely on simple logging information.

Logs and Interactions. First, application logs are modelled as facts like

```
log(SName, SInstance, Timestamp, Event, Message, Severity).
```

where the name SName and the instance identifier SInstance of the logging service are followed by the log Timestamp, the type of the logged Event, the associated log Message (if any), and its Severity level. Our methodology currently handles the following types of event:

- internal, which denotes logs related to the internal business logic of the considered service,
- sendTo(DstService, SessionId), which denotes that a request was sent to an instance of DstService with an associated SessionId,[2]
- received(SessionId), which denotes reception of a message by an instance of the destination service within the interaction identified by SessionId,
- timeout(DstService, SessionId), which denotes that the interaction started towards DstService, identified by SessionId, incurred in a timeout, and
- errorFrom(DstService, SessionId), which denotes that the destination service replied with an error code within the interaction identified by SessionId.

Finally, logged severity levels are expressed according to the Syslog standard [7]:

---

[1] A Prolog program is a finite set of *clauses* of the form a :- b1, ..., bn. stating that a holds when b1 ∧ ⋯ ∧ bn holds, where n ≥ 0 and a, b1, ..., bn are atomic literals. The logical or of two literals b1 ∨ b2 can be expressed as b1; b2. Clauses with empty condition are also called *facts*. Prolog variables begin with upper-case letters, lists are denoted by square brackets, and negation by \+.

[2] To easily identify messages pertaining to the same interaction, we assume that the code performing a request generates fresh session identifiers for each interaction.

```
severity(emerg, 0).    severity(err, 3).       severity(info, 6).
severity(alert, 1).    severity(warning, 4).   severity(debug, 7).
severity(crit, 2).     severity(notice, 5).
```

Note that Syslog severity levels can be mapped onto other existing industry standards (e.g., Log4J), and compared one another via a predicate like

```
moreSevere(Sev1,Sev2) :- severity(Sev1,A), severity(Sev2,B), A<B.
```

which holds when the severity level identified by Sev1 is more severe than the one identified by Sev2.

Based on this simple modelling, we can identify any completed interaction between instance I of service SI and instance J of service SJ, that happened between time Ts and time Te. Predicate interaction/5 infers that instance I of service SI performed a request towards instance J of service SJ and that, in turn, instance J of SJ logged reception of such request. Such interaction is identified by its unique session Id and happened at time Tr, between Ts and Te:

```
interaction(Id,(SI,I),(SJ,J),Ts,Te) :-
    log(SI,I,Ts,sendTo(SJ,Id),_,_), log(SJ,J,Tr,received(Id),_,_),
    Ts < Tr, Tr < Te.
```

Dually, predicate nonReceivedRequest/5 covers the case in which a request sent by instance I of SI incurred in a timeout event and its reception was not logged by any instance of SJ between Ts and Te:

```
nonReceivedRequest(Id,I,SJ,Ts,Te) :-
    log(SI,I,Ts,sendTo(SJ,Id),_,_), log(SI,I,Te,timeout(SJ,Id),_,_),
    \+ ( log(SJ,_,Tr,received(Id),_,_), Ts =< Tr, Tr =< Te ).
```

By relying on interaction/5, predicate failedInteraction/5 identifies interactions that – despite being correctly received at the destination service – failed either due to a logged error or to an expired timeout:

```
failedInteraction(Id,(SI,I),(SJ,J),Ts,Te) :-
    errorInteraction(Id,(SI,I),(SJ,J),Ts,Te) ;
    timedOutInteraction(Id,(SI,I),(SJ,J),Ts,Te).
```

On the one hand, errorInteraction/5 identifies that the invoked service instance J of SJ terminated the interaction identified by Id by returning an error response to the source service instance I:

```
errorInteraction(Id,(SI,I),(SJ,J),Ts,Te) :-
    log(SI,I,Te,errorFrom(SJ,Id),_,_),
    interaction(Id,(SI,I),(SJ,J),Ts,Te).
```

On the other hand, predicate timedOutInteraction/5 handles the case in which the interaction was interrupted by the invoking service instance I of SI, since the corresponding request's timeout expired:

```
timedOutInteraction(Id,(SI,I),(SJ,J),Ts,Te) :-
  log(SI,I,Te,timeout(SJ,Id),_,_),
  interaction(Id,(SI,I),(SJ,J),Ts,Te).
```

Explanations. Predicate `causedBy/3` is the core that our methodology exploits to determine explanations for root causes. A call to `causedBy(Log, Explanation, RootCause)` inputs an event `Log` to be explained and recursively builds an `Explanation`, represented as a list of logs, until it determines `RootCause` as the name of the service that started the failure cascade. Predicate `causedBy/3` distinguishes 8 cases – 5 recursive and 3 base cases – corresponding to different possible cascading or root failures, respectively. For each case, we illustrate the Prolog code and offer a graphical sketch to epitomise recursive cases.

The first case (lines 1–7) infers that event `E` logged by instance `I` of service `SI` (line 2), currently being explained, has been caused by an *internal error of the invoked service instance* `J` of `SJ`. Event `E` is either an error or a timeout (line 3), resulting from an interaction between `I` and `J` that failed or timed-out between time `Ts` and `Te` (line 4). If `J` logged an internal error more severe than a warning in the same time period (line 5–6), then the `Log` currently being explained is added to the explanation (line 1), and `causedBy/3` recurs to possibly explain the internal error of `J` (line 7).

```
1  causedBy(Log,[Log|Xs],Root) :-
2    Log=log(SI,I,T,E,M,Sev),
3    (E=errorFrom(SJ,Id);E=timeout(SJ,Id)),
4    failedInteraction(Id,(SI,I),(SJ,J),Ts,Te),
5    L=log(SJ,J,U,internal,MJ,SevJ),
6    moreSevere(SevJ,warning), Ts =< U, U =< Te,
7    causedBy(L,Xs,Root).
```

The second case (lines 8–15) infers that event `E` logged by instance `I` of service `SI` (line 9), currently being explained, has been caused by a cascading *failed interaction of the invoked service instance* `J` of `SJ`. Event `E` is either an error or a timeout (line 10) resulting from an interaction between `I` and `J` that failed between time `TsIJ` and `TeIJ` (line 11). In turn, such failure has been caused by a failed interaction of `J` with a third service between time `TsJK` and `TeJK` (line 12), within `TsIJ` and `TeIJ` (line 13). If `J` logged an event `F` at time `TeJK` (line 14) more severe than a warning (line 15), then the `Log` currently being explained is added to the explanation (line 8), and `causedBy/3` recurs to possibly explain the log `L` related to event `F` (line 16).

```
 8  causedBy(Log,[Log|Xs],Root) :-
 9    Log=log(SI,I,T,E,M,Sev),
10    (E=errorFrom(SJ,Id);E=timeout(SJ,Id)),
11    failedInteraction(Id,(SI,I),(SJ,J),TsIJ,TeIJ),
12    failedInteraction(_,(SJ,J),(_,_),TsJK,TeJK),
13    TsIJ =< TsJK, TeJK =< TeIJ,
14    L=log(SJ,J,TeJK,F,MJ,SevJ),
15    moreSevere(SevJ,warning),
16    causedBy(L,Xs,Root).
```

The third case (lines 17–23) infers that event E logged by instance I of service SI (line 18), currently being explained, has been caused by the *timed-out interaction of the invoked service instance* J of SJ. Event E is a timeout resulting from an interaction between I and J timed out at time TeIJ (line 19). In turn, such timeout has been caused by a timed out interaction of J with a third service SK between time TsJK and TeJK (line 20), started before the previous interaction and timed out afterwards (line 21). If J logged a timeout event at time TeJK related to an interaction IdJK with SK (line 22), then the Log currently being explained is added to the explanation (line 17), and causedBy/3 recurs to possibly explain the timeout of interaction IdJK (line 23).

```
17  causedBy(Log,[Log|Xs],Root) :-
18    Log=log(SI,I,T,timeout(SJ,Id),M,Sev),
19    timedOutInteraction(Id,(SI,I),(SJ,J),_,TeIJ),
20    timedOutInteraction(_,(SJ,J),(SK,_),TsJK,TeJK),
21    TsJK =< TeIJ, TeIJ < TeJK,
22    L=log(SJ,J,TeJK,timeout(SK,IdJK),MJ,SevJ),
23    causedBy(L,Xs,Root).
```

The fourth case (lines 24–31) infers that event E logged by instance I of service SI (line 25), currently being explained, has been caused by the *unreachability of a service called by the invoked service instance* J of SJ. Event E is either an error or a timeout (line 26) resulting from a failed interaction Id between I and J between time TsIJ and TeIJ (line 27). In turn, such an event has been caused by a request of J towards service SK, happening between TsIJ and TeIJ, which was never received by any instance of SK (lines 28–29). If J logged a timeout event at time TeJK related to interaction IdJK with SK (line 30), then the Log currently being explained is added to the explanation (line 24), and causedBy/3 recurs to possibly explain the time out of interaction IdJK (line 31).

```
24  causedBy(Log,[Log|Xs],Root) :-
25    Log=log(SI,I,T,E,M,Sev),
26    (E=errorFrom(SJ,Id);E=timeout(SJ,Id)),
27    failedInteraction(Id,(SI,I),(SJ,J),TsIJ,TeIJ),
28    nonReceivedRequest(IdJK,J,SK,TsJK,TeJK),
29    TsIJ =< TsJK, TsJK =< TeIJ,
30    L=log(SJ,J,TeJK,timeout(SK,IdJK),MJ,SevJ),
31    causedBy(L,Xs,Root).
```

The fifth case (lines 32–35) infers that event E logged by instance I of service SI (line 33), currently being explained, has been caused by the *unreachability of the invoked service instance* J of SJ. Indeed, I incurred in a timeout during an interaction Id with SJ (line 33), which was caused by a request that was never received at any instance of SJ (line 34). Then, the Log currently being explained is added to the explanation (line 32), and causedBy/3 recurs to possibly explain an abducted piece of knowledge, i.e. that SJ was unreachable (line 35).

```
32   causedBy(Log,[Log|Xs],Root) :-
33     Log = log(SI,I,T,timeout(SJ,Id),M,Sev),
34     nonReceivedRequest(Id,I,SJ,_,T),
35     causedBy(unreachable(SJ),Xs,Root).
```

The sixth case (line 36) explains an internal event R logged by a service, identifying the service itself as the Root cause for R. Recursion ends.

```
36   causedBy(Log,[Log],Root) :- Log = log(Root,R,T,internal,M,Sev).
```

The seventh case (line 37) explains an abducted unreachable(Root) fact, identifying that such a service was temporarily unreachable as it previously logged some information. Recursion ends.

```
37   causedBy(Log,[Log],Root) :- Log = unreachable(Root), log(Root,_,_,_,_,_).
```

The last case (lines 38–39) explains an abducted unreachable(Root) fact (line 34), identifying that such a service never logged any information (line 39). Recursion ends, by adding the fact that Root was possibly never started (line 40).

```
38   causedBy(unreachable(Root),[Log],Root) :-
39     \+ log(Root,_,_,_,_,_),
40     Log = neverStarted(Root).
```

Last, but not least, xfail(Event,Explanations,RootCause) exploits causedBy/3 to determine all distinct Explanations starting from the service RootCause, as in:

```
xfail(Event,Explanations,RootCause) :-
   findall(E,distinct(causedBy(Event,E,RootCause)),Explanations).
```

It is worth noting that, thanks to Prolog resolution mechanisms, our methodology permits instantiating the RootCause parameter to a specific service name so to restrict the obtained explanations only to those that have such a service as the failure cascade root cause. If, conversely, RootCause is left unbound, it determines all explanations for all possible values that can be unified with RootCause. This enables using our methodology both as an explainer working in pipeline with other existing tools for root caused identification and as a standalone tool.

4   Prototype Implementation

We developed an open source prototype of our explainable analysis technique, called yRCA.[3] yRCA embeds the Prolog reasoner presented in the previous section in a Python-based command-line tool, which can be run as follows:

```
python3 yrca.py [-r S] [-v] EVENT LOGS TEMPLATES
```

where EVENT and LOGS are two JSON files containing the failure event to be explained and a dump of the distributed logs of all service instances in an application. In both JSON files, log entries are expected to be in GELF (*Graylog Extended Log Format* [5]). TEMPLATES is instead a YAML file specifying the templates to parse log messages, with each template being a regular expression to match log messages to determine whether they correspond to client-side events (viz., request sent, successful/error response received, or timeout expired) or server-side events (viz., request received, response sent). Finally, option -r S enables focusing on explanations having S as the root causing service, e.g., to explain how its failure – identified with another root cause analysis technique – caused that in EVENT. Option -v instead allows running yRCA in *verbose* mode, namely by printing all possible explanations, rather than grouping them based on their structure, as yRCA does by default.

An example of output returned by yRCA is shown hereafter, with possible explanations for the failure mentioned in our motivating scenario (Sect. 2):

```
[0.615]: edgeRouter: Error response (code: 500) received from frontend
(request_id: [<requestId>])
    -> frontend: Error response (code: 500) received from orders (request_id:
       [<requestId>])
    -> orders: Failing to contact carts (request_id: [<requestId>]). Root
       cause: <exception>
    -> carts: unreachable
[0.385]: edgeRouter: Error response (code: 500) received from frontend
(request_id: [<requestId>])
    -> frontend: Failing to contact carts (request_id: [<requestId>]). Root
       cause: <exception>
    -> carts: unreachable
```

Note that, by default, yRCA groups the possible explanations based on the structure of the failure cascade, and it ranks the different explanations based on the frequency with which they occur in all identified failure cascades —with such frequency indicated between square brackets at the beginning of each explanation. The idea is that the more frequent is an explanation, the higher is the probability that it corresponds to the true explanation for an observed failure. This is inspired by other existing analysis techniques, which rank the identified root causes by giving higher ranks to those found with a higher rate [28].

---

[3] https://github.com/di-unipi-socc/yrca

5   Evaluation

To assess the practical applicability of our root cause analysis technique, we run yRCA in controlled experiments.[4] Their objective was to evaluate the performances of our technique in determining the failure cascades that may have caused an observed failure, namely whether the true cause is among those returned, how many possible explanations were returned, and the elapsed time.

In our experiments, we exploited the CHAOS ECHO testbed [27] to obtain a reference application. CHAOS ECHO enables deploying interconnected services to mirror the architecture of an existing application, while replacing each of its services with a CHAOS ECHO service. A CHAOS ECHO service simulates the behaviour of an existing service by interacting with its backend services (if any) to process incoming requests, and by possibly failing in doing so. Whenever it receives a request, it interacts with a randomly selected subset of its backend services, each invoked with a given probability. The CHAOS ECHO service forwards them the incoming request's message and waits for their answer. If any of the invoked backend services returns an error response, or if a request timeout expires, the CHAOS ECHO service considers the interaction as failed. It then fails in cascade, by replying to the request under processing with an error response. A CHAOS ECHO service may also fail on its own, with a given probability, either returning an error response (even if all its backend services successfully replied to its requests) or by suddenly crashing, hence not replying at all. By differently configuring the CHAOS ECHO services in a reference application, we can control how their services interact, fail, and propagate failures. This, together with the workload generator available in the CHAOS ECHO testbed, enable assessing tools for analysing failures in multi-service applications, like yRCA.

The reference application we used in our experiments mirrors *Sock Shop* (Fig. 1), by replacing each of its components by a CHAOS ECHO service. The CHAOS ECHO service replacing edgeRouter was then configured to always invoke frontend and to never fail on its own, but only in cascade to the service it interacts with, viz., frontend. Our objective was indeed to assess yRCA's ability to determine the root causing failures and the cascades that resulted in failures observed on edgeRouter. All other CHAOS ECHO services were then differently configured to analyze the performances of yRCA when varying four different parameters, viz., (a) end-user load, (b) service interaction rate, (c) failure cascade length, and (d) service failure rate. More precisely:

(a) We configured all services (but edgeRouter) to invoke their backend services with probability 0.5. We also set them to never fail on their own, with the only exception of carts, which was set to fail with probability 0.5. We then varied the end-user load from 1 to 100 req/s.
(b) We varied the probability with which all services (but edgeRouter) invoked their backend services from 0.1 to 1. We also set them to never fail on their

---

[4] The sources of the controlled experiments are publicly available at https://github.com/di-unipi-socc/yrca/tree/main/data/experiments/sock-echo.

own (except for `carts`, which was set to fail with probability 0.5) and we fixed the end-user load to 10 req/s.

(c) We configured all services (but `edgeRouter`) to invoke their backend services with probability 0.5 and set the end-user load to 10 req/s. We then varied the length of the considered failure cascade by considering the different cases of `frontend`, `orders`, `shipping`, or `rabbitMq` being the *only* services set to fail on their own with probability 0.5. This enabled us to generate failure cascades of length 1, 2, 3, or 4, respectively.

(d) We configured the services to invoke their backend services with probability 0.5 and set the end-user load to 10 req/s. We then set all services (but `edgeRouter`) to fail with a probability varying from 0.1 to 1.

In all cases, to also account for service instances, all services (but `edgeRouter`) were set to be replicated over two instances. Overall, we hence always had 27 deployed service instances.

We run the differently configured deployments to generate logs, ensuring that each deployment was generating at least 200 failures in `edgeRouter`. We then run yRCA to explain a random sample of 200 `edgeRouter`'s failures in the logs of each case, repeating the run 5 times for each failure, so as to measure the average time yRCA took to explain a failure in each case. As a result, we observed that the results returned by yRCA contained the true root cause and the corresponding explanation in 99.74% of the times. The effectivenss of our technique however not only depends on this, but also on the number of returned false positives, viz., failure cascades considered to have possibly caused the observed failure, even if this was not the case. False positives should be kept low, as they require application operators to waste time and resources in unnecessarily checking them [28]. We therefore measured the average number of failure cascades identified by yRCA, one being the right solution and the other being false positives.[5]

Number of Identified Failure Cascades. The results of our measurements are shown in Fig. 2. We can readily observe that in cases (a–c), where there was only one service set to possibly fail (and to cause subsequent failure cascades), yRCA correctly determined only one possible root cause. The latter effectively corresponded to the known ground truth in all the three cases, viz., `carts` in cases (a) and (b), and each service set to fail in each different cascade for case (c). yRCA also identified a number of possible explanations originating from carts that slightly increased when we increased (a) the load rate, (b) the rate with which each service was invoking its backend services, and (c) the length of the failure cascade. This is mainly because the increasing load/interactions in (a–b) resulted in an increasing number of service interactions, whilst in (c) we had an increasing number of services failing in cascade. For this reasons, (a–c) resulted in an increasing number of possible paths for the root causing failure to propagate up to `edgeRouter`, which is reflected by the plots (a–c) in Fig. 2.

The results were instead quite different when we increased the probability with which each service (but `edgeRouter`) could have failed, as shown in Fig. 2(d).

---

[5] All experiments reported in this section were executed on a Ubuntu 20.04.3 LTS virtual machine, with four vCPUs and 32 GB of RAM.

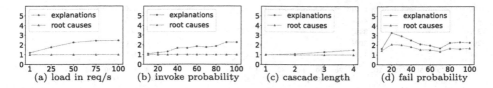

Fig. 2. Average number (y-axis) of identified explanations and root causes.

In this case, all instances of the services in Fig. 1 (but queueMaster) not only get invoked to process an end-user request received by edgeRouter, but they may also fail on their own with increasing probability. Their failures may then propagate and cause that observed on edgeRouter. Even in such a complex scenario, with all instances of 12 services possibly being the root cause of an observed failure, the average numbers of root causes and explanations returned by yRCA were (in the worst case) around two and three, respectively. Out of those, one always corresponded to the true root cause and failure cascade that happened in our reference application deployment.

The above discussed experiments (a–d) show that yRCA not only effectively identified the failure cascades that caused an observed failure, but also that it was able of restricting such cascades to quite a few. This hence reduces the number of false positives returned by yRCA, which is a plus when enacting root cause analysis in applications composed of many interacting microservices [28].

Average Processing Time. Figure 3 shows the average time required by yRCA to explain each failure in each experiment, normalised in milliseconds for processing a megabyte of logs. We can observe that the average processing time depends on how much services interacts. Indeed, elapsed time significantly grew with (a) the load rate, whose increase results more service interactions due to a higher number of end users' requests to be processed, and with (b) the probability of each service invoking its backend services. This is to be expected, given that our Prolog reasoner first identifies and classifies service interactions, to then process classified interactions to reconstruct possible failure cascades (Sect. 3). It is anyhow worth noting that, even in the cases of heavy load, yRCA took 104.04 s to process 381.21 MBs of logs. Such an amount of time is acceptable for an offline task as that of failure root cause analysis [37]. It is also much less than that we would need to elicit the failure cascades that may have caused a failure by manually inspecting the same logs, even in the case when the possible root causing failures have already been identified with some existing technique (like those discussed in Sect. 6).

Figure 3 also shows that the average processing time instead kept stable when we increased (c) the length of failure cascades or (d) the services' failure rate. This suggests that our root cause analysis is independent from how long is a failure cascade or how many services failed, as it would require the same processing time. This is a desiderata when having big enterprise applications where a failure cascade may involve tens of services [30].

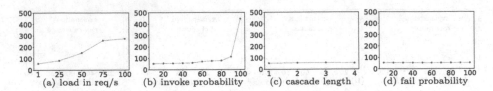

Fig. 3. Average elapsed time (y-axis) for each experiment, in ms/MB.

6   Related Work

Various techniques have been proposed to identify the possible root causes of failures in multi-service applications [28]. This is typically done by relying on applications being instrumented to feature distributed tracing or to monitor specific Key Performance Indicators (KPIs) on their services. For instance, Zhou *et al.* [37] and Guo *et al.* [6] propose two methodologies to systematically identify the root cause of a failure observed on the frontend of an application, based on manually inspecting its distributed traces with the support of visualisation tools. Similarly to our technique, their methodologies enable identifying not only the possible root causing failures, but also the cascades that made such failures propagate up to that observed on the application frontend. They however differ from our technique, since we enable identifying the possible root causes for failures happening on any service in an application, whilst also fully automating the root cause analysis.

CloudDiag [18], TraceAnomaly [13], MonitorRank [8], and MicroHECL [12] are other examples of distributed tracing-based root cause analysis techniques, yet fully automating the analysis. CloudDiag [18] and TraceAnomaly [13] directly analyse the distributed traces and consider as possible root causes for a failure those services whose response time was anomalous. MonitorRank [8] and Micro-HECL [12] instead process the distributed traces to obtain a graph representing the services forming the application and their interactions, which they then visit guided by the correlation between service performances. The services corresponding to the nodes where their visits stop are considered as possible root causes for the considered failure. A first difference between the above techniques (but MicroHECL [12]) resides in the fact that they focus on analysing the possible root causes of failures happening on the application frontend, whilst we enable analysing those for failures happening on any service. In addition, all the above techniques differ from ours since they require application to feature distributed tracing, and since they return the possible root causes for a failure, but without explaining how they propagated and caused the observed failure. Our technique can hence complement their results, by not only returning the possible root causes of an observed failure, but also the cascades that made root causing failures propagate to that observed.

Similar considerations apply to the root cause analysis techniques requiring to instrument applications to monitor specific KPIs on their services. For instance, ϵ-diagnosis [26], PAL [21], Wang *et al.* [31], and FChain [22] enable determining the possible root causes for a service's failure, based on the correlation between anomalous KPI values monitored on the failing service and on other services. They all differ from our technique since, even if identifying the possible root causes for an observed failure (which must be a frontend failure in the case ϵ-diagnosis [26], PAL [21], and FChain [22]), they are not providing explanations on how the root causing failures propagated to that observed. We instead enable identifying the failure cascades that caused a failure observed on any service. We can thus complement the results obtained with ϵ-diagnosis [26], PAL [21], Wang et al. [31], or FChain [22], by allowing to determine how the root causing failures – identified with such techniques – propagated and caused that observed.

MicroRCA [35], Wu et al. [36], Sieve [30], and Brandón et al. [2], and DLA [25] exploit monitored KPIs to drive the search for the possible root causes of a failure in a graph-based modelling of the architecture of an application. The latter is automatically reconstructed by MicroRCA [35], Wu et al. [36], Sieve [30], and Brandón et al. [2] from monitored KPIs themselves, and it is instead an input for DLA [25]. Despite relying different methods to visit the graph, they can all effectively determine the possible root causes for an observed failure. At the same time, they all differ from our technique since they return the possible root causing failures, without eliciting how such failures propagated and caused that observed. We instead enable identifying the whole failure cascades that caused an observed failure, also allowing to explain how the root causing failures identified with MicroRCA [35], Wu et al. [36], Sieve [30], Brandón et al. [2], or DLA [25] caused that observed.

Similar considerations apply to CauseInfer [4], Microscope [10], Qiu et al. [23], CloudRanger [32], MS-Rank [14], AutoMap [15], MicroCause [17], FacGraph [11], and LOUD [16]. They all exploit monitored KPIs to infer a causality graph, whose nodes model the services forming an application and whose arcs model causal relationships between the performances of its services. Most of them then exploit KPIs to identify the possible root causes of a failure by visiting the causality graph, with CauseInfer [4], Microscope [10], and Qiu et al. [23] enacting a KPI-driven BFS, whereas CloudRanger [32], MS-Rank [14], AutoMap [15], MicroCause [17] enact a random walk similar to that of MonitorRank [8]. FacGraph [11] and LOUD [16] instead analyze the graph structure to determine the possible root causes for a failure. Again, the main difference between such techniques and ours resides in explainability. The above techniques indeed effectively identify the possible root causes for an observed failure, without explaining how the root causing failures propagated to that observed. Our technique instead determines the failure cascades that may have possibly caused an observed failure, hence also enabling to complement the results that can be obtained with the above discussed techniques.

Finally, it is worth positioning our work with respect to Aggarwal et al. [1] and our previous work [29], which both process the logs produced by the services in an application, instead of requiring it to feature distributed tracing or to get instrumented with monitoring probes. Aggarwal et al. [1] model the logs of the services forming an application as multivariate time series, and it then exploits Granger causality tests to derive a causality graph. In the latter, nodes model services, whilst arcs model causal dependencies among the errors logged by services. The causality graph is then visited by enacting a random walk similar to MonitorRank [8], in order to determine the highest probable root cause for a failure observed on the application frontend. Aggarwal *et al.* [1] hence differ from our technique since they return one possible root cause for a frontend failure, without explaining how such root causing failure propagated to the application frontend. We instead enable determining the possible root causes for failures observed on any service, while also eliciting the failure cascades that may have caused root causing failures to propagate to the observed ones.

In this perspective, the root cause analysis technique we proposed in our previous work [29] is closer to that in this paper, given that it identifies the possible root causes and explains how they propagated to cause an observed failure. Our previous work [29] however relies on a specification of the application architecture and of the failure behaviour of each of the service therein, given by associating each service to its fault-aware management protocol [3]. We indeed exploited such specification to drive the search for failure cascades in the application logs. The technique presented in this paper hence differs from that in our previous work [29], given that we now directly process the application logs, without requiring any specification of the application.

In summary, to the best of our knowledge, ours is the first explainable root cause analysis technique, which not only determines the possible root causes for a failure, as typically done in literature, but also the cascades due to which the root causing failures propagated and caused that observed. It is the first doing it in a fully automated manner, and without requiring other inputs than the logs produced by the services forming an application. Our technique can also complement the results obtained with other existing techniques, by explaining how the root causing failures they identify propagated and caused that observed.

7   Conclusions

We presented an explainable technique for determining the possible root causes of cascading failures in any microservice-based application, provided that its services suitably log their interaction and failure events (Sect. 5). Our technique can be used to determine the failure cascades that possibly caused an observed failure, either also eliciting the possible root causes or starting from a given set of possible root causes. It can hence complement existing root cause analysis techniques, providing explanations of how the root causing failures they identify propagated and caused that observed.

We also presented a prototype implementation of our technique, called yRCA, which we used to assess it based on controlled experiments run on an existing chaos testbed. The results of our experiments showed that yRCA features good time performances, and that it effectively determined the root cause of a failure in 99.74% of the cases. This happened whilst returning around 3 possible explanations in the worst case. yRCA hence kept the number of false negatives low, thus limiting the efforts hat should be spent by application administrators in checking failure cascades that did not truly caused an observed failure.

The failure cascades explaining an observed failure can help application administrators in identifying where to enact suitable countermeasures (e.g., circuit breakers and bulkheads [20]) to avoid the occurrence of those failure cascades. One natural direction for future work is the prototyping of a tool supporting the visualization of failure cascades explaining observed failures, together with suggestions of possible countermeasures.

Another interesting future work direction is experimenting our technique on industrial applications, based on different chaos testing approaches (e.g., Netflix's Chaos Monkey [19]). We also plan to extend the scope of our explainable root cause analysis to deal with incomplete logs, e.g., in case the logging driver fails or a service instance gets suddenly killed without flushing all its logs.

References

1. Aggarwal, P., et al.: Localization of operational faults in cloud applications by mining causal dependencies in logs using golden signals. In: Hacid, H., et al. (eds.) ICSOC 2020. LNCS, vol. 12632, pp. 137–149. Springer, Cham (2021). https://doi.org/10.1007/978-3-030-76352-7_17
2. Brandón, A., et al.: Graph-based root cause analysis for service-oriented and microservice architectures. J. Syst. Soft. **159**, 110432 (2020). https://doi.org/10.1016/j.jss.2019.110432
3. Brogi, A., et al.: Fault-aware management protocols for multi-component applications. J. Syst. Softw. **139**, 189–210 (2018). https://doi.org/10.1016/j.jss.2018.02.005
4. Chen, P., et al.: Causeinfer: automatic and distributed performance diagnosis with hierarchical causality graph in large distributed systems. In: INFOCOM 2014, pp. 1887–1895. IEEE (2014). https://doi.org/10.1109/INFOCOM.2014.6848128
5. Graylog Extend Log Format: Graylog (2022). https://www.graylog.org/
6. Guo, X., et al.: Graph-based trace analysis for microservice architecture understanding and problem diagnosis. In: ESEC/FSE 2020, pp. 1387–1397. ACM (2020). https://doi.org/10.1145/3368089.3417066
7. IETF: The Syslog protocol. RFC 5424, Network Working Group (2009)
8. Kim, M., et al.: Root cause detection in a service-oriented architecture. SIGMETRICS Perform. Eval. Rev. **41**(1), 93–104 (2013). https://doi.org/10.1145/2494232.2465753
9. Kratzke, N., Quint, P.: Understanding cloud-native applications after 10 years of cloud computing - a systematic mapping study. J. Syst. Soft. **126**, 1–16 (2017). https://doi.org/10.1016/j.jss.2017.01.001
10. Lin, J., Chen, P., Zheng, Z.: Microscope: pinpoint performance issues with causal graphs in micro-service environments. In: Pahl, C., Vukovic, M., Yin, J., Yu, Q. (eds.) ICSOC 2018. LNCS, vol. 11236, pp. 3–20. Springer, Cham (2018). https://doi.org/10.1007/978-3-030-03596-9_1
11. Lin, W., et al.: FacGraph: frequent anomaly correlation graph mining for root cause diagnose in micro-service architecture. In: IPCCC 2018, pp. 1–8. IEEE (2018). https://doi.org/10.1109/PCCC.2018.8711092

12. Liu, D., et al.: MicroHECL: high-efficient root cause localization in large-scale microservice systems. In: ICSE-SEIP 2021, pp. 338–347. IEEE (2021). https://doi.org/10.1109/ICSE-SEIP52600.2021.00043
13. Liu, P., et al.: Unsupervised detection of microservice trace anomalies through service-level deep Bayesian networks. In: ISSRE 2020, pp. 48–58. IEEE (2020). https://doi.org/10.1109/ISSRE5003.2020.00014
14. Ma, M., et al.: MS-rank: multi-metric and self-adaptive root cause diagnosis for microservice applications. In: ICWS 2019, pp. 60–67. IEEE (2019). https://doi.org/10.1109/ICWS.2019.00022
15. Ma, M., et al.: AutoMAP: diagnose your microservice-based web applications automatically. In: WWW 2020, pp. 246–258. ACM, New York (2020). https://doi.org/10.1145/3366423.3380111
16. Mariani, L., et al.: Localizing faults in cloud systems. In: ICST 2018, pp. 262–273. IEEE (2018). https://doi.org/10.1109/ICST.2018.00034
17. Meng, Y., et al.: Localizing failure root causes in a microservice through causality inference. In: IWQoS 2020, pp. 1–10. IEEE (2020). https://doi.org/10.1109/IWQoS49365.2020.9213058
18. Mi, H., et al.: Toward fine-grained, unsupervised, scalable performance diagnosis for production cloud computing systems. IEEE Trans. Par. Dist. Sys. 24(6), 1245–1255 (2013). https://doi.org/10.1109/TPDS.2013.21
19. Netflix: Chaos monkey. https://netflix.github.io/chaosmonkey/. Accessed 13 Aug 2022
20. Newman, S.: Building Microservices, 2 edn. O'Reilly Media, Sebastopol (2021)
21. Nguyen, H., et al.: PAL: propagation-aware anomaly localization for cloud hosted distributed applications. In: Managing Large-Scale Systems via the Analysis of System Logs and the Application of Machine Learning Techniques. ACM (2011). https://doi.org/10.1145/2038633.2038634
22. Nguyen, H., et al.: FChain: toward black-box online fault localization for cloud systems. In: ICDCS 2013, pp. 21–30. IEEE (2013). https://doi.org/10.1109/ICDCS.2013.26
23. Qiu, J., et al.: A causality mining and knowledge graph based method of root cause diagnosis for performance anomaly in cloud applications. App. Sci. 10(6) (2020). https://doi.org/10.3390/app10062166
24. Richardson, C.: Microservices Patterns, 1 edn. Manning Publications, Shelter Island (2018)
25. Samir, A., Pahl, C.: DLA: detecting and localizing anomalies in containerized microservice architectures using Markov models. In: FiCloud 2019, pp. 205–213. IEEE (2019). https://doi.org/10.1109/FiCloud.2019.00036
26. Shan, H., et al.: ε-diagnosis: unsupervised and real-time diagnosis of small-window long-tail latency in large-scale microservice platforms. In: WWW 2019, pp. 3215–3222. ACM (2019). https://doi.org/10.1145/3308558.3313653
27. Soldani, J., Brogi, A.: Automated generation of configurable cloud-native chaos testbeds. In: Adler, R., et al. (eds.) EDCC 2021. CCIS, vol. 1462, pp. 101–108. Springer, Cham (2021). https://doi.org/10.1007/978-3-030-86507-8_10
28. Soldani, J., Brogi, A.: Anomaly detection and failure root cause analysis in (micro) service-based cloud applications: a survey. ACM Comput. Surv. 55(3) (2022). https://doi.org/10.1145/3501297
29. Soldani, J., Montesano, G., Brogi, A.: What went wrong? Explaining cascading failures in microservice-based applications. In: Barzen, J. (ed.) SummerSOC 2021. CCIS, vol. 1429, pp. 133–153. Springer, Cham (2021). https://doi.org/10.1007/978-3-030-87568-8_9

30. Thalheim, J., et al.: Sieve: actionable insights from monitored metrics in distributed systems. In: Middleware 2017, pp. 14–27. ACM (2017). https://doi.org/10.1145/3135974.3135977
31. Wang, L., et al.: Root-cause metric location for microservice systems via log anomaly detection. In: ICWS 2020, pp. 142–150. IEEE (2020). https://doi.org/10.1109/ICWS49710.2020.00026
32. Wang, P., et al.: CloudRanger: root cause identification for cloud native systems. In: CCGRID 2018, pp. 492–502. IEEE (2018). https://doi.org/10.1109/CCGRID.2018.00076
33. Waseem, M., et al.: Design, monitoring, and testing of microservices systems: the practitioners' perspective. J. Syst. Soft. **182**, 111061 (2021). https://doi.org/10.1016/j.jss.2021.111061
34. Weaveworks: Sock shop (2017). https://microservices-demo.github.io
35. Wu, L., et al.: MicroRCA: root cause localization of performance issues in microservices. In: NOMS 2020, pp. 1–9. IEEE (2020). https://doi.org/10.1109/NOMS47738.2020.9110353
36. Wu, L., Bogatinovski, J., Nedelkoski, S., Tordsson, J., Kao, O.: Performance diagnosis in cloud microservices using deep learning. In: Hacid, H., et al. (eds.) ICSOC 2020. LNCS, vol. 12632, pp. 85–96. Springer, Cham (2021). https://doi.org/10.1007/978-3-030-76352-7_13
37. Zhou, X., et al.: Fault analysis and debugging of microservice systems: industrial survey, benchmark system, and empirical study. IEEE Trans. Soft. Eng. **47**(2), 243–260 (2021). https://doi.org/10.1109/TSE.2018.2887384

Trusted Execution, Deep Learning, and IoT

Attestation Mechanisms for Trusted Execution Environments Demystified

Jämes Ménétrey[1]([✉]) [ID], Christian Göttel[1] [ID], Anum Khurshid[2] [ID],
Marcelo Pasin[1] [ID], Pascal Felber[1] [ID], Valerio Schiavoni[1] [ID], and Shahid Raza[2] [ID]

[1] University of Neuchâtel, Neuchâtel, Switzerland
{james.menetrey,christian.gottel,marcelo.pasin,pascal.felber,
valerio.schiavoni}@unine.ch
[2] RISE Research Institutes of Sweden, Stockholm, Sweden
{anum.khurshid,shahid.raza}@ri.se

Abstract. Attestation is a fundamental building block to establish trust over software systems. When used in conjunction with trusted execution environments, it guarantees the genuineness of the code executed against powerful attackers and threats, paving the way for adoption in several sensitive application domains. This paper reviews remote attestation principles and explains how the modern and industrially well-established trusted execution environments Intel SGX, Arm TrustZone and AMD SEV, as well as emerging RISC-V solutions, leverage these mechanisms.

Keywords: Trusted execution environments · Attestation · Intel SGX · Arm TrustZone · AMD SEV · RISC-V

1 Introduction

Confidentiality and integrity are essential features when building secure computer systems. This is particularly important when the underlying system cannot be fully trusted or controlled. For example, video broadcasting software can be tampered with by end-users to circumvent digital rights management, or virtual machines are candidly open to the indiscretion of their cloud-based untrusted hosts. The introduction of Trusted Execution Environments (TEEs), such as Intel SGX, AMD SEV, RISC-V and Arm TrustZone-A/-M, into commodity processors, significantly mitigates the attack surface against powerful attackers. In a nutshell, TEEs let a piece of software be executed with stronger security guarantees, including privacy and integrity properties, without relying on a trustworthy operating system. Each of these enabling technologies offers different degrees of guarantees that can be leveraged to increase the confidentiality and integrity of applications.

Published by Springer Nature Switzerland AG 2022
D. Eyers and S. Voulgaris (Eds.): DAIS 2022, LNCS 13272, pp. 95–113, 2022.
https://doi.org/10.1007/978-3-031-16092-9_7

Remote attestation allows establishing a trusting relationship with a specific software by verifying its authenticity and integrity. Through remote attestation, one ensures to be communicating with a specific, trusted (attested) program remotely. TEEs can support and strengthen the attestation process, ensuring that programs are shielded against many powerful attacks by isolating critical security software, assets and private information from the rest of the system. However, to the best of our knowledge, there is not a clear systematisation of attestation mechanisms supported by modern and industrially well-established TEEs. Hence, the main contribution of this work is to describe the state-of-the-art best practices regarding remote attestation mechanisms of TEEs, covering a necessarily incomplete selection of TEEs, which includes the four major technologies available for commodity hardware, which are Intel SGX, Arm TrustZone-A/-M, AMD SEV and many emerging TEEs using the open ISA RISC-V. We complement previous work [36,37] with an updated analysis of TEEs (e.g., introduction of Intel SGX and Arm TrustZone variations), a thorough analysis of remote attestation mechanisms and coverage of the upcoming TEEs of Intel and Arm.

2   Attestation

2.1   Local Attestation

Local attestation enables a trusted environment to prove its identity to any other trusted environments hosted on the same system, respectively, on the same CPU if the secret provisioned for the attestation is bound to the processor. The target environment that receives the local attestation request can assess whether the issued proof is genuine by verifying its authentication, usually based on a symmetric-key scheme, using a *message authentication code* (MAC). This mechanism is required to establish secure communication channels between trusted environments, often used to delegate computing tasks securely. As an example, Intel SGX's remote attestation (detailed in Sect. 3.3) leverages the local attestation to sign proofs in another trusted environment through a secure communication channel.

2.2   Remote Attestation

Remote attestation allows to establish trust between different devices and provides cryptographic proofs that the executing software is genuine and untampered [18]. In the remainder, we adopt the terminology proposed by the IETF to describe remote attestation and related architectures [13]. Under these terms, a *relying party* wishes to establish a trusted relationship with an *attester*, thanks to the help of a *verifier*. The attester provides the state of its system, indicating the hardware and the software stack that runs on its device by collecting a set of *claims* of trustworthiness. A claim is a piece of asserted information collected by an attesting environment, e.g., a TEE. An example of claims is the code *measurement*, (i.e., a cryptographic hash of the application's code) of an executing program within a TEE. TEEs also create additional claims that identify the *trusted computing base* (TCB is the amount of hardware and software that needs to be trusted), so verifiers are able to evaluate the genuineness of the platform. Claims are collected and cryptographically signed to form *evidence*, later observed and accepted (or denied) by the verifier. Once the attester is proven genuine, the relying party can safely interact with it and transfer confidential data or delegate computations.

The problem of remotely attesting software has been extensively studied in academia, and industrial implementations already exist. Three leading families of remote attestation methods exist: (i) software-based, (ii) hardware-based, and (iii) hybrid (software- and hardware-based). Software-based remote attestation [47] does not depend on any particular hardware. This method is particularly adapted to low-cost use cases. Hardware-based remote attestation relies on a *root of trust*, which is one or many cryptographic values rooted in hardware to ensure that the claims are trustworthy. Typically, a root of trust can be implemented using tamper-resistant hardware, such as a *trusted platform module* (TPM) [55], a *physical unclonable function* (PUF) that prevents impersonations by using unique hardware marks produced at manufacture [30], or a hardware secret fused in a die (e.g., CPU) exposed exclusively to the trusted environment. Hybrid solutions combine hardware devices and software implementations [21], in an attempt to leverage advantages from both sides. Researchers used hardware/software co-design techniques to propose a hybrid design with a formal proof of correctness [40]. Finally, remote attestation mechanisms are popular among the TEEs due to their carefully controlled environments and their ability to generate code measurements. Section 3 delivers extensive analysis of the state of the art of the TEEs, including their support for remote attestation.

2.3   Mutual Attestation

Trusted applications may need stronger trust assurances by ensuring both ends of a secure channel are attested. For example, when retrieving confidential data from a sensing IoT device (where data is particularly sensitive), the device must authenticate the remote party, while the latter must ensure the sensing device has not been spoofed or tampered with. Mutual attestation protocols have been designed to appraise the trustworthiness of both end devices involved in a communication. We also report how mutual attestation has also been studied in the context of TEEs [51], as we further detail in Sect. 3.

3 Issuing Attestations Using TEEs

Several solutions exist to implement hardware support for trusted computing, and TEEs are particularly promising. Typically, a TEE consists of isolating critical components of the system, (e.g., portions of the memory), denying access to more privileged but untrusted systems, such as kernel and machine modes. Depending on the implementation, it guarantees the confidentiality and the integrity of the code and data of trusted applications, thanks to the assistance of CPU security features. This work surveys modern and prevailing TEEs from processor designers and vendors with remote attestation capabilities for commodity or server-grade processors, namely Intel SGX [19], AMD SEV [3], and Arm TrustZone [42]. Besides, RISC-V, an open ISA with multiple open-source core implementations, ratified the *physical memory protection* (PMP) instructions, offering similar capabilities to memory protection offered by aforementioned technologies. As such, we also included many emerging academic and proprietary frameworks that capitalise on standard RISC-V primitives, which are Keystone [33], Sanctum [20], TIMBER-V [54] and LIRA-V [49]. Finally, among the many other technologies in the literature, we omitted the TEEs lacking remote attestation mechanisms (e.g., IBM PEF [26]) as well as the TEEs not supported on currently available CPUs (e.g., Intel TDX [27], Realm [11] from Arm CCA [8]).

Table 1. Comparison of the state-of-the-art TEEs.

Features	SGX Client SGX	SGX Scalable SGX	TrustZone TrustZone-A	TrustZone TrustZone-M	SEV Vanilla	SEV SEV-ES	SEV SEV-SNP	RISC-V Keystone	RISC-V Sanctum	RISC-V TIMBER-V	RISC-V LIRA-V
Integrity	●	◐	○	○	○	○	◐	●	●	○	○
Freshness	●	◐	○	○	○	○	◐	●	○	○	○
Encryption	●	●	○	○	●	●	●	●	○	○	○
Unlimited domains	●	●	○	●	◐	●	●	●	●	●	○
Open source	○	○	◐	◐	○	○	○	●	●	●	●
Local attestation	●	●	○	○	○	○	○	○	●	●	●
Remote attestation	●	●	◐	◐	●	●	●	●	●	●	●
API for attestation	●	●	◐	◐	●	●	●	●	●	●	●
Mutual attestation	○	○	◐	○	○	○	○	○	○	○	●
User-mode support	●	●	●	●	●	●	●	●	●	●	○
Industrial TEE	●	●	●	●	●	●	●	○	○	○	○
Isolation and attestation granularity	Intra-address space		Secure world		VM			Secure world	Intra-address space		
System support for isolation	μcode + XuCode		SMC	MPU	Firmware			SMC + PMP		Tag + MPU	PMP

Table 2. Features of the state-of-the-art TEEs.

Feature	Description
Integrity	An active mechanism preventing DRAM of TEE instances from being tampered with. Partial fulfilment means no protection against physical attacks.
Freshness	Protecting DRAM of TEE instances against replay and rollback attacks. Partial fulfilment means no protection against physical attacks.
Encryption	DRAM of TEE instances is encrypted to assure that no unauthorised access or memory snooping of the enclave occurs.
Unlimited domains	Many TEE instances can run concurrently, while the TEE boundaries (e.g.,isolation, integrity) between these instances are guaranteed by hardware. Partial fulfilment means that the number of domains is capped.
Open source	Indicate whether the solution is either partially or fully publicly available.
Local attestation	A TEE instance attests running on the same system to another instance.
Remote attestation	A TEE instance attests genuineness to remote parties. Partial fulfilment means no built-in support but is extended by the literature.
API for attestation	An API is available by the trusted applications to interact with the process of remote attestation. Partial fulfilment means no built-in support but is extended by the literature.
Mutual attestation	The identity of the attester and the verifier are authenticated upon remote attestations. Partial fulfilment means no built-in support but is extended by the literature.
User mode support	State whether the trusted applications are hosted in user mode, according to the processor architecture.
Industrial TEE	Contrast the TEEs used in production and made by the industry from the research prototypes designed by the academia.
Isolation and attestation granularity	The level of granularity where the TEE operates for providing isolation and attestation of the trusted software.
System support for isolation	The hardware mechanisms used to isolate trusted applications.

3.1   TEE Cornerstone Features

We propose a series of cornerstone features of TEEs and remote attestation capabilities and compare many emerging and well-established state-of-the-art solutions in Table 1. Each feature is detailed in Table 2 and can either be missing (○), partially (◔) or fully (●) available. Besides, we elaborate further on each TEE in the remainder of the section.

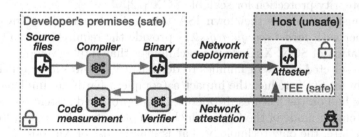

Fig. 1. The workflow of deployment and attestation of TEEs.

3.2 Trusted Environments and Remote Attestation

The attestation of software and hardware components requires an environment to issue evidence securely. This role is usually assigned to some software or hardware mechanism that cannot be tampered with. These environments rely on the code measurement of the executed software and combine that claim with cryptographic values derived from the root of trust. We analysed today's practices for the leading processor vendors for issuing cryptographically signed evidence.

Figure 1 illustrates the generic workflow TEE developers usually follow for the deployment of trusted applications. Initially, the application is compiled and measured on the developers' premises. It is later transferred to an untrusted system, executed in the TEE facility. Once the trusted application is loaded and required to receive sensitive data, it communicates with a verifier to establish a trusted channel. The TEE environment must facilitate this transaction by exposing evidence to the trusted application, which adds key material to bootstrap a secure channel from the TEE, thus preventing an attacker from eavesdropping on the communication. The verifier examines the evidence, maintaining a list of reference values to identify genuine instances of trusted applications. If recognised as trustworthy, the verifier can proceed to data exchanges.

3.3 Intel SGX

Intel Software Guard Extensions (SGX) [19] introduced TEEs for mass-market processors in 2015. Figure 2a illustrates the high-level architecture of SGX. Specifically, Intel's Skylake architecture introduced a new set of processor instructions to create encrypted regions of memory, called *enclaves*, living within the processes of the user space. Intel SGX exist in two flavours: *client* SGX and *scalable* SGX [12]. The former is the technology released in 2015, designed and implemented into consumer-grade processors, while the latter was released in 2021, focusing on server-grade processors. The key differences between the two variants are: (i) the volatile memory available to enclaves, 128 MB and 512 GB, respectively, (ii) the multi-socket support and (iii) the lack of integrity and replay protections against hardware attacks for the latter. Researchers conduct work to bring integrity protection for scalable SGX [12].

These instructions are their own ISA that is implemented in XuCode [28] and together with *model specific registers* provide the requirements to form the implementation of SGX. XuCode is a technology that Intel developed and integrated into selected processor families to deliver new features more quickly and, particularly for SGX, reduce the impact a (complex) hardware implementation would have had on the features. It operates from protected system memory in a special execution mode of the CPU, which are both set up by system firmware. SGX is, to date, the only technology that is making use of XuCode.

A memory region is reserved at boot time for storing code and data of encrypted enclaves. This memory area, called the *enclave page cache* (EPC), is inaccessible to other programs running on the same machine, including the operating system and the hypervisor. The traffic between the CPU and the system

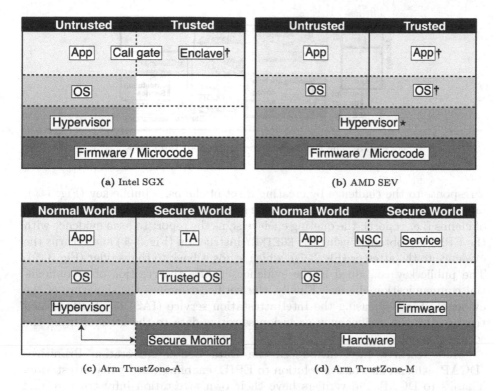

Fig. 2. Overview of the industrial TEE architectures. († denotes the attested elements) (* means trusted for SEV/SEV-ES, untrusted for SEV-SNP)

memory remains confidential thanks to the *memory encryption engine* (MEE). The EPC also stores verification codes to ensure that the DRAM corresponding to the EPC was not modified by any software external to the enclave.

A trusted application executing in an enclave may establish a local attestation with another enclave running on the same hardware. Toward this end, Intel SGX issues a set of claims, called *report*, that contains identities, attributes (i.e., modes and other properties), the trustworthiness of the TCB, additional information for the target enclave and a MAC. Unlike local attestation, remote attestation uses an asymmetric-key scheme, which is made possible by a special enclave, called *quoting enclave*, that has access to the device-specific private key. Intel designed their remote attestation protocol based on the SIGMA protocol [31] and extended it to the *enhanced privacy ID* (EPID). The EPID scheme does not identify unique entities, but rather a group of attesters. Each attester belongs to a group, and the verifier checks the group's public key. Evidence is signed by the EPID key, which guarantees the trustworthiness of the hardware and is bound to the firmware version of the processor.

In a remote attestation scenario, a verifier submits a challenge to the attester (i.e., application enclave) with a nonce (Fig. 3-①). The attester prepares

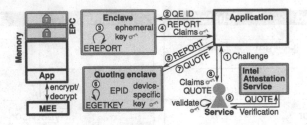

Fig. 3. The remote attestation flow of Intel SGX.

a response to the challenge by creating a set of claims, a public key (Fig. 3-③), and performs a local attestation with the quoting enclave. After verifying the set of claims (i.e., report), the quoting enclave signs the report to form evidence with the EPID key obtained using the EGETKEY instruction (Fig. 3-⑥) and returns the evidence to the attester (Fig. 3-⑦), which sends it back to the verifier (Fig. 3-⑧). The public key contained in the evidence enables the creation of a confidential communication channel. Finally, the verifier examines the signature of the evidence (Fig. 3-⑨) using the Intel attestation service (IAS) [5,14]. If deemed trustworthy, the verifier may provision sensitive data to the attester using the secure channel.

More recently, Intel introduced the Data Center Attestation Primitives (DCAP) [46], an alternative solution to EPID, enabling third-party attestation. Thanks to DCAP, the verifiers have their own attestation infrastructure and prevent depending on external dependencies (e.g., IAS) during the attestation procedure. DCAP introduces an additional step, where the quote (Fig. 3-⑦) is signed using *elliptic curve digital signature algorithm* (ECDSA) by the attestation collateral of the attestation infrastructure. Instead of contacting the IAS (Fig. 3-⑨), the service retrieves the attestation collateral associated with the received evidence from the attestation infrastructure in order to validate the signature.

While the quoting enclave, the microcode and XuCode are closed-source, recent work analysed the TEE and its attestation mechanism formally [45,50]. The other components of SGX (i.e., kernel driver and SDK) are open source. MAGE [16] further extended the remote attestation scheme of Intel SGX by offering mutual attestation for a group of enclaves without trusted third parties. Similarly, OPERA [17] proposes a decentralised attestation scheme, unchaining the attesters from the IAS while conducting attestation.

Intel SGX has many advantages but suffers from a few limitations as well. First, most of the SGX implementation limits the EPC size to 93.5 MB [52]. While smaller programs offer smaller attack surfaces, exceeding this threshold increases the memory access latency because of its pagination mechanism. Newer Intel Xeon processors extend that limit to 512 GB, but drop integrity protection and freshness against physical attacks. Besides, the enclave model prevents performing system calls and direct hardware access since the threat model distrusts the outer world, leading to the development of partitioned applications.

3.4   Arm TrustZone Architectures

Depending on the architecture of Arm's processors, TrustZone comes in two flavours: TrustZone-A (for Cortex-A) and TrustZone-M (for Cortex-M). While they share many design aspects, we detail how different they are in the remainder.

Arm TrustZone-A provides the hardware elements to establish a single TEE per system [42]. Figure 2c illustrates the high-level architecture of TrustZone-A. Broadly adopted by commodity devices, TrustZone splits the processor into two states: the secure world (TEE) and the normal world (untrusted environment). A *secure monitor* (SMC) is switching between worlds, and each world operates with its own user and kernel spaces. The trusted world uses a trusted operating system (e.g., OP-TEE) and runs *trusted applications* (TAs) as isolated processes. The normal world uses a traditional operating system (e.g., Linux).

Despite the commercial success of TrustZone-A, it lacks attestation mechanisms, preventing relying parties from validating and trusting the state of TrustZone-A remotely. Nevertheless, researchers proposed several variants of one-way remote attestation protocols for Arm TrustZone [34,56], as well as mutual remote attestation [2,48], thus extending the built-in capabilities of the architecture for attestation. All of these propositions require the availability of hardware primitives on the *system-on-chip* (SoC): (i) a root of trust in the secure world, (ii) a secure source of randomness for cryptographic operations, and (iii) a secure boot mechanism, ensuring the sane state of a system upon boot. Indeed, devices lacking built-in attestation mechanisms may rely on a root of trust to derive private cryptographic materials (e.g., a private key for evidence issuance). Secure boot measures the integrity of individual boot stages on devices and prevents tampered systems from being booted. As a result, remote parties can verify issued evidence in the TEE and ensure the trustworthiness of the attesters.

We describe the remote attestation mechanism of Shepherd et al. [48] as a study case. This solution establishes mutually trusted channels for bi-directional attestation, based on a *trusted measurer* (TM), which is a software component located in the trusted world and authenticated by the TEE's secure boot, to generate claims and issue evidence based on the OS and TA states. A private key is provisioned and sealed in the TEE's secure storage and used by the TM to sign evidence, similarly to a firmware TPM [43]. Using a dedicated protocol for remote attestation, the bi-directional attestation is accomplished in three rounds:

1. The attester sends a handshake request to the verifier containing the identity of both parties and the cryptographic materials to initiate keys establishment.
2. The verifier answers to the handshake by including similar information (i.e., both identifies and cryptographic materials), as well as evidence of the verifier's TEE, based on the computed common secret (i.e., using Diffie-Hellman).
3. Finally, the attester sends back signed evidence of the attester's TEE, based on the same common secret.

Once the two parties validated the genuineness of the evidence, they can derive further shared secrets to establish a trusted communication channel.

Arm TrustZone-A also presents some advantages and drawbacks. Hardware is independently accessible by both worlds, which is helpful for TEE applications utilising peripherals. On the other hand, the reference and open-source trusted OS, i.e., OP-TEE, limits the memory available to TAs by a few MB [24]. Due to this constraint, software needs to be partitioned to leverage TrustZone. Besides, the system must be installed in a particular way: a trusted OS is required, instead of creating TEE instances directly in the regular OS, bringing more complexity. Finally, OP-TEE is small and does not implement a POSIX API, making developing TAs difficult, notably when porting legacy code. While most components of TrustZone have open-source alternatives (e.g., the firmware and the trusted OS), many vendors do not disclose the implementation of the secure monitor.

Arm TrustZone-M (TZ-M) much like its predecessor TrustZone-A, provides an efficient mechanism to isolate the system into two distinct states/processing environments [7]. The TZ-M extension brings trusted execution into resource-constrained IoT devices (e.g., Cortex-M23/M33/M35P/M55). When a TZ-M enabled device boots up, it always starts in the secure world, where the memory is initialised before transferring the control to the normal world. Despite the similarity regarding the high-level concept, TrustZone-M differs from TrustZone-A in low-level implementation of some features. The switch between the secure and the normal world is embedded in hardware and is much faster than the secure monitor [6]. This makes the context switching efficient and suitable for constrained devices. The normal world applications directly call the secure world functions using the *non-secure callable* (NSC) region (Fig. 2d). TrustZone-M lacks complex memory management operations like the *memory management unit* (MMU) and only supports the *memory protection unit* (MPU) to enforce even finer levels of access control and memory protection [9]. In TZ-M enabled IoT devices, the secure world runs a concise trusted firmware which provides secure processing in the form of secure services (e.g., TrustedFirmware-M), which is a reference implementation of Platform Security Architecture (PSA) [10]) and the normal world supports real-time operating systems (e.g., Zephyr OS, Arm MBED OS, FreeRTOS).

Since TZ-M is a relatively new addition, recently available for the IoT infrastructure, existing work on attestation mechanisms for the hardware/software is scarce. Nonetheless, TZ-M fulfils some basic requirements for attestation like (i) secure storage, (ii) secure boot, (iii) secure inter-world communication and (iv) isolation of software. Thus, schemes like [1] have leveraged TZ-M to develop attestation and use TZ-M's TEE capabilities to establish a chain of trust. TrustedFirmware-M, following the guidelines of PSA, also supports initial attestation of device-specific data in the form of a secure service. We provide further details of the remote attestation mechanism introduced in DIAT [1]. It aims at providing run-time attestation of on-device data integrity in autonomous embedded systems in the absence of a central verifier. They provide attestation of the data integrity by identifying the software components (or modules), i.e., the claims, that process the data of concern, verifying that the modules are not modified, ensuring that all modules of software that influence data are benign. Data integrity is provided by attestation, ensuring correct processing of the sensitive data. The main steps of the protocol are described below:

- The verifier sends a request for data to the attester along with a nonce. The data can represent collected environmental (e.g., a sensing edge device) or compute-bound (e.g., machine learning) information.
- The attester generates the requested data and issues evidence, called the *attestation results*, which are the list of all the software modules that affect the data, and the control flow of each module is derived using the control flow graph. The attester signs the data and the evidence with its secret key and sends the authenticated data to the verifier.
- The verifier assesses the authenticity and integrity of the data by tracing the software modules from the evidence. Since the evidence is comprised of software modules that process the data and the frequency of execution of a module, unauthorised data modifications and code reuse attacks are detected and prevented.

TrustZone-M provides several advantages as a TEE to support remote attestation but also has a few drawbacks. It provides efficient isolation of the software modules and a faster context switch between the secure and normal world. This is advantageous as it is critical to have minimum attestation latency in the real-time operations of embedded systems like autonomous vehicles, industrial control systems, unmanned aerial vehicles, etc. The availability of hardware-unique keys in TZ-M enabled devices further ensures that the evidence generated by the TCB cannot be forged. Besides, the software stack may be fully open source, thanks to the absence of a secure monitor. On the other hand, since the components involved in measuring, attesting, and verifying the data/system need to be protected as part of the TCB, it increases the TCB size on the attested devices, raising the attack surface.

3.5   AMD SEV

AMD Secure Encrypted Virtualization (SEV) [3] allows isolating virtualised environments (e.g., containers and virtual machines) from trusted hypervisors. Figure 2b illustrates the high-level architecture of SEV. SEV uses an embedded hardware AES engine, which relies on multiple keys to encrypt memory seamlessly. It exploits a closed Arm Cortex-v5 processor as a secure co-processor, used to generate cryptographic materials kept in the CPU. Each virtual machine (VM) and hypervisor is assigned a particular key and tagged with an *address space identifier* (ASID), preventing cross-TEE attacks. The tag restricts the code and data usage to the owner with the same ASID and protects from unauthorised usage inside the processor. Code and data are protected by AES encryption with a 128-bit key based on the tag outside the processor package.

The original version of SEV could leak sensitive information during interrupts from guests to the hypervisor through registers [25]. This issue was addressed with SEV Encrypted State (SEV-ES) [29], where register states are encrypted, and the guest operating system needs to grant the hypervisor access to specific guest registers. Register states are stored with SEV-ES for each VM in a *virtual machine control block* (VMCB) that is divided into an unencrypted control area and an encrypted *virtual machine save area*. The hypervisor manages the control area to indicate event and interrupt handling, while VMSA contains register states. Integrity protection ensures that encrypted register values in the VMSA cannot be modified without being noticed and VMs resume with the same state. Requesting services from the hypervisor due to interrupts in VMs are communicated over the *guest hypervisor communication block* (GHCB) that is accessible through shared memory. Hypervisors do not need to be trusted with SEV-ES because they no longer have access to guest registers. However, the remote attestation protocol was recently proven unsecure [15], exposing the system to rollback attacks and allowing a malicious cloud provider with physical access to SEV machines to easily install malicious firmware and be able to read in clear the (otherwise protected) system. Future iterations of this technology, i.e., SEV Secure Nested Paging (SEV-SNP) [4], plan to overcome these limitations, typically by means of in-silico redesigns.

At its core, SEV leverages a root of trust, called *chip endorsement key*, a secret fused in the die of the processor and issued by AMD for its attestation mechanism. The three editions of SEV may start the VMs from an unencrypted state, similarly to Intel SGX enclaves. In such cases, the secrets and confidential data must then be provisioned using remote attestation. The AMD secure processor creates a claim based on the measurement of the content of the VM. In addition, SEV-SNP measures the metadata associated with memory pages, ensuring the digest also considers the layout of the initial guest memory. While SEV and SEV-ES only support remote attestation during the launch of the guest operating system, SEV-SNP supports a more flexible model. That latter bootstraps private communication keys, enabling the guest VM to request evidence at any time and obtain cryptographic materials for data sealing, i.e., storing data securely at rest.

The remote attestation process takes place when SEV is starting the VMs. First, the attester, called *hypervisor*, executes the LAUNCH_START command (Fig. 4-❶) which creates a guest context in the firmware with the public key of the verifier, called *guest owner*. As the attester is loading the VM into memory, the LAUNCH_UPDATE_DATA/LAUNCH_UPDATE_VMSA commands (Fig. 4-❷) are called to encrypt the memory and calculate the claims. When the VM is loaded, the attester calls the LAUNCH_MEASURE command (Fig. 4-❸), which produces evidence of the encrypted VM. The SEV firmware provides the verifier with evidence of the state of the VM to prove that it is in the expected state. The verifier examines the evidence to determine whether the VM has not been interfered with. Finally, sensitive data, such as image decryption keys, is provisioned through the LAUNCH_SECRET command (Fig. 4-❹) after which the attester calls

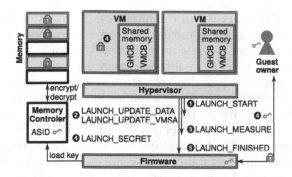

Fig. 4. The remote attestation flow of AMD SEV.

the LAUNCH_FINISHED command (Fig. 4-❺) to indicate that the VM can be executed.

Software development is eased, as AMD SEV protects the whole VM, which comprises the operating system, unlike Intel SGX, where the applications are split into untrusted and trusted parts. Nonetheless, this approach increases the attack surface of the secure environment since the TCB is enlarged. The guest operating system must also support SEV, cannot access host devices (PCI passthrough), and the first edition of SEV (called *vanilla* in Table 1) is limited to 16 VMs.

3.6   RISC-V Architectures

There exist several proposals for TEEs designs for RISC-V based on PMP instructions. These proposals include support for remote attestation, such as those previously described. We survey the most important ones in the following.

Keystone [33] is a modular framework that provides the building blocks to create trusted execution environments, rather than providing an all-in-one solution that is inflexible and is another fixed design point. Instead, they advocate that hardware should provide security primitives instead of point-wise solutions. Keystone implements a secure monitor at machine mode (M-mode) and relies on the RISC-V PMP instructions to provide isolated execution and, therefore, does not require any hardware change. Since Keystone leverages features composition, the framework users can select their own set of security primitives, e.g., memory encryption, dynamic memory management and cache partitioning. Each trusted application executes in user mode (U-mode) and embeds a runtime that executes in supervisor mode (S-mode). The runtime decouples the infrastructure aspect of the TEE (e.g., memory management, scheduling) from the security aspect handled by the secure monitor. As such, Keystone programmers can roll their custom runtime to fine-grained control of the computer resources without managing the TEE's security. Keystone utilises a secure boot mechanism that measures the secure monitor image, generates an attestation key and signs them using a root of trust. The secure monitor exposes a *supervisor system interface* (SBI) for the enclaves to communicate. A subset of the SBI is dedicated to issue evidence signed by provisioned keys (i.e., endorsed by the verifier), based on the measurement of the secure monitor, the runtime and the enclave's application. Arbitrary data can be attached to evidence, enabling an attester to create a secure communication channel with a verifier using key establishment protocols (e.g., Diffie-Hellman). When a remote attestation request takes place, the verifier sends a challenge to the trusted application. The response contains evidence with the public session key of the attester. Finally, the verifier examines the evidence based on the public signature and the claims (i.e., measurements of components), leading to establishing a secure communication channel. While Keystone does not describe in-depth the protocol, the authors provide a case study of remote attestation.

Sanctum [20] has been the first proposition with support for attesting trusted applications. It offers similar promises to Intel's SGX by providing provable and robust software isolation, running in enclaves. The authors replaced Intel's opaque microcode/XuCode with two open-source components: the *measurement root* (`mroot`) and a secure monitor to provide verifiable protection. A remote attestation protocol is proposed, as well as a comprehensive design for deriving trust from a root of trust. Upon booting the system, `mroot` generates the cryptographic materials for signing if started for the first time and hands off to the secure monitor. Similarly to SGX, Sanctum utilises a *signing enclave*, that receives a derived private key from the secure monitor for evidence generation. The remote attestation protocol requires the attester, called *enclave*, to establish a session key with a verifier, called *remote party*. Afterwards, an enclave can request evidence from the signing enclave based on multiple claims, such as the hash of the code of the requesting enclave and some information coming from the key exchange messages. The evidence is then forwarded to the verifier through the secure channel for examination. This work has been further extended to establish a secure boot mechanism and an alternative method for remote attestation by deriving a cryptographic identity from manufacturing variation using a PUF, which is useful when a hardware secret is not present [32].

TIMBER-V [54] achieved the isolation of execution on small embedded processors thanks to hardware-assisted memory tagging. Tagged memory transparently associates blocks of memory with additional metadata. Unlike Sanctum, they aim to bring enclaves to smaller RISC-V featuring only limited physical memory. Similarly to TrustZone, the user mode (U-mode) and the supervisor mode (S-mode) are split into a secure and normal world. The secure supervisor mode runs a trust manager, called *TagRoot*, which manages the tagging of the memory. The secure user mode improves the model of TrustZone, as it can handle multiple concurrent enclaves, which are isolated from each other. They combine tagged memory with an MPU to support an arbitrary number of processes while avoiding the overhead of large tags. The trust manager exposes an API for the enclaves to retrieve evidence, based on a given enclave identity, a root of trust, called the *secret platform key*, and an arbitrary identifier provided by the enclave. The remote attestation protocol is twofold: the verifier (i.e., remote party) sends a challenge to the attester (i.e., enclave). Next, the challenge is forwarded to the trust manager as an identifier to issue evidence, which is authenticated using a MAC. The usage of symmetric cryptography is unusual in remote attestation because the verifier requires to own the secret key to verify the evidence. The authors added that TIMBER-V could be extended to leverage public-key cryptography for remote attestation.

LIRA-V [49] drafted a mutual remote attestation for constrained edge devices. While this solution does not enable the execution of arbitrary code in a TEE, it introduces a comprehensive remote attestation mechanism that leverages PMP for code protection of the attesting environment and the availability of a root of trust to issue evidence. The proposed protocol relies exclusively on machine mode (M-mode) or machine and user mode (M-mode and U-mode). The claim, which is the code measurement, is computed on parts of the physical memory regions by a program stored in the ROM. LIRA-V's mutual attestation protocol works similarly to the protocol illustrated in TrustZone-A, in three rounds and requires provisioned keys as a root of trust. The first device (i.e., verifier) sends a challenge with a public session key. Next, the second device (i.e., attester) answers with a challenge and public session key, as well as evidence bound to that device and encrypted using the established shared session key. Finally, if the first device validates the evidence, it becomes the attester and issues evidence for the second device, which becomes the verifier. This protocol has been formally verified and enables the creation of a trusted communication channel upon the validation of evidence.

Lastly, we omitted some other emerging TEEs leveraging RISC-V as they lack remote attestation mechanisms. These technologies are yet to be researched for bringing such capabilities. We briefly introduce them here for completeness. SiFive, the provider of commercial RISC-V processor IP, proposes Hex-Five MultiZone [23], a zero-trust computing architecture enabling the isolation of software, called *zones*. The multi zones kernel ensures the sane state of the system using secure boot and PMP and runs unmodified applications by trapping and emulating functionality for privileged instructions. HECTOR-V [39] is a design for developing hardened TEEs with a reduced TCB. Thanks to a tight coupling of the TEE and the SoC, the authors provide runtime and peripherals services directly from the hardware and leverage a dedicated processor and a hardware-based security monitor, which ensure the isolation and the control-flow integrity of the trusted applications, called *trustlets*. Finally, Lindemer et al. [35] enable simultaneous thread isolation and TEE separation on devices with a flat address space (i.e., without an MMU), thanks to a minor change in the PMP specification.

4 Future Work

TEEs and remote attestation are fast-moving research areas, where we expect many technological and paradigm enhancements in the next decades. This section introduces the next trusted environments announced by Intel and Arm.

Besides, we also describe a shift to VM-based TEEs and conclude on attestation uniformity.

Intel unveiled Trust Domain Extensions (TDX) [27] in 2020 as its upcoming TEE, introducing the deployment of hardware-isolated virtual machines, called *trust domains*. Similarly to AMD SEV, Intel TDX is designed to isolate legacy applications running on regular operating systems, unlike Intel SGX, which requires tailored software working on a split architecture (i.e., untrusted and trusted parts). TDX leverages Intel Virtual Machine Extensions and Intel Multi-Key Total Memory Encryption, as well as proposes an attestation process to guarantee the trustworthiness of the trust domains for relying parties. In particular, it extends the remote attestation mechanisms of Intel SGX to issue claims and evidence, which has been formally verified by researchers [44].

Arm announced Confidential Compute Architecture (CCA) [8] as part of their future Armv9 processor architecture, consolidating TrustZone to isolate secure virtual machines. With this aim in mind, Arm CCA leverages Arm Realm Management Extension [11] to create a trusted third world called *realm*, next to the existing normal and secure worlds. Arm designed CCA to provide remote attestation mechanisms, assuring that relying parties can trust data and transactions.

These two recent initiatives highlight a convergence into the VM-based isolation paradigm. Initially started by AMD, that architecture of TEEs has many advantages. In particular, it reduces the developers' friction in writing applications, since the underlying operating system and API are standard and no different compared to the outside of the TEE. Furthermore, a convergence of the paradigm may ease the development of unified and hardware-agnostic solutions for trusted software deployment, such as Open Enclave SDK [41] or the recent initiatives promoting WebAssembly as an abstract portable executable code running in TEEs [22,38,53]. Remote attestation may also benefit from these unified solutions by abstracting the attestation process behind standard interfaces.

5   Conclusion

This work compares state-of-the-art remote attestation schemes, which leverage hardware-assisted TEEs, which help deploy and run trusted applications from commodity devices to cloud providers. TEE-based remote attestation has not yet been extensively studied and remains an industrial challenge.

Our survey highlights four architectural extensions: Intel SGX, Arm Trust-Zone, AMD SEV, and upcoming RISC-V TEEs. While SGX competes with SEV, the two pursue significantly different approaches. The former provides a complete built-in remote attestation protocol for multiple, independent, trusted applications. The latter is designed for virtualised environments, shielding VMs from untrusted hypervisors, and provides instructions to help the attestation of independent VMs. Arm TrustZone and native RISC-V do not provide means for attesting software running in the trusted environment, relying on the community to develop alternatives. However, TrustZone-M supports a root of trust, helping to develop an adequately trusted implementation. RISC-V extensions differ a lot, offering different combinations of software and hardware extensions, some of which support a root of trust and multiple trusted applications.

Whether provided by manufacturers or academia, remote attestation remains an essential part of trusted computing solutions. They are the foundation of trust for remote computing where the target environments are not fully trusted. Current solutions widely differ in terms of maturity and security. Whereas some TEEs are developed by leading processor companies and provide built-in attestation mechanisms, others still lack proper hardware attestation support and require software solutions instead. Our study sheds some light on the limitations of state-of-the-art TEEs and identifies promising directions for future work.

Acknowledgments. This publication incorporates results from the VEDLIoT project, which received funding from the European Union's Horizon 2020 research and innovation programme under grant agreement No 957197, and from the Swedish Foundation for Strategic Research (SSF) aSSIsT.

References

1. Abera, T., Bahmani, R., Brasser, F., et al.: DIAT: data integrity attestation for resilient collaboration of autonomous systems. In: NDSS 2019 (2019)
2. Ahn, J., Lee, I.-G., Kim, M.: Design and implementation of hardware-based remote attestation for a secure internet of things. Wireless Pers. Commun. **114**(1), 295–327 (2020)
3. AMD: Secure encrypted virtualization API: technical preview. Technical report 55766 (2019)
4. AMD: Strengthening VM isolation with integrity protection and more. White Paper (2020)
5. Anati, I., Gueron, S., Johnson, S., et al.: Innovative technology for CPU based attestation and sealing. In: HASP 2013 (2013)
6. ARM: ARM TrustZone technology for the Armv8-M architecture. Technical report 100690 (2016)
7. ARM:. Armv8-M Architecture Reference Manual. DDI0553 (2016)
8. ARM: Introducing ARM confidential compute architecture. Technical report, DEN0125 (2021)
9. ARM: Memory protection unit. Technical report, 100699, version 2.1 (2018)
10. ARM: Platform security architecture application guide. Technical report, version 2 (2019)
11. ARM: The realm management extension (RME), for Armv9-A. DDI0615 (2021)
12. Aublin, P.L., Mahhouk, M., Kapitza, R.: Towards TEEs with large secure memory and integrity protection against HW attacks. In: SysTEX 2022 (2022)
13. Birkholz, H., Thaler, D., Richardson, M., et al.: Remote attestation procedures architecture. Technical report. draft-ietf-rats-architecture-12, Internet Engineering Task Force (2021)
14. Brickell, E., Li, J.: Enhanced privacy ID: a direct anonymous attestation scheme with enhanced revocation capabilities. In: WPES 2007 (2007)

15. Buhren, R., Werling, C., Seifert, J.-P.: Insecure until proven updated: analyzing AMD SEV's remote attestation. In: CCS 2019. ACM (2019)
16. Chen, G., Zhang, Y.: Mage: mutual attestation for a group of enclaves without trusted third parties. arXiv preprint arXiv:2008.09501 (2020)
17. Chen, G., Zhang, Y., Lai, T.-H.: Opera: open remote attestation for Intel's secure enclaves. In: CCS 2019. ACM (2019)
18. Coker, G., Guttman, J., Loscocco, P., et al.: Principles of remote attestation. Int. J. Inf. Secur. **10**(2), 63–81 (2011)
19. Costan, V., Devadas, S.: Intel SGX explained. Cryptology ePrint Archive
20. Costan, V., Lebedev, I., Devadas, S.: Sanctum: minimal hardware extensions for strong software isolation. In: USENIX Security 2016 (2016)
21. De Oliveira Nunes, I., Jakkamsetti, S., Rattanavipanon, N., et al.: On the TOCTOU problem in remote attestation. In: CCS 2021. ACM (2021)
22. Enarx. https://enarx.dev
23. Garlati, C., Pinto, S.: A clean slate approach to Linux security RISC-V enclaves. In: EW 2020 (2020)
24. Göttel, C., Felber, P., Schiavoni, V.: Developing secure services for IoT with OP-TEE: a first look at performance and usability. In: Pereira, J., Ricci, L. (eds.) DAIS 2019. LNCS, vol. 11534, pp. 170–178. Springer, Cham (2019). https://doi.org/10.1007/978-3-030-22496-7_11
25. Hetzelt, F., Buhren, R.: Security analysis of encrypted virtual machines. In: VEE 2017. ACM (2017)
26. Hunt, G.D.H., Pai, R., Le, M.V., et al.: Confidential computing for OpenPOWER. In: EuroSys 2021. ACM (2021)
27. Intel: Trust domain extensions (2020). https://intel.ly/3L901wS
28. Intel: XuCode (2021). https://intel.ly/3rYAhMI
29. Kaplan, D.: Protecting VM register state with SEV-ES. Technical report (2017)
30. Kong, J., Koushanfar, F., Pendyala, P.K., et al.: PUFatt: embedded platform attestation based on novel processor-based PUFs. In: DAC 2014. IEEE (2014)
31. Krawczyk, H.: SIGMA: The 'SIGn-and-MAc' approach to authenticated Diffie-Hellman and its use in the IKE protocols. In: Boneh, D. (ed.) CRYPTO 2003. LNCS, vol. 2729, pp. 400–425. Springer, Heidelberg (2003). https://doi.org/10.1007/978-3-540-45146-4_24
32. Lebedev, I., Hogan, K., Devadas, S.: Invited paper: secure boot and remote attestation in the Sanctum processor. In: CSF 2018. IEEE (2018)
33. Lee, D., Kohlbrenner, D., Shinde, S., et al.: Keystone: an open framework for architecting trusted execution environments. In: EuroSys 2020. ACM (2020)
34. Li, W., Li, H., Chen, H., et al.: AdAttester: secure online mobile advertisement attestation using TrustZone. In: MobiSys 2015. ACM (2015)
35. Lindemer, S., Midéus, G., Raza, S.: Real-time thread isolation and trusted execution on embedded RISC-V. In: SECRISC-V 2020 (2020)
36. Maene, P., Götzfried, J., de Clercq, R., et al.: Hardware-based trusted computing architectures for isolation and attestation. IEEE Trans. Comput. **67**(3), 361–374 (2018)
37. Ménétrey, J., Pasin, M., Felber, P., et al.: An exploratory study of attestation mechanisms for trusted execution environments. In: SysTEX 2022 (2022)
38. Ménétrey, J., Pasin, M., Felber, P., et al.: TWINE: an embedded trusted runtime for WebAssembly. In: ICDE 2021. IEEE (2021)
39. Nasahl, P., Schilling, R., Werner, M., et al.: HECTOR-V: a heterogeneous CPU architecture for a secure RISC-V execution environment. In: ASIA CCS 2021. ACM (2021)

40. Nunes, I.D.O., Eldefrawy, K., Rattanavipanon, N., et al.: VRASED: a verified hardware/software co-design for remote attestation. In: USENIX Security 2019 (2019)
41. Open Enclave SDK. https://openenclave.io
42. Pinto, S., Santos, N.: Demystifying ARM TrustZone: a comprehensive survey. ACM Comput. Surv. **51**(6), 1–36 (2019)
43. Raj, H., Saroiu, S., Wolman, A., et al.: fTPM: a Software-Only implementation of a TPM chip. In: USENIX Security 2016 (2016)
44. Sardar, M.U., Musaev, S., Fetzer, C.: Demystifying attestation in Intel Trust Domain Extensions via formal verification. IEEE Access **9**, 83067–83079 (2021)
45. Sardar, M.U., Quoc, D.L., Fetzer, C.: Towards formalization of enhanced privacy ID (EPID)-based remote attestation in Intel SGX. In: DSD 2020. IEEE (2020)
46. Scarlata, V., Johnson, S., Beaney, J., et al.: Supporting third party attestation for Intel SGX with Intel data center attestation primitives. White paper (2018)
47. Seshadri, A., Luk, M., Shi, E., et al.: Pioneer: verifying integrity and guaranteeing execution of code on legacy platforms. In: SOSP 2005. ACM (2005)
48. Shepherd, C., Akram, R.N., Markantonakis, K.: Establishing mutually trusted channels for remote sensing devices with trusted execution environments. In: ARES 2017. ACM (2017)
49. Shepherd, C., Markantonakis, K., Jaloyan, G.-A.: LIRA-V: lightweight remote attestation for constrained RISC-V devices. In: SPW 2021. IEEE (2021)
50. Subramanyan, P., Sinha, R., Lebedev, I., et al.: A formal foundation for secure remote execution of enclaves. In: CCS 2017. ACM (2017)
51. Turan, F., Verbauwhede, I.: Propagating trusted execution through mutual attestation. In: SysTEX 2019. ACM (2019)
52. Vaucher, S., Pires, R., Felber, P., et al.: SGX-aware container orchestration for heterogeneous clusters. In: ICDCS 2018. IEEE (2018)
53. Veracruz. https://veracruz-project.com
54. Weiser, S., Werner, M., Brasser, F., et al.: TIMBER-V: tag-isolated memory bringing fine-grained enclaves to RISC-V. In: NDSS 2019 (2019)
55. Xu, W., Zhang, X., Hu, H., et al.: Remote attestation with domain-based integrity model and policy analysis. IEEE TDSC **9**(3), 429–442 (2012)
56. Zhao, S., Zhang, Q., Qin, Y., et al.: SecTEE: a software-based approach to secure enclave architecture using TEE. In: CCS 2019. ACM (2019)

Accelerate Model Parallel Deep Learning Training Using Effective Graph Traversal Order in Device Placement

Tianze Wang$^{(\boxtimes)}$, Amir H. Payberah, Desta Haileselassie Hagos,
and Vladimir Vlassov

KTH Royal Institute of Technology, Stockholm, Sweden
{tianzew,payberah,destah,vladv}@kth.se

Abstract. Modern neural networks require long training to reach decent performance on massive datasets. One common approach to speed up training is model parallelization, where large neural networks are split across multiple devices. However, different device placements of the same neural network lead to different training times. Most of the existing device placement solutions treat the problem as sequential decision-making by traversing neural network graphs and assigning their neurons to different devices. This work studies the impact of neural network graph traversal orders on device placement. In particular, we empirically study how different graph traversal orders of neural networks lead to different device placements, which in turn affects the training time of the neural network. Our experiment results show that the best graph traversal order depends on the type of neural networks and their computation graphs features. In this work, we also provide recommendations on choosing effective graph traversal orders in device placement for various neural network families to improve the training time in model parallelization.

Keywords: Device Placement · Model Parallelization · Deep Learning · Graph Traversal Order

1 Introduction

Recent years have seen the prevalence of Deep Learning (DL) with larger and deeper models with billions of neurons [2,29]. Together with the performance boost of DL models comes the increasing computation demand for model training. Most solutions seek to parallelize the training on GPU clusters to meet the requirement of computation power. *Data parallelization* [27] and *model parallelization* [29] of DL models are the most common parallelization strategies. In data parallelization, data are distributed among several servers (a.k.a. devices) in a GPU cluster. In contrast, in model parallelization, the DL model is split into multiple parts and distributed among devices. Assigning different parts of a DL model to different devices is known as *device placement*.

© IFIP International Federation for Information Processing 2022
Published by Springer Nature Switzerland AG 2022
D. Eyers and S. Voulgaris (Eds.): DAIS 2022, LNCS 13272, pp. 114–130, 2022.
https://doi.org/10.1007/978-3-031-16092-9_8

Finding the optimal device placement of DL models in model parallelization is a challenging task. It is mainly due to the large search spaces of potential parallelization strategies, model architectures, and device characteristics [38]. Despite lots of efforts to improve device placements, it still takes a long time for device placement methods to train [1,3,4,19,38]. The first effort in automating device placement combines global partitioning and local scheduling by using heuristic strategies to first partition the DL model into smaller parts and then determine the execution schedule of neurons within each part [17].

The state-of-the-art device placement methods use a combination of Graph Neural Network (GNN) and Reinforcement Learning (RL) to find the placement of DL models [1,38]. In these solutions, a DL neural network graph is represented as a Directed Acyclic Graph (DAG), in which each node of the DAG represents a single operation or a group of operations, e.g., convolutions. In a typical setting, a GNN takes a DAG of a DL model and its nodes' features as input and generates node embeddings, which summarize the attributes and neighborhood topology of each node [1,38]. An RL agent then processes the node embeddings and uses a policy to predict device placements for all nodes in the DAG on the given device cluster. To this end, the RL agent needs to *traverse* all the nodes in the DAG and learn to propose placements to reduce the training time of the DL model.

Identifying a good *graph traversal order* can decrease the time to train the RL agent and potentially help the RL agent to find better placements to reduce the DL model training time. In this work, we empirically study the relationship between graph traversal orders and the learning efficiency of the RL agent for finding device placement during the training process. We look into six different graph traversal orders and show how they affect the training process of Placeto [1], a state-of-the-art device placement method on three different families of neural networks. Each family of neural networks contains structurally similar DL models [25]. Our initial results suggest that different traversal orders are better suited for different types of neural networks, and the best graph traversal order to use depends on the attributes of the DL model.

We also explain how our traversal order recommendation can be used in DL models built for Remote Sensing (RS) and Earth Observation (EO) applications. RS and EO are domains where there is a need to provide near real-time services and products for global monitoring of planet earth. EO satellites developed over the years have provided an unprecedented amount of data that need to be processed [6,40]. Model parallelization methods can contribute to these domains by distributing the computation and memory requirement for training large models on large datasets.

Our contributions are summarized as follows.

1. We empirically study the impact of the graph traversal orders on finding the best device placement for the model parallelization of DL models and, consequently, their training times. In this study, we consider different architectures of DL models, such as Convolutional Neural Network (CNN) and Recurrent Neural Network (RNN). Our study shows that different graph traversal orders

triumph at finding the best device placements efficiently for different types of DL models.

2. Based on our empirical evaluation of graph traversal orders in device placement for different model parallelization of DL architectures, we summarize and provide guidelines on identifying the best graph traversal order for a given DL model based on its characteristics. For example, we recommend using Breadth-First Search (BFS) traversal order for model parallelization of RNNs with large average degrees to perform device placement.

3. In the context of RS and EO, we show how our methods on identifying the best graph traversal order can be used on different DL models, e.g., CNN models for satellite image classification and RNN models for sequence classification. Choosing a proper graph traversal method in device placement improves the DL models' training time and enables us to train them on larger datasets within a certain (the same) amount of time. The above two-fold benefit enables real-time online training of model parallelization of DL models with time deadlines.

2   Preliminaries

In this section, we discuss the problem formulation of device placement and present Placeto [1] as a state-of-the-art device placement method and show how it uses GNN and RL for device placement. Moreover, we review the graph traversal order methods we use in this work.

2.1   Device Placement

Let $G(V, E)$ be a DAG that represents the computation graph of a neural network. Each node $v \in V$ describes a single computation operation (e.g., convolution) or a predefined small group of operations (e.g., groups of convolutions nearby) that we are interested in predicting its device placement. Each edge $e \in E$ models the data dependencies between the vertices. Let D denote a given device cluster (e.g., GPU clusters) where $d \in D$ characterizes a single device in D. A placement $p : V \rightarrow D$ assigns each node $v \in V$ to a device $d \in D$. Our goal in device placement is to find a placement p to minimize the training time of G (i.e., the DL model) on the given device cluster D while satisfying the memory constraints of every device in the cluster. When given a fixed number of devices, we can treat the device placement task as a classification problem by considering each device identifier as a label. The classification model takes the DAG of a computation graph G as input and classifies every node or group of nodes of G into devices in D.

2.2   Placeto

Placeto [1] models a device placement task as finding a sequence of iterative placement improvements. In each training round, Placeto takes the current placement of the DAG and the representation of one of its nodes as input and predicts that node's placement. Each training episode lasts until the placements of all the nodes have been updated once. The Placeto method, in general, consists of two parts, (i) using GNN [26] for making node embeddings of the input DAG, and (ii) using RL for assigning nodes of the DAG to devices. The Placeto model's parameters are shared across episodes, allowing to learn placement policies that generalize well to unseen graphs [1]. Below, we elaborate on these two parts in more detail.

Graph Neural Network. What matters in node embeddings of a computation graph is not only the features of the nodes but also their topological relationship. If two connected nodes are placed on two different devices, there will be data transfer between two devices in both the forward and backward path of model training, which is expensive. Things become even more complicated when there are more complex graph and sub-graph structures. For example, convolution blocks [30] contain parallel computation threads that depend on the same node for input data and send the result to another node for intermediate result concatenation, or temporal dependency [8] during the training of recurrent neural networks can also incur a lot of data communication if the nodes that construct the recurrent unit are located on different devices. Thus, it is crucial to consider the relationships among the nodes while making graph representations.

   GNN [26] can generate graph embeddings for each node in a given graph that can generalize to unseen graphs. Placeto [1] uses a graph embedding architecture that computes node attributes (e.g., the execution time of operation, total size of output tensor), summarizes the topology of a local neighborhood through message passing, and uses pooling operations for creating a global summary of the entire graph. Mitropolitsky et al. [22] study the impact of different graph embedding techniques on the training time of DL models. By explicitly modeling the relationships between nodes in a computation graph, better placement can be found by auto device placement methods.

Reinforcement Learning. After generating node embeddings of the input DAG, Placeto uses a RL agent to predict the device placement of the DAG's nodes. The RL agent takes the node embeddings of the DAG as input and generates the probability distribution of the current node over candidate devices as the output. During the training process, the RL agent interacts with the training environment and uses the training time of the input DL model as a reward function to guide the training process. Thus, the RL agent aims to minimize the training time of the DL model across different episodes of training. In each episode of training, Placeto updates the placement of each node one time. Placeto uses REINFORCE policy-gradient method [34] to train the RL agent. Placeto also has a simulator to predict the training time of the DL model, which helps to speed up the training process of RL agent by avoiding taking DL model training time measurement of placements on real hardware.

2.3   Graph Traversal Order

Since the device placement problem is treated as a sequential decision-making task [19], we need to convert the computation graph into a sequence of node embeddings. Placeto formulated the device placement problem as Markov Decision Process (MDP), where the RL agent selects to update the placement for a node in the computation graph in each state. Thus, we need to form a sequence by traversing the computation graph, which is represented as a DAG. Below, we review some of the graph traversal orders on DAG that one can consider using.

Topological. Topological ordering [9] on the DAG of a computation graph defines a graph traversal order such that for every directed edge $u \rightarrow v$ from node u to node v, u must appear before v in the traversal order. Topological ordering can be used to represent dependencies in a DAG where we only visit a node once all its dependencies have been met.

Reversed Topological. A reversed topological ordering of a DAG of a computation graph is simply the reversed order of its topological ordering.

Depth-First Search. Depth-First Search (DFS) is a graph traversal method that starts at source nodes (input nodes of a DAG) and explores the DAG as far as possible by continuously visiting the children nodes of the current node first before visiting the sibling nodes. A DFS ordering is an enumeration of the nodes that is a possible output of applying DFS on the graph. A DFS preorder is a list of nodes that are in the order of when they are first visited by DFS. A DFS postorder is a list of nodes that are in the order of when they are last visited by DFS.

Breadth-First Search. Breadth-First Search (BFS) is a graph traversal method that starts at source nodes (input nodes of a DAG) and explores the DAG by first visiting all the sibling nodes of the current nodes before moving to children nodes. A BFS order of a graph is an enumeration of its nodes that is one possible output of applying BFS on the graph.

Lexicographical. Lexicographical order is an order where the strings are placed in order based on the position of each character in the string and their position in the alphabet. For example, given the names of two nodes in a DAG are $a = a_1 a_2 \cdots a_k$ and $b = b_1 b_2 \cdots b_k$, the order of the name of the two nodes depends on the alphabetical order of the characters in the first place i that a and b differs. If $a_i < b_i$ then $a < b$, otherwise $a > b$.

3   Graph Traversal Orders in Device Placement

In this section, we discuss challenges in device placement and the impact of graph traversal orders.

3.1   Challenges in Device Placement

Finding a good placement for model parallelization is challenging. Most of the state-of-the-art methods use RL to find placements; however, RL agents still require a long time to train before they can find suitable placements. Mirhoseini et al. [21] find that it takes 12 to 27 hours for their RL method to find the best placement. Although lots of efforts have been made in reducing the complexity of the problem [19], making the training method more efficient [3,4], and generalizing them better on unseen computation graph [1,38,39], the RL agent still needs a long time to train.

One of the challenges in device placement is defining order for nodes in a DAG. Unlike text and image data, the nodes in DAGs reside in a multi-dimensional space that are linked by edges to represent connectivity [36]. Since a node in a graph might have an arbitrary number of edges, it is challenging for a DL model to encode the structural information of a graph. Recent work in graph representation learning [36] has shown that successfully learning structural information of graphs helps better represent them, which in turn leads to performance improvement of downstream tasks that utilize the graph representations. In Placeto [1], the structural information is (partially) reflected in the sequential order that the device placement method iterates through the nodes of the DAG.

Another challenge in device placement concerns the expressiveness of GNN that are used to generate node embeddings. The GNN that are used by state-of-the-art device placement methods mostly follow the message-passing paradigm, which is known to have inherent limitations. For example, the expressiveness of such GNN is bounded by the Weisfeiler-Lehman isomorphism hierarchy [14]. Also, GNNs are known to suffer from over-squashing [32], where there is a distortion of information propagation between distant nodes. Due to these limitations, the node embeddings created by GNN have limited expressiveness. In such cases, different graph traversal orders in device placement can lead to placements with different DL model training time.

3.2   Impact of Graph Traversal Orders

A graph traversal order determines the order where an RL agent learns the placement of each node in a DAG. We believe that a proper graph traversal order can help the RL agent to learn appropriate placements with a lower DL training time faster. One approach to help the RL agent finds better placements is to prioritize learning the placement of important nodes that have more impact on the DL model training time, e.g., to place the nodes with heavy communications first. On the other hand, misplacement of such nodes can lead to longer DL model training time due to extra data communications between different devices. The placement order in a local neighborhood could also play an important role in finding a suitable device placement. Apart from the straggler problem caused by the unbalanced distribution of computation where all the other devices will have to wait for the slowest device, data communication is also challenging.

Table 1. Computation Graph Datasets Summary

Features	Dataset		
	nmt	ptb	cifar10
#nodes (avg)	179.44	500.75	303.44
#edges (avg)	476.25	1285.44	444.22
node degree (avg)	2.65	2.56	1.47
diameter (avg)	63.13	316.09	95.63
diameter (min, max)	(41, 69)	(216, 450)	(74, 154)

For example, many of the modern DL models consist of several computation blocks, where each block has multiple parallel threads sharing the same input and whose output should be concatenated to serve as the input for the next computation block [8,30,33]. Suppose these computation threads are placed on different devices; thus, the input of a computation block needs to be replicated and sent to these parallel threads to perform the computation independently. All the intermediate results from these parallel threads are later concatenated that will serve as the input of the next computation block. If the RL agent can not anticipate the concatenation of results from parallel computation threads, it might misplace the threads on different devices, which incurs a lot of data transfer for the concatenation node. However, if the RL agent learns the placement of the concatenation node first, it can anticipate placements of predecessor nodes in the computation block to better balance computation and communication.

4   Evaluation

In this section, we present the details of the empirical evaluation setup, results, experiment analysis, and guidelines for choosing an effective graph traversal order for a given DL model.

4.1   Datasets

We conduct our experiments on three different datasets nmt, ptb, and cifar10 as in [1,22]. The nmt dataset contains 32 variations of Neural Machine Translation (NMT) [35] with different number of unrolled steps. The computation graphs in nmt are a family of encoder-decoder networks with attention structures. The ptb and cifar10 are generated using an RL-based method ENAS [25] that finds the optimal subgraph within a larger graph search space. The ptb dataset consists of 32 computation graphs for language modeling tasks, and the cifar10 dataset consists of 32 computation graphs of CNNs for image classification tasks. The nodes of computation graphs are pre-grouped together in all three datasets to reduce graph sizes in the same way as in [21]. The computation graphs in nmt, ptb, and cifar10 have on average 180, 500, and 300 nodes. Table 1 summarizes the three datasets.

Overall, the datasets we are studying for device place are similar to the models in EO. For example, CNN models are used for satellite image classification and detection tasks. RNN models are used to learn from time series of satellite data to monitor an area over different times of the year. Based on the results of our empirical evaluation, we provide guidelines on choosing graph traversal orders for EO tasks in Sect. 4.4.

4.2   Experiment Setup

We implement all the graph traversal orders in Sect. 2.3 using NetworkX [5] and refer to them as `topo`, `reversed-topo`, `dfs-preorder`, `dfs-postorder`, `bfs`, and `lexico` hereafter for Topological, Reversed Topological, DFS preorder, DFS postorder, BFS, and Lexicographical, respectively. For the implementation of Placeto, we use the implementation provided in [22], which is based on the original implementation [1]. We use the same simulator in the original implementation to simulate the physical execution environment with different numbers of devices that a neural network can be placed on. We use the same graph traversal order in one experiment, and this order is fixed across different episodes that happened in the experiment.

We conduct experiments on the graphs from each of the three datasets with three, five, and eight devices, in line with [22]. We run independent experiments with the same setting (dataset and number of devices) to account for the stochastic and randomness that might lead to differences in experiment results. We compare different settings for the number of repeated runs on a subset of the whole datasets and found that 10 repeated runs offer a good balance between computation load and the reproducibility of the result.

The experiments are run on a standalone benchmark machine with AMD Ryzen Threadripper 2920X 12-Core Processor and 128 GB of RAM. Since we have $3 \times 32 \times 3 \times 6 \times 10 = 17280$ (3 datasets, 32 graphs in each dataset, 3 different number of devices, 6 graph traversal orders, and 10 repeat for each experiment) experiments to run, we use parallel Docker containers that each have one experiment to speed up the process. We give each graph traversal order the same number of training episodes to run, and it approximately takes a few hours to finish each experiment on the CPU. We empirically found that the metrics we measure in the experiment are not sensitive to the number of parallel Docker containers running simultaneously. We use TensorFlow and NetworkX libraries for the experiment, and we refer the readers to this repository[1] for experiment code and the specific version of the libraries and other software settings.

4.3   Results and Analysis

Through the training process of device placement, the RL agent aims to find device placements with lower training times for the input DL models (i.e., the DAGs). However, the device placement processes might have different learning

---

[1] https://github.com/bwhub/Graph_Traversal_Order_in_Device_Placement.

speeds using different graph traversal orders, meaning that the RL agent can find a placement with lower training times for the input DL model faster if it uses a proper graph traversal order.

Table 2. The number of times graph traversal orders find the placement with the lowest training time on the nmt dataset.

nmt		Graph Traversal Order					
#dev	episode	lexico	topo	dfs-preorder	reversed-topo	dfs-postorder	bfs
3 dev	9	0	2	0	**22**	1	7
	19	0	0	1	**23**	1	7
	49	0	0	1	**24**	1	6
5 dev	9	0	0	1	**24**	1	6
	19	0	0	2	**26**	0	4
	49	0	0	0	**27**	0	5
8 dev	9	0	0	0	**23**	3	6
	19	0	0	0	**24**	1	7
	49	0	0	0	**24**	3	5

We empirically observe that the training process of the RL agent is roughly divided into three phases: (i) episodes 1 to 9, (ii) episodes 10 to 19, and (iii) episodes 20 to 49. In the first phase (episode 1 to 9), the RL agent learns efficiently and finds a better placement across different training episodes. This can be explained by the fact that the learning process just started, and finding a good enough placement that is better than a random strategy is not very hard. In the second phase (episode 10 to 19), the learning process slows down, and the RL agent cannot always find drastically better placements than in the first phase. This reflects that the learning process plateaus, and we see diminishing returns. In the third phase (episode 20 to 49), the RL agent overcomes the plateau and finds better placements thanks to the more extended training budget and the knowledge learned through the process. In the rest of the experiments, we compare the best placement training time of different graph traversal orders at these three episodes: 9, 19, and 49.

We report the number of times each graph traversal order finds the placement with the lowest training time for the input DL models in the given dataset. Table 2 shows the result of experiments on the nmt dataset. Each row shows the number of times each graph traversal order, compared to other graph traversal orders, finds placements with the lowest training time of the DL model at the given training episode (i.e., 9, 19, or 49) and the number of devices (i.e., 3, 5, or 8). Since there are 32 computation graphs of DL models in each dataset, each row in the table should sum to 32. The comparison between training time is based on 10 repeated experiments to minimize random factors in the training process.

As Table 2 shows, in the nmt dataset, the reversed-topo order dominates and gives the best result. This can be explained by the fact that the reversed-topo order considers how intermediate results are concatenated in the DAG. The RL agent can decide the placement of the concatenation operation first. Then it is easier for the RL agent to collocate the input operations nodes to the concatenation node to minimize expensive data transfer and synchronization between devices during training. In such cases, starting from the nodes in the output layers of the DAG also helps. The dfs-postorder order does not work well on the nmt dataset (unlike on the cifar10 dataset that we show) as it has a larger average node degree of 2.65 compared to the average node degree of 1.47 of cifar10. This increases the effort for the RL agent to collocate the sibling nodes that are far away in the placement sequence generated using the dfs-postorder order. Better collocation of sibling nodes can also potentially explain why the bfs order is the graph traversal order that finds the placement with the lowest training time.

Table 3 shows the result of experiments on the ptb dataset. The bfs order is the graph traversal order that achieves the best learning efficiency on this dataset. This can be explained by the fact that the DAGs in the ptb dataset have more nodes and edges than the cifar10 and nmt datasets. There are potentially more sibling nodes that the RL agent needs to consider when performing the placement. Since sibling nodes in a local neighborhood will be put close together in the traversal sequence generated by bfs, it is easier for the RL agent to learn to collocate these nodes together to avoid unnecessary data transfer between devices. In this way, the RL agent does not need to worry too much about long-range dependencies in large DAGs.

Table 3. The number of times graph traversal orders find the placement with the lowest training time on the ptb dataset.

ptb				Graph Traversal Order			
#dev	episode	lexico	topo	dfs-preorder	reversed-topo	dfs-postorder	bfs
3 dev	9	0	1	6	1	0	**24**
	19	0	1	10	1	2	**18**
	49	0	1	8	5	2	**16**
5 dev	9	0	0	3	0	2	**27**
	19	0	1	3	2	2	**24**
	49	0	1	2	6	5	**18**
8 dev	9	0	0	2	1	1	**28**
	19	0	0	2	5	4	**21**
	49	0	0	2	**13**	5	12

Table 4 shows the result of experiments on the cifar10 dataset. Unlike in the nmt and ptb dataset, where only one graph traversal order dominates the contest for the optimal graph traversal order, the results are more diverse in the cifar10 dataset. For example, the topo order achieves the best result in experiments on three devices at episode nine, and the dfs-preorder on five devices at episode nine. However, most of the time the reversed-topo and

Table 4. The number of times graph traversal orders find the placement with the lowest training time on the `cifar10` dataset.

cifar10				Graph Traversal Order			
#dev	episode	lexico	topo	dfs-preorder	reversed-topo	dfs-postorder	bfs
3 dev	9	1	6	**10**	**10**	4	1
	19	3	3	7	8	**11**	0
	49	5	4	5	**8**	**8**	2
5 dev	9	0	**9**	6	6	**9**	2
	19	0	9	3	**10**	8	2
	49	2	6	6	**9**	6	3
8 dev	9	0	8	3	10	**11**	0
	19	1	4	2	8	**17**	0
	49	0	5	1	11	**15**	0

`dfs-postorder` orders are the best traversal orders to use since they are the orders that find the placements of DL models with the lowest training time (e.g., experiments on five and eight devices). This can be explained by the fact that there are structures of parallel convolutions in the DAG of the `cifar10` dataset where the intermediate results for parallel convolutions are concatenated for later use. In such cases, it is better to start the learning process from the nodes in the output layer of the model. Once the placement of concatenation nodes located near the output layer is settled, it will be easier for the RL agent to optimize the placement for the parallel convolutions. Also, we observe that with more training episodes, the `topo` and `dfs-preorder` start to show fewer advantages as the number of times they find the best placement with the lowest training time decreases.

We also find out that the diameter of the input DAG affects which graph traversal order is performing the best in the `cifar10` dataset. With a smaller diameter (e.g., diameters smaller than 100), the `dfs` family (`dfs-preorder` and `dfs-postorder`) performs the best. With a larger diameter (e.g., diameters larger than 100), the `topo` family (`topo` and `reversed-topo`) tends to find better placements. This could be explained by the fact that the `dfs` family forms longer sequences of consecutive nodes on the diameter with a larger diameter. This can be hard for the RL agent to learn the placement of sibling nodes in the DAG as they are far away from each other in the sequence. This might require the RL agent to learn placement collocation of sibling nodes far away from each other.

4.4   Discussion and Guidelines

In the previous subsection, we show that graph traversal orders affect the training time of parallelized DL models. It means that a proper graph traversal order can help the RL agent to find better placements for DL models to reduce DL models' training time. Nevertheless, in Table 5 we show that if we give enough budget (time) to the RL agent to find the placements, then different graph traversal orders lead to placements of similar qualities (i.e., similar DL training time). Table 5 compares the ratio of the DL training speed found by different graph traversal orders versus the fastest training speed at episode 49, which is enough training budget based on our empirical study. For example, for cifar10 dataset with eight devices, the placements found using dfs-postorder have an average training speed of one epoch per time unit, while the placements found using dfs-preorder have an average training speed of 0.97 epoch per time unit. The values of each row are normalized by the fastest training speed (i.e., the values are between zero and one, where one is the fastest). However, the efficiencies are different when the training budget is limited in real-world settings where larger DL models take much longer to find placement. Furthermore, the time saved for training DL models with a 5% speedup is still not negligible when the DL model would take weeks, if not months, to train on a GPU cluster.

Identifying the proper graph traversal order for a DAG can improve the training efficiency that leads to better placements with lower training time on distributed hardware. However, finding the optimal graph traversal order for a given DL model is not an easy task as many factors are involved in the process, e.g., the topology of the DAG, the ratio of computation, and the communication during training. Although one cannot always quickly find the best graph traversal order for a DAG, we can still provide some guidelines based on our experience.

Table 5. The placement training time comparison between different graph traversal orders. Each row shows a comparison of the average training speed of the DL model according to the placement found by different graph traversal orders at episode 49.

episode 49		\multicolumn{6}{c}{Graph Traversal Order}					
dataset	#dev	lexico	topo	dfs-preorder	reversed-topo	dfs-postorder	bfs
nmt	3	0.931	0.922	0.948	1.000	0.963	0.978
	5	0.869	0.863	0.929	1.000	0.954	0.966
	8	0.849	0.831	0.953	1.000	0.960	0.972
ptb	3	0.969	0.980	0.990	0.986	0.981	1.000
	5	0.953	0.962	0.969	0.976	0.974	1.000
	8	0.953	0.953	0.977	0.983	0.983	1.000
cifar10	3	0.975	0.982	1.000	0.997	0.990	0.978
	5	0.976	0.989	0.999	1.000	0.994	0.974
	8	0.945	0.970	0.970	0.995	1.000	0.929

In general, it is good to start experiments with graph traversal orders that traverse the nodes in a DAG in a backward fashion, i.e., start from the nodes in the final layer of the graph, gradually go through the nodes in the previous layers, and finish with the nodes in the first layer of the model. For example, when using the **reversed-topo** order, the RL agent in the device placement method can first learn the placement of the nodes in the last layers and then on the nodes that are input to nodes that the RL agent already find placements for. By starting from backward, the RL agent can learn to better collocate parent and children nodes.

If a DAG has a large diameter and a large number of nodes or groups of nodes, then a graph traversal order that can put sibling nodes near each other in the one-dimensional sequence is a better candidate for the optimal graph traversal order. For example, when facing a large DL model with more than 200 nodes, the bfs order can put sibling nodes close to each other in the one-dimensional sequence. Thus, the RL agent can learn to better place the sibling nodes consecutively, instead of having to remember the placements of sibling nodes that are far away from each other in a long sequence.

In the context of the ExtremeEarth project [6,12,13], different types of models are used to provide EO products. While hyperparameter tuning [18] and ablation studies [28] can help to improve model performance, identifying proper graph traversal order can improve the model parallel training performance. For example, for Synthetic Aperture Radar (SAR) image classification [10,11], the reversed-topo and dfs-postorder would be good traversal orders to start the experiment, as the models are similar to those in cifar10 model datasets. For sequence classification tasks [24], the bfs order would be a good traversal order to start with, as they are sequence to sequence models, which are similar to those in the ptb model datasets. The bfs order can help the RL agent to collocate better the placements of sibling operations in the DL model.

5   Related Work

In this section, we discuss related work in device placement. We start with a general overview of methods in device placement and then focus on those more related to graph traversal orders.

The first effort in device placement uses partition methods. For example, Mayer et al. [17] use a two-step approach that first partition the computation graph and then locally schedule the operations in each partition on each device. In another work, Tanaka et al. [31] present RaNNC that uses a three-step approach to partition the computation graph by first distinguishing atomic components, then coarsely partitioning the graph, and finally searching for the combination of the coarse partitions to find the final partition.

Mirhoseini et al. [19,21] are the first to use RL approaches for device placement. In [19], they present HDP to find the placement by jointly learning the grouping operations in a computation graph and placement of the groups. This way, they improve the device placement time. Similarly, Lan et al. [16] present EAGLE that combines the automatic grouping of operations and finding placement for each group that improves the speed of finding better placements.

For making the device placement methods more generalized, Addanki et al. [1] introduce Placeto, which uses a graph embedding method for representing nodes in the graph and placing them iteratively. GPD [38], which is a single-shot device placement method, and Mars [15], which uses self-supervised pre-training to capture the topological relations between nodes in the computation graph, are other examples of generalized device placement methods. Gao et al. [4] present Spotlight that improves the training time of device placement methods by introducing a new RL algorithm based on proximal policy optimization. Later, they introduce Post [3] that further improves training efficiency by combining cross-entropy minimization and proximal policy optimization.

Some of the previous works study the relationship between graph traversal orders and the training time of the final placement found. For example, HDP [19] randomizes the order of predicting placements for each group of operations in a DL model. The authors find that the difference between the fastest and slowest placements is less than 7% in 10 experiments. Placeto [1] uses GNN to eliminate the need to assign indices when embedding graph features. Experiment results show that the predicted placement of Placeto is more robust to graph traversal orders than the RNN-based approaches. REGAL [23] uses topological order to convert a graph into a sequence. Mitropolitsky et al. [22] study how different graph embedding techniques affect the execution time of the final placement and show that position-aware graph embedding improves the training time of the placement found compared to Placeto-GNN [1] and GraphSAGE [7]. GPD [38] removes the positional embedding in the transformer model to prevent overfitting.

Some work in other domains also studies graph traversal orders. In chip placement, Mirhoseini et al. [20] find that topological order can help the RL agent to place connected nodes close to each other. In the domain of generating graphs with DL models, GraphRNN [37] uses BFS order for graph generation to reduce the complexity of learning over all possible node sequences. The only possible edges for a new node are those connecting to nodes in the "frontier" of the BFS order. To the best of our knowledge, our work is the first to study how the graph traversal orders affect device placement training efficiency in device placement.

6   Conclusion

This work studies the impact of graph traversal orders on device placement for accelerating model parallel deep learning training. We empirically show that graph traversal orders affect the device placement and, consequently, the training time of deep learning models. A device placement method can learn more efficiently during the training process by finding placement strategies with lower training time faster when given a proper graph traversal order. Specifically, we find that traversing the computation graph from the nodes in the output layer of a deep learning model to the nodes in the input layer helps device placement methods find good placements efficiently. Moreover, we observe that for larger computation graphs, traversing orders that can better collocate sibling nodes, e.g., breadth-first search, in the traversal sequence is more efficient than its depth-first counterparts. We also provide practical guidelines on choosing traversal orders for device placement.

We believe that our study can help researchers and practitioners better understand the relationship between types of network and graph traversal orders. Several potential extensions and improvements to this work exist, including jointly learning graph traversal orders, graph embedding, and the policy network in the

RL agent. Another possible direction is to study graph traversal orders based on the graph structures and features of individual nodes (e.g., input and output size and computation intensity of the given node). We can also investigate other optimization techniques, such as constraint programming, to solve device placement in future work.

Acknowledgements. This work was supported by the ExtremeEarth project funded by European Union's Horizon 2020 Research and Innovation Programme under Grant agreement No. 825258.

References

1. Addanki, R., Bojja Venkatakrishnan, S., Gupta, S., Mao, H., Alizadeh, M.: Placeto: Learning generalizable device placement algorithms for distributed machine learning. Advances in Neural Information Processing Systems 32 (NIPS 2019) (2019)
2. Brown, T.B., Mann, B., Ryder, N., Subbiah, M., Kaplan, J., Dhariwal, P., Neelakantan, A., Shyam, P., Sastry, G., Askell, A., et al.: Language models are few-shot learners. arXiv preprint arXiv:2005.14165 (2020)
3. Gao, Y., Chen, L., Li, B.: Post: Device placement with cross-entropy minimization and proximal policy optimization. In: Advances in Neural Information Processing Systems. pp. 9971–9980 (2018)
4. Gao, Y., Chen, L., Li, B.: Spotlight: Optimizing device placement for training deep neural networks. In: International Conference on Machine Learning. pp. 1676–1684 (2018)
5. Hagberg, A., Swart, P., S Chult, D.: Exploring network structure, dynamics, and function using networkx. Tech. rep., Los Alamos National Lab. (LANL), Los Alamos, NM (United States) (2008)
6. Hagos, D.H., Kakantousis, T., Vlassov, V., Sheikholeslami, S., Wang, T., Dowling, J., Paris, C., Marinelli, D., Weikmann, G., Bruzzone, L., et al.: Extremeearth meets satellite data from space. IEEE Journal of Selected Topics in Applied Earth Observations and Remote Sensing **14**, 9038–9063 (2021)
7. Hamilton, W.L., Ying, R., Leskovec, J.: Inductive representation learning on large graphs. In: Proceedings of the 31st International Conference on Neural Information Processing Systems. pp. 1025–1035 (2017)
8. Hochreiter, S., Schmidhuber, J.: Long short-term memory. Neural computation **9**(8), 1735–1780 (1997)
9. Kahn, A.B.: Topological sorting of large networks. Communications of the ACM **5**(11), 558–562 (1962)
10. Khaleghian, S., Kramer, T., Everett, A., Kiarbech, A., Hughes, N., Eltoft, T., Marinoni, A.: Synthetic aperture radar data analysis by deep learning for automatic sea ice classification. In: EUSAR 2021; 13th European Conference on Synthetic Aperture Radar. pp. 1–6. VDE (2021)
11. Khaleghian, S., Ullah, H., Kræmer, T., Hughes, N., Eltoft, T., Marinoni, A.: Sea ice classification of sar imagery based on convolution neural networks. Remote Sensing **13**(9), 1734 (2021)
12. Koubarakis, M., Bereta, K., Bilidas, D., Giannousis, K., Ioannidis, T., Pantazi, D.A., Stamoulis, G., Haridi, S., Vlassov, V., Bruzzone, L., et al.: From copernicus big data to extreme earth analytics. Open Proceedings pp. 690–693 (2019)

13. Koubarakis, M., Stamoulis, G., Bilidas, D., Ioannidis, T., Mandilaras, G., Pantazi, D.A., Papadakis, G., Vlassov, V., Payberah, A.H., Wang, T., et al.: Artificial intelligence and big data technologies for copernicus data: The extremeearth project. In: Proceedings of the 2021 conference on Big Data from Space. Publications Office of the European Union (2021)

14. Kreuzer, D., Beaini, D., Hamilton, W.L., Létourneau, V., Tossou, P.: Rethinking graph transformers with spectral attention. arXiv preprint arXiv:2106.03893 (2021)

15. Lan, H., Chen, L., Li, B.: Accelerated device placement optimization with contrastive learning. In: 50th International Conference on Parallel Processing. pp. 1–10 (2021)

16. Lan, H., Chen, L., Li, B.: Eagle: Expedited device placement with automatic grouping for large models. In: 2021 IEEE International Parallel and Distributed Processing Symposium (IPDPS). pp. 599–608 (2021). DOI: https://doi.org/10.1109/IPDPS49936.2021.00068

17. Mayer, R., Mayer, C., Laich, L.: The tensorflow partitioning and scheduling problem: it's the critical path! In: Proceedings of the 1st Workshop on Distributed Infrastructures for Deep Learning. pp. 1–6 (2017)

18. Meister, M., Sheikholeslami, S., Payberah, A.H., Vlassov, V., Dowling, J.: Maggy: Scalable asynchronous parallel hyperparameter search. In: Proceedings of the 1st Workshop on Distributed Machine Learning. pp. 28–33 (2020)

19. Mirhoseini, A., Goldie, A., Pham, H., Steiner, B., Le, Q.V., Dean, J.: A hierarchical model for device placement. In: International Conference on Learning Representations (2018)

20. Mirhoseini, A., Goldie, A., Yazgan, M., Jiang, J.W., Songhori, E., Wang, S., Lee, Y.J., Johnson, E., Pathak, O., Nazi, A., et al.: A graph placement methodology for fast chip design. Nature 594(7862), 207–212 (2021)

21. Mirhoseini, A., Pham, H., Le, Q.V., Steiner, B., Larsen, R., Zhou, Y., Kumar, N., Norouzi, M., Bengio, S., Dean, J.: Device placement optimization with reinforcement learning. In: International Conference on Machine Learning. pp. 2430–2439. PMLR (2017)

22. Mitropolitsky, M., Abbas, Z., Payberah, A.H.: Graph representation matters in device placement. In: Proceedings of the Workshop on Distributed Infrastructures for Deep Learning. pp. 1–6 (2020)

23. Paliwal, A., Gimeno, F., Nair, V., Li, Y., Lubin, M., Kohli, P., Vinyals, O.: Reinforced genetic algorithm learning for optimizing computation graphs. In: International Conference on Learning Representations (2020)

24. Paris, C., Weikmann, G., Bruzzone, L.: Monitoring of agricultural areas by using sentinel 2 image time series and deep learning techniques. In: Image and Signal Processing for Remote Sensing XXVI. vol. 11533, p. 115330K. International Society for Optics and Photonics (2020)

25. Pham, H., Guan, M., Zoph, B., Le, Q., Dean, J.: Efficient neural architecture search via parameters sharing. In: International Conference on Machine Learning. pp. 4095–4104. PMLR (2018)

26. Scarselli, F., Gori, M., Tsoi, A.C., Hagenbuchner, M., Monfardini, G.: The graph neural network model. IEEE transactions on neural networks 20(1), 61–80 (2008)

27. Shallue, C.J., Lee, J., Antognini, J., Sohl-Dickstein, J., Frostig, R., Dahl, G.E.: Measuring the effects of data parallelism on neural network training. Journal of Machine Learning Research 20(112), 1–49 (2019)

28. Sheikholeslami, S., Meister, M., Wang, T., Payberah, A.H., Vlassov, V., Dowling, J.: Autoablation: Automated parallel ablation studies for deep learning. In:

Proceedings of the 1st Workshop on Machine Learning and Systems. pp. 55–61 (2021)

29. Shoeybi, M., Patwary, M., Puri, R., LeGresley, P., Casper, J., Catanzaro, B.: Megatron-lm: Training multi-billion parameter language models using model parallelism. arXiv preprint arXiv:1909.08053 (2019)

30. Szegedy, C., Liu, W., Jia, Y., Sermanet, P., Reed, S., Anguelov, D., Erhan, D., Vanhoucke, V., Rabinovich, A.: Going deeper with convolutions. In: Proceedings of the IEEE conference on computer vision and pattern recognition. pp. 1–9 (2015)

31. Tanaka, M., Taura, K., Hanawa, T., Torisawa, K.: Automatic graph partitioning for very large-scale deep learning. arXiv preprint arXiv:2103.16063 (2021)

32. Topping, J., Di Giovanni, F., Chamberlain, B.P., Dong, X., Bronstein, M.M.: Understanding over-squashing and bottlenecks on graphs via curvature. arXiv preprint arXiv:2111.14522 (2021)

33. Vaswani, A., Shazeer, N., Parmar, N., Uszkoreit, J., Jones, L., Gomez, A.N., Kaiser, Ł., Polosukhin, I.: Attention is all you need. In: Advances in neural information processing systems. pp. 5998–6008 (2017)

34. Williams, R.J.: Simple statistical gradient-following algorithms for connectionist reinforcement learning. Machine learning 8(3), 229–256 (1992)

35. Wu, Y., Schuster, M., Chen, Z., Le, Q.V., Norouzi, M., Macherey, W., Krikun, M., Cao, Y., Gao, Q., Macherey, K., et al.: Google's neural machine translation system: Bridging the gap between human and machine translation. arXiv preprint arXiv:1609.08144 (2016)

36. Ying, C., Cai, T., Luo, S., Zheng, S., Ke, G., He, D., Shen, Y., Liu, T.Y.: Do transformers really perform bad for graph representation? arXiv preprint arXiv:2106.05234 (2021)

37. You, J., Ying, R., Ren, X., Hamilton, W., Leskovec, J.: Graphrnn: Generating realistic graphs with deep auto-regressive models. In: International conference on machine learning. pp. 5708–5717. PMLR (2018)

38. Zhou, Y., Roy, S., Abdolrashidi, A., Wong, D., Ma, P.C., Xu, Q., Zhong, M., Liu, H., Goldie, A., Mirhoseini, A., et al.: Gdp: Generalized device placement for dataflow graphs. arXiv preprint arXiv:1910.01578 (2019)

39. Zhou, Y., Roy, S., Abdolrashidi, A., Wong, D.L.K., Ma, P., Xu, Q., Mirhoseini, A., Laudon, J.: A single-shot generalized device placement for large dataflow graphs. IEEE Micro 40(5), 26–36 (2020)

40. Zhu, X.X., Tuia, D., Mou, L., Xia, G.S., Zhang, L., Xu, F., Fraundorfer, F.: Deep learning in remote sensing: A comprehensive review and list of resources. IEEE Geoscience and Remote Sensing Magazine 5(4), 8–36 (2017)

Analysis of the Impact of Interaction Patterns and IoT Protocols on Energy Consumption of IoT Consumer Applications

Rodrigo Canek[✉], Pedro Borges, and Chantal Taconet

SAMOVAR, Télécom SudParis, Institut Polytechnique de Paris, Paris, France
rodrigo.canek@telecom-sudparis.eu

Abstract. Nowadays, it is estimated that half the connected devices are related to the Internet of Things (IoT). The IoT paradigm contributes to the increase of the Information Technology energy demand. The energy demand is due on one side to the huge number of IoT devices, and on the other side to the plethora of IoT end user applications consuming data produced by those devices. However, taking into account energy consumption in the development of such applications, consuming data produced by IoT devices is still challenging. There is a lack of knowledge on what are the best practises to develop green IoT applications. The work presented in this paper aims to raise the awareness of application designers concerning the impact of the choice of IoT protocols and interaction patterns on the energy consumption of the applications. For this purpose, we have experimentally analysed the energy consumption of HTTP and MQTT, which are two of the most popular, mature and stable protocols for IoT consumer applications. For the HTTP protocol, we have studied both the publish-subscribe and the request-reply interaction patterns. For MQTT, we have studied the publish-subscribe interaction pattern with the three available Quality of Services. We also examine the impact of message payload on energy consumption. The results show that the publish/subscribe interaction pattern has lower energy consumption (around 92% less) than the synchronous interaction pattern and HTTP consumes 20% more energy than the MQTT protocol for the publish/subscribe interaction pattern. Finally, we show that the payload has a low impact on energy consumption, having a 9% overhead on payloads ranging from 24 to 3120 bytes.

This work is a contribution to the Energy4Climate Interdisciplinary Center (E4C) of IP Paris and Ecole des Ponts ParisTech, supported by 3rd Programme d'Investissements d'Avenir [ANR-18-EUR-0006-02]. It has been funded by the "Futur & Ruptures" program from Institut Mines Télécom, Fondation, Fondation Mines-Télécom and Institut Carnot.

© IFIP International Federation for Information Processing 2022
Published by Springer Nature Switzerland AG 2022
D. Eyers and S. Voulgaris (Eds.): DAIS 2022, LNCS 13272, pp. 131–147, 2022.
https://doi.org/10.1007/978-3-031-16092-9_9

Keywords: Middleware · Internet of Things applications · IoT protocols · Interaction patterns · IoT Platforms · Energy Consumption · Green IT

1   Introduction

It is estimated that the number of Internet-connected devices will be 29.3 billion in 2023, among them 50% will be IoT devices and 23% smartphones [4]. As the number of IoT systems is one of the main causes of the growth of IT energy consumption [9], handling IoT systems energy-efficiency is from now on a first class imperative [20].

Because of their limited battery lifetime, energy-efficiency has firstly been taken into account in the design of software deployed on IoT devices [12]. However, reducing software energy consumption should not be limited to IoT devices. It has been estimated that around 67 zettabytes of data were generated by IoT devices in 2020 [9]. Part of this volume of data has been consumed by IoT applications. Thus, carefully designing interactions between IoT applications and IoT systems with a energy-efficiency concern is also essential.

Developers still lack knowledge about software energy consumption [18]. Measuring experimentally software and hardware energy consumption participates in providing this knowledge. Several approaches may be used for energy measurement [15]. As most of the libraries that measure energy consumption at the process level only consider the impact of CPU and memory (e.g., [1]), measuring the cost of the interaction between distributed components is still a difficult task. In this study, we propose to experimentally measure the cost of the interactions between IoT consumer applications and IoT systems. These measures will guide IoT consumer application developers in their design choices in terms of energy consumption.

In our experiments, we consider consumer IoT applications connected with a WiFi (802.11n) interface and that use MQTT and HTTP protocols. Those technologies are commonly used for IoT consuming applications placed in different networks from the connected object ones, whereas other networks (e.g. Bluetooth) and protocols (e.g. Zigbee, COAP) are used on the connected object side. The conducted analysis answers the following questions: What is the energy consumption impact of (RQ1) the publish/subscribe interaction pattern vs request/reply, (RQ2) the HTTP protocol vs MQTT for the publish subscribe interaction pattern, (RQ3) the Quality of service (QoS) level (in the case of MQTT) and (RQ4) the size of the payload. From the analysis of the results of the experiments, we propose guidelines to help developers to build low energy consuming IoT applications.

The rest of this paper is structured as follows. Section 2 provides important background concepts on IoT architectures, interaction patterns and IoT protocols. Section 3 investigates the related works concerning the energy consumption of the studied IoT protocols. Section 4 shows the setup of the hardware and software for the experiments and discusses the threats to validity. Section 5 presents the results of the experiments, analyses the results according to the four introduced research questions and provides guidelines for IoT consuming application developers. Finally, Sect. 6 draws conclusions and perspectives.

2 Consuming IoT Applications: Architecture, Interaction Patterns and Protocols

This section introduces the main concepts that will be used throughout the article, concerning IoT distributed architecture and IoT protocols.

2.1 Distributed IoT Architecture

Figure 1 presents a classical IoT system architecture. According to the ISO-IEC IoT reference architecture [10], an IoT system consists of (1) IoT devices (sensors and actuators), (2) end user applications that may consume sensor data (called *IoT consumer applications* in this paper), (3) IoT platforms and IoT gateways, standardized intermediates for interacting with IoT devices that deal with the high degree of hardware and software heterogeneity in IoT environments.

The usage of IoT platforms to support IoT systems is a recent trend: they provide services to deploy and run applications on top of a hardware and/or software suite in different application domains [13]. Their role is to decouple producers from consumers by providing an intermediary layer. Among the platforms, we can cite FIWARE/Orion [6], an IoT platform supported by the European Community, and OneM2M [17] a Machine-2-Machine standard.

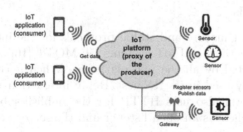

Fig. 1. IoT distributed architecture

2.2 Interaction Patterns

An interaction pattern, or a Message Exchange Pattern [7], defines the structure of the interactions between the two sides engaged in a communication. In the IoT, two high level interaction patterns are commonly used between the consumers of data and the providers of data [3]: Publish-Subscribe and Request-Reply.

Request-Reply. As shown in Fig. 2, the consumer (i.e. IoT consumer application), sends a request message to the producer (e.g., the IoT platform). The consumer is waiting for a reply from the producer (or a timeout). The producer receives and processes the request and sends the consumer a reply message with a given payload.

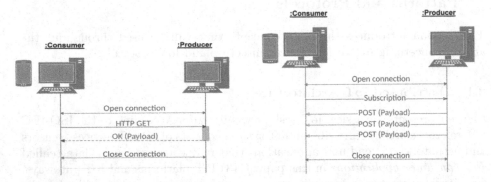

Fig. 2. Request-Reply Pattern   **Fig. 3.** Publish-Subscribe Pattern

Publish-Subscribe. As shown in Fig. 3 the consumer defines, with a subscription, what kind of data it is interested in. The consumer is notified whenever there is a message matching the subscription.

2.3 IoT Protocols

We consider the most mature and stable protocols for the interaction between IoT consumer applications and IoT systems [5]: MQTT [16] and HTTP [14].

HTTP is supported by all the IoT platforms. When it comes to using the protocol, it is mostly used in its Request/Reply interaction pattern. However, the FIWARE platform also uses HTTP for the publish-subscribe interaction pattern, where the client is an open listener and the server posts available data (as shown in Fig. 3).

MQTT is a lightweight protocol with the publish/subscribe interaction pattern. IoT platforms host MQTT brokers that receive publications from connected objects or gateways. Brokers are responsible to filter incoming messages and distribute them properly according to the message topics. MQTT implements three different models of message exchange known as Quality of Service, where the delivery with QoS 0 being at most once, QoS 1 being at least once, and QoS 2 being exactly once.

In our experiments, MQTT and HTTP are above TCP/IP. TCP handles the connections between the remote processes and reassembles the data in the correct order. The Internet Protocol (IP) [19] is responsible for routing data. It provides fragmentation and reassembly of long datagrams, if necessary according to the

Maximum Transmission Unit (MTU). We investigate in our experiments whether having a message payload below or above the MTU impacts the energy consumption.

3 Related Work

In this section, we present an analysis of the related works concerning the efficiency of IoT protocols used by IoT consumer applications. We have selected research papers that include energy consumption measures in the evaluation of HTTP and/or MQTT. We have to mention that, to the best of our knowledge, the number of papers on this subject is low, we only found 4 papers and the measures do not isolate the consumption on the consumer side. Furthermore, none of them study the impact of the interaction pattern.

A synthesis of the study is presented in Table 1. For those related works, the following points have been analyzed. Since our objective is to study the consumer side of an IoT architecture, we indicate whether the study is conducted on the producer side (P), on the consumer side (C), or on both sides. We mention which IoT protocols were compared in the work. We also indicate the experimental conditions: the device where the measure was conducted and the type of network. The last aspect concerns type of the evaluation, analytical or experimental energy evaluation and, if experimental, the tool they have used to measure the energy consumption.

Bandyopadhyay and Bhattacharyya present an analysis of MQTT and CoAP [2]. They examine the resource usage including energy consumption according to the message size and the packet loss ratio. The energy consumption of the most reliable configurations was measured on a Wide Area Network: CoAP and MQTT with QoS 2. They show that with a perfect network without any loss, MQTT with QoS2 is more than ten times more consuming than CoAP. Concerning energy efficiency, they only study MQTT with QoS2. They do not define whether the measures are done on the producer or/and consumer side, which makes it difficult to know which side of the architecture was studied. They also do not mention how the energy consumption was measured.

Toldinas et al. perform a dedicated study of MQTT QoS levels and their energy consumption [21]. They use a ESP-WROOM-02 hardware device connected to the network through Wifi 802.11 and acting both as producer and consumer. For each level of QoS, the remaining battery voltage level was measured using a digital multimeter as an indicator of energy consumption. This study provides a good indication of the percentage increase in energy consumption for each level of the QoS compared to the previous one. However, it does not allow effective energy-consumption conclusions to be drawn about the behavior of a consumer or a producer as the same device is used for both tasks.

Hofer and Pawaska studied the impact of MQTT and HTTP protocols on CPU, RAM, and energy consumption [8]. The device used is a Raspberry Pi connected by Ethernet, that acts both as a producer and a consumer, as a consequence they can not isolate the energy consumption on the consumer side.

They do not mention what QoS was used for MQTT. For the energy evaluation, the authors studied the Ampere per second in the device using an oscilloscope. The study proved that MQTT outperformed HTTP RESTful in terms of data overhead which is the amount of extra data needed to be sent to a client (e.g. HTTP Headers, MQTT headers, etc.), a nearly four times higher throughput. Furthermore, MQTT also had lower resource consumption and significantly lower energy consumption. As HTTP is used with the synchronous interaction pattern and MQTT is used with the publish/subscribe interaction pattern, it is not possible to isolate the impact of the interaction pattern from the impact of the protocol.

Joshi et al. presented a comparison in terms of protocol impact on throughput and battery consumption between MQTT (QoS not specified), CoAP and HTTP RESTful [11]. The device used was a Raspberry Pi, which acted only as a producer. For energy consumption, the percentage of battery consumption per hour was taken as a reference. However, it was not mentioned how it was calculated. The conclusions are: (i) HTTP consumes more energy than MQTT, and (ii) with the same amount of battery it is possible to send 100 times more messages with MQTT compared to HTTP. Although the work was not dedicated to the study of energy consumption, it lacks details on how the measures were implemented as well as the conditions of the experiment (e.g. network type).

Table 1. Synthesis of the related work

Ref	Network	P/C	MQTT QoS			HTTP		Evaluation
			0	1	2	Sync	Pub/sub	
[2]	WAN em.	?	×	×	√	×	×	?
[21]	Wifi	P+C	√	√	√	×	×	simulation
[8]	Ethernet	P+C	?	?	?	√	×	oscilloscope
[11]	Wifi	P	√	×	×	√	×	calculated
this	Wifi	C	√	√	√	√	√	wattmeter

Compared to the presented works, the experiments we have conducted allow to isolate the cost of the consumer application side of an IoT architecture. Furthermore as we test the HTTP protocol with the request/reply and publish/subscribe interaction patterns, we are able to study the impact of the interaction pattern separately from the impact of the protocol.

4   Experimental Methodology

This section presents the methodology used in the experiments. We present the experimental conditions in terms of computer, network, energy measurement tool, software and algorithms in Sect. 4.1. We continue by presenting the process allowing to isolate the energy consumption of the communication part in

Sect. 4.2. Then we present the experimental plan in Sect. 4.3. Finally, we discuss the threats that may affect the validity of the experimentation in Sect. 4.4.

4.1   Experimental Setup

Computers and Network. As shown in Fig. 4, three computers were used to perform the experiments. 1) The **Consumer Computer** used for running the consumer application. A wattmeter measures its energy consumption. The Consumer is connected to the network through a Wifi interface. The characteristics of this computer are the following: Dell Latitude E6320 v:01 with 5.68 GiB of RAM, a Broadcom (BCM4313 802.11 bgn) Wireless Network Adapter driver and Ubuntu 20.10 Operating system. Furthermore, the battery was fully charged and the computer was always plugged to the electricity. 2) The **Producer Computer** used for simulating an IoT platform. It runs a process that produces data. It is a fixed computer connected to the Internet through an Ethernet interface. 3) The **Script Computer** was used (i) running the scripts responsible for starting all applications on the client and server computers, and (ii) for reading the energy consumption measures.

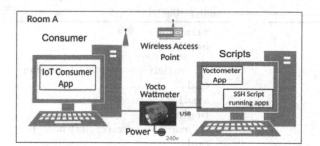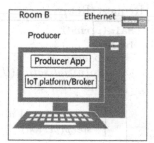

Fig. 4. Experimental setup

For **MQTT**, we use the Mosquitto broker version 3. The producer and the consumer were developed using the open-source Eclipse Paho library for Java. For **HTTP Request/Reply**, the consumer use HTTP/1.1 with the *java.net.http.HttpClient* Java library. For **HTTP Publish/Subscribe** we also use HTTP/1.1 and the consumer includes an Undertow Server to receive HTTP publications. We have to mention that in a real scenario, the consumer application does not choose the version of the HTTP protocol used by the server neither the configuration of the server concerning the connection management. In this context, the usage of HTTP/1.1 is widely supported by servers and clients whereas other versions such as HTTP//2 are still less common.

Energy Consumption Measurements. Currently there is no library that includes the consumption of the network interface in the energy consumption measurements. Some libraries such as RAPL are able to make energy measurements, but are limited to the CPU and memory consumption. In the case for communications over the internet, the hardware that need to have its energy-consumption measured is the network interface, making it difficult the usage of RAPL in our case. As a consequence, it was decided to use a Yocto wattmeter [22] to measure the energy consumption of the consuming application.

As shown in Fig. 4, the Yocto-wattmeter is located between the consumer computer power cable and the wall power outlet. The Yocto-wattmeter is connected to the energy measurement computer via a USB cable. It uses the Yocto software API to read energy consumption measures.

Algorithms. We provide below the algorithms used in the experiments.

On the consumer side, Algorithm 1 is used for the Request/Reply interaction pattern, it takes as an input parameter the period between two requests. Algorithm 2 is used for the publish/subscribe interaction pattern and registers the handler to be called on the reception of a notification and runs forever.

Algorithm 1: Consumer Request/Reply

```
Main(period)
begin
    producer ←
    httpInitialisation(URI)
    while true do
        value ←
        producer.getValue()
        sleep(period)
    end
end
```

Algorithm 2: Consumer publish/subscribe

```
Main(void)
begin
    server ←
    initializeServer(URI, handler)
end
handler(receiver)
begin
    value ← receiver.getValue()
end
```

On the producer side, the Algorithm 3 is used to simulate IoT data publications. It takes as input the period between two publications and the size of the payload to be sent periodically.

Finally a script runs on the measuring computer. It takes as input the period between two publications, the payload size and the duration of the experiment. The script starts the consumer and the producer, then sleeps for one minute for initialization and consumer warmup purposes. Then, the energy meter on the wattmeter is reset and is ready to start gathering new energy measures for the duration of the experiment. Finally, the script reads the consumed energy on the consumer application from the wattmeter and stops the producer and the consumer.

Algorithm 3: Producer

Main(*period, payload*)

begin

    dest=initializeServer(URI)

    while *true* **do**

        dest.send(payload)

        sleep(period)

    end

end

4.2   Process to Isolate the Communication Energy Consumption

Using a wattmeter has the following disadvantage: There is no isolation of the application or any particular process in the measurement, as the wattmeter measures the energy consumption of the computer as a whole. For a proper measurement of the impact of an application, it is necessary to make two measures: (1) the measure of the energy consumption without the application and (2) the measure of the energy consumption with the application.

In Fig. 5, we present, for the 5 families of experiments in Table 2, the following measures of energy consumption of the consumer computer:

- $M_{idle+jvm}$: we start the Consumer computer with the consumer application but without any interaction with the producer application (blue + orange on Fig. 5)
- $M_{idle+jvm+interactions}$: we start the Consumer computer with the full consumer application (blue + orange + green on Fig. 5)

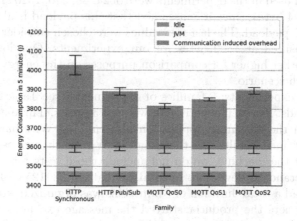

Fig. 5. Energy consumption measures (Color figure online)

The results that are presented in Sect. 5 only show the interaction cost (the upper part in green on Fig. 5). We obtain this value with this formula:

$M_{idle+jvm+interactions} - M_{idle+jvm}$. As a consequence, the standard deviation of the result is the addition of the standard deviation of the two measures.

4.3   Experimental Plan

Table 2 presents the combinations of interaction patterns and protocols for which we have handled the experiments. That gives 5 families of experiments. We measure: (1) the impact of the interaction pattern through families F1 and F2; (2) the impact of the protocol with families F2 and F3 and (3) the impact of the QoS for MQTT with families F3, F4 and F5.

Table 2. Families of experiments

Family	Interaction pattern	Protocol
F1	Synchronous	HTTP
F2	Publish/Subscribe	HTTP
F3	Publish/Subscribe	MQTT QoS0
F4	Publish/Subscribe	MQTT QoS1
F5	Publish/Subscribe	MQTT QoS2

The message rates used in the experiments were of 1, 2, 4, 8 and 16 messages by second. The tests at 32, 64 and 128 messages per second with both interaction patterns using HTTP started to receive a significantly lower amount of messages, as a consequence we did not keep those results.

The payload used in the experiments were of 24, 48, 240, 1320 and 1560 bytes. We start with 24 bytes, since it is assumed that this payload is about the usual value for an IoT payload. The last two values were chosen considering the MTU, which was measured at 1500 bytes for our experiments. One lower than this value and the other higher for comparison purposes on the energy-consumption influence of such scenario.

We did 125 experiments: 5 families of experiments (see Table 2)* 5 message rates * 5 payloads. For each experiment, we used 30 tests. Three more measures were done with the consumer application also running Wireshark in order to explain the obtained results. As the usage of Wireshark increases the energy consumption of the machine, we do not include those tests for computing the mean and the standard deviation. In total we realized 33*125 = 4 125 tests.

Each test had a total duration of 8 min. This was organized with one minute for warm up, where the producer started the message exchange with the consumer. Followed by a measurement of the energy consumption for 5 min while the producer was exchanging data with the consumer. Finally, two more minutes of sleep time to reset the experiment and the network conditions before starting the following test. 4 125 tests of duration 8 min necessitate around one full month of experiments. Additionally, for $M_{idle+jvm}$, 60 tests were realized, we double the number of tests to obtain low standard deviation and confidence intervals.

4.4   Threats to Validity

We present below potential threats to the validity of our study and how we propose to minimize their effects.

Computer conditions: The activity of the computer can not be totally controlled, as a consequence we report some discrepancies in the measured values. To reduce these discrepancies, we have shut down or disabled all unnecessary processes of the operating system as well as using the lowest brightness and connecting to the device via ssh to reduce user tampering. In order to minimize the standard deviation and obtain a more consistent result, each of the experiments were run a total of 30 times.

Network conditions: The conditions of the network while doing the tests were optimal. The gathered data showed that there was no packet loss during the tests and the latency remained low and stable at around 23 ms.

Temperature at which the experiments are conducted: During the initial experiments, the climate did not rise above 25 °C. However, on some days when the external temperature rose between 28 and 32°C, the fluctuations in energy consumption increased. These fluctuations may be due to the need for the equipment cooling systems to increase their output in order to keep the components of the equipment in the correct temperature conditions. To address this threat, the client computer was moved to an air-conditioned room where the computer was always at a cold temperature. This resulted in a reduction of the standard deviations of the measurements, making the results more stable. The experiments realized in the air-conditioned room were for the message rate of 8 m/s and the payloads of 1320 B, 1560 B, and 3120 B.

5   Analysis

We organize the analysis of the results of the experiments according to the four tackled research questions presented in the introduction. As an outcome of the analysis, Sect. 5.5 presents guidelines dedicated to developers of IoT consumer applications.

5.1   (RQ1) Impact of the Interaction Pattern

For a fair comparison of the interaction patterns, we compared only the results obtained with the HTTP protocol for which we have measured the two interaction patterns.

Figure 6 presents the results of the energy consumption for a 24 Bytes payload for both interaction patterns. Table 3 presents in percentage the synchronous pattern overhead over the publish/subscribe pattern. This is a synthesis of all the realized measures (all the message rates).

The results of the experiments show that with the same number of received observations, the synchronous pattern consumes around 92% (mean of all the message rates and payloads results) more energy than the publish/subscribe interaction pattern, being almost two times less efficient. This happens as the client needs to process the request for the server and wait for a reply whereas in pub/sub it will only need to wait for notifications from the server.

5.2   (RQ2) Impact of the Application Protocol

For the comparison of the protocols, it was desired to do a fair comparison of the two protocols, comparing the MQTT QoS 0 and HTTP Pub/Sub as they both propose an "at most once" semantics. As observed in Fig. 7 and in Table 4, MQTT outperforms HTTP in terms of energy consumption and number of bytes by Joule.

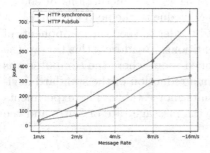

Fig. 6. Energy consumption 24 B, Interaction Pattern Comparison

Table 3. Synchronous pattern average overhead over the publish/subscribe pattern

Payload	Overhead in %
24 B	+94.03%
48 B	+89.96%
240 B	+106.90%
1320 B	+85.16%
1560 B	+85.50%
Mean	+92.31%

We observe that in terms of energy, the MQTT protocol outperforms HTTP by 20% on average while having the same interaction pattern and the same semantics. This happens because of the purpose of each protocol. While HTTP has more processing on top of the data received by the client, as it needs to look into further validations (e.g. size variable header, parameters, etc.), MQTT is proposed with a more lightweigth structure that, for example, has fixed headers, enabling a less intensive processing by the client.

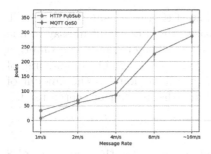

Fig. 7. Energy consumption for a 24 B payload, Protocol Comparison

Table 4. HTTP vs MQTT average overhead with all the message rates

Payload	HTTP vs MQTT in %
24 B	+28.07%
48 B	+23.40%
240 B	+31.05%
1320 B	+2.58%
1560 B	+18.63%
Mean	+20.75%

5.3   (RQ3) Impact of the QoS in MQTT

In Fig. 8, we compare the measures of energy consumption for the three MQTT QoS with the 24 B payload. Table 5 presents a synthesis of the overheads for all the payloads.

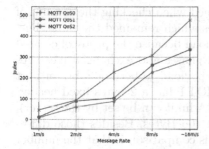

Fig. 8. Energy consumption for a 24 B payload, QoS Comparison

Table 5. MQTT QoS overheads

Payload	QoS1/QoS0	QoS2/QoS1	QoS2/QoS0
24 B	+24.64%	+46.58%	+79.72%
48 B	+17.76%	+51.09%	+78.20%
240 B	+58.67%	+27.08%	+104.46%
1320 B	+12.16%	+88.10%	+111.76%
1560 B	+21.83%	+53.31%	+86.45%
Mean	+27.01%	+59.77 %	+92.12%

Taking into consideration all the measures realized, meaning all the message rates and payloads, the comparison of the QoS shows that QoS 0 consumes around 27% less energy than QoS 1 and 92% compared to QoS 2 with the same number of received observations. QoS 2 consumes 60% more energy than QoS 1. Having similar results in the comparisons of QoS 0, QoS 1 and QoS 2, to what was observed in the related work [21]. The difference is that we are able to measure the consumer side only while they use the same device as producer and consumer and as a result can not differentiate consumer from producer energy consumption.

A deeper look at the results shows that the impact of the QoS using MQTT is related to the amount of messages exchanged during the experiment. QoS 0 had the smallest amount of messages exchanged between the broker and the consumer because of the fire and forget mechanism (Sending messages and not verifying the arrival) it implements and resulted in the lowest energy consumption. MQTT QoS 1 followed a similar path but as it increased the amount of messages, due to the acknowledgments of the client, it resulted in a bigger energy consumption when compared to MQTT QoS 0. Finally, QoS 2 with its bigger amount of messages exchanged between the broker and the client doubled the amount of packets exchanged and ended up almost doubling the amount of energy used.

5.4   (RQ4) Impact of the Payload

Figure 9 presents the bytes/Joule for different payloads for the fixed rate of 8 messages per second for the 5 families of experiments.

The usage of a payload up to 3120 bytes, presented a moderate increase in the experiments (mean 9%), having cases with even lower consumption for HTTP. The fragmentation of the messages according to the MTU (1500 bytes) does not seem to have a relevant impact on the energy consumption. The experiment impacted the most by the increase was MQTT QoS 0, having up to 21.89% more energy consumption. Concerning HTTP publish-subscribe and request-reply, both seemed unaffected by the changes in the payload as the payload of 24 B was slightly higher than the one with 3120 B (Table 6), which had the message broken into 3 fragments according to the size of the MTU. The behaviour of the payload seen in HTTP is further confirmed when checking the amount of TCP connections with 24 bytes and 3120 bytes which remained the same. Furthermore, MQTT is more impacted by the payload because the protocol created only one TCP connection through all the test phases and exchanged messages in this established connection. This causes the payload to become a bigger part of the energy consumption considering that MQTT has a 2 bytes fixed header, while the HTTP header does not have a limit (A limit can be set by the server), but in the case of the tests done, it is around 106 Bytes. Besides those differences by family of experiment, the lesson of this comparison is that the number of Bytes by Joule is augmented significantly for all the families while augmenting the payload. An explanation for this result comes from the cost of the software call stack necessary to handle one message whatever the size of the message is.

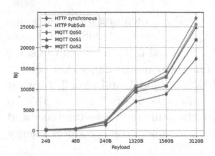

Fig. 9. Bytes Received by Joule Payload Comparison

Table 6. Payload overhead from 24 Bytes to 3120 Bytes

Family of experiment	Overhead in %
HTTP synchronous	−1.36%
HTTP Pub/sub	−1.32%
MQTT QoS0	+21.89%
MQTT QoS1	+15.45%
MQTT QoS2	+11.24%
Mean	+9,18%

5.5 Guidelines for IoT Consumer Application Designers

We provide in this section guidelines for IoT consumer application designers to reduce the energy consumption at the end user device side.

Group Several Observations in One Message. We have shown that using different payloads, from 24 up to 3120 bytes, has a small impact on the energy consumption of the application. If the application necessitates multiple sensor observations, we advise combining the different observations into one single message. Some IoT platforms, such as Fiware/Orion, provide the possibility to query (or subscribe to) a group of sensors. This possibility has clearly to be chosen by application developers.

Favor the Publish-Subscribe Interaction Pattern. The comparison of interaction patterns showed that for the same frequency of requests and notifications, the publish/subscribe pattern consumed on average 92% less energy than the request/reply pattern. As a consequence, we advise to favor the publish/subscribe pattern.

We have to mention that this advice may depend on the IoT application and the IoT platform. If the frequency of requests is far lower than the frequency of publications, the synchronous pattern can be an option because the client can better control the amount of messages being exchanged.

Favor the MQTT Protocol over the HTTP Protocol. For the publish/subscribe pattern, the comparison of the MQTT and HTTP protocols shows that MQTT has 20% less energy overhead in comparison to HTTP. The advice is then to favor the MQTT protocol for the publish/subscribe pattern.

Choose the QoS Appropriate for Your Application. If your IoT application supports losing some observations, prefer QoS 0 since it involves less energy consumption. If the application cannot afford to lose observations, use QoS 1 instead of QoS 0 as it provides a complementary service to TCP's reliability by ensuring that each message is received at least once. Keep the QoS2 for exactly once semantics requirement as it presents an overhead of 92% and should be used in conditions that require no duplication of messages.

Guideline Example. The benefits of guidelines to develop IoT applications can be better seen when viewing with a bigger space of time. As an example, an IoT application running for one year using HTTP pub/sub sending 4 messages per second with a payload of 24 B will consume around 31,01 MegaJoules while another application running with the same parameters but using MQTT QoS 0 will consume around 8,40 MegaJoules. Furthermore, if the messages are grouped into a single message, and sent once per second, we can achieve a consumption of around 4,20 MegaJoules for both HTTP pub/sub and MQTT QoS 0 with a payload of 24 Bytes. As an example, for a regular notebook battery with around 360 KiloJoules, an IoT application using HTTP or MQTT and grouping messages could lead to a lifetime of around 31 h, on the other hand, without grouping and using HTTP synchronous we have around 9 h of battery (71% less).

6   Conclusions

Energy consumption is a first class concern in the development of future IoT applications. As the amount of devices and the amount of applications related to IoT will keep growing in the near future, there is a new requirement for the developers and the users to regulate and improve the energy consumption of IoT applications not only on the connected object side but also on the consumer application side.

In this paper, we have measured the energy consumption of IoT consumer applications on user devices connected with WiFi (802.11n). We have been able to show the impact on energy consumption on different interaction choices summarized below. The results show that for the same amount of received observations, the publish/subscribe interaction pattern has lower energy consumption (around 92% lower) than the synchronous interaction pattern. We have also shown that, for the publish/subscribe interaction pattern, MQTT consumes less than the HTTP protocol (around 20% less). Finally, we have shown that the payload has a low impact on energy consumption having a 9% overhead from 24 to 3120 bytes payloads. From the above results, we have been able to provide guidelines for IoT consumer application designers, for example we advise developers to favor the publish/subscribe pattern and to group several observations in one message when possible.

As a future work, we plan to investigate the cost of the software call stack to better guide the developers of IoT consumer applications. We plan to investigate the impact of data representation on the cost of marshalling and unmarshalling data in IoT applications. We also plan to follow the guidelines for the design of a middleware used by IoT applications to transparently interact with multiple IoT platforms. Implementing those strategies at the middleware level may have a strong impact for reducing IoT application energy consumption while keeping a low development effort.

References

1. PowerAPI. http://powerapi.org/. Accessed 15 Feb 2022
2. Bandyopadhyay, S., Bhattacharyya, A.: Lightweight internet protocols for web enablement of sensors using constrained gateway devices. In: 2013 International Conference on Computing, Networking and Communications (ICNC), pp. 334–340 (2013). https://doi.org/10.1109/ICCNC.2013.6504105
3. Bouloukakis, G., Georgantas, N., Ntumba, P., Issarny, V.: Automated synthesis of mediators for middleware-layer protocol interoperability in the IoT. Future Gener. Comput. Syst. **101**, 1271–1294 (2019). https://doi.org/10.1016/j.future.2019.05.064

4. Cisco Annual Internet Report (2018–2023). https://www.cisco.com/c/en/us/solutions/collateral/executive-perspectives/annual-internet-report/white-paper-c11-741490.html (2020)
5. Dizdarević, J., Carpio, F., Jukan, A., Masip-Bruin, X.: A survey of communication protocols for internet of things and related challenges of fog and cloud computing integration, vol. 51. Association for Computing Machinery, NY (2019). https://doi.org/10.1145/3292674
6. FIWARE: What is fiware? https://www.fiware.org/
7. Garbarino, E.: Message exchange patterns (MEPs) (2013). https://garba.org/article/general/soa/mep.html#top
8. Hofer, J., Pawaskar, S.: Impact of the application layer protocol on energy consumption, 4G utilization and performance. In: 2018 3rd Cloudification of the Internet of Things (CIoT), pp. 1–7 (2018). https://doi.org/10.1109/CIOT.2018.8627133
9. Directed by Hugues Ferreboeuf, S.P.: Lean ICT - towards digital sobriety (2019). https://theshiftproject.org/wp-content/uploads/2019/03/Lean-ICT-Report_The-Shift-Project_2019.pdf
10. ISO/IEC: Internet of Things (IoT) - reference architecture. ISO/IEC JTC 1/SC 41 - Internet of Things and Digital Twin, p. 84 (2018)
11. Joshi, J., et al.: Performance enhancement and IoT based monitoring for smart home. In: 2017 International Conference on Information Networking (ICOIN), pp. 468–473 (2017). https://doi.org/10.1109/ICOIN.2017.7899537
12. Munoz, D.J., Montenegro, J.A., Pinto, M., Fuentes, L.: Energy-aware environments for the development of green applications for cyber-physical systems. Future Gener. Comput. Syst. **91**, 536–554 (2019). https://doi.org/10.1016/j.future.2018.09.006
13. Nakhuva, B., Champaneria, T.: Study of various internet of things platforms. Int. J. Comput. Sci. Eng. Surv. **6**(6), 61–74 (2015)
14. Nielsen, H., et al.: Hypertext Transfer Protocol - HTTP/1.1. RFC 2616 (1999). https://doi.org/10.17487/RFC2616, https://rfc-editor.org/rfc/rfc2616.txt
15. Noureddine, A., Rouvoy, R., Seinturier, L.: A review of energy measurement approaches. ACM SIGOPS Oper. Syst. Rev. **47**(3), 42–49 (2013)
16. OASIS: MQTT version 3.1.1 plus errata 01 (2015). https://docs.oasis-open.org/mqtt/mqtt/v3.1.1/mqtt-v3.1.1.pdf. Accessed 21 May 2021
17. oneM2M: Who we are. https://www.onem2m.org/harmonization-m2m
18. Pang, C., Hindle, A., Adams, B., Hassan, A.E.: What do programmers know about software energy consumption? IEEE Softw. **33**(3), 83–89 (2016). https://doi.org/10.1109/MS.2015.83
19. Postel, J.: Internet Protocol. RFC 791, RFC Editor (1981). https://doi.org/10.17487/RFC0791, https://www.rfc-editor.org/info/rfc791
20. Shaikh, F.K., Zeadally, S., Exposito, E.: Enabling technologies for green internet of things. IEEE Syst. J. **11**(2), 983–994 (2017). https://doi.org/10.1109/JSYST.2015.2415194
21. Toldinas, J., Lozinskis, B., Baranauskas, E., Dobrovolskis, A.: MQTT quality of service versus energy consumption. In: 2019 23rd International Conference Electronics, pp. 1–4 (2019). https://doi.org/10.1109/ELECTRONICS.2019.8765692
22. YoctoPuce: Who are we? https://www.yoctopuce.com/EN/aboutus.php. Accessed 17 Oct 2021

Elastic and Scalable Systems

The HDFS Replica Placement Policies: A Comparative Experimental Investigation

Rhauani Weber Aita Fazul$^{(\boxtimes)}$ (iD) and Patrícia Pitthan Barcelos (iD)

Federal University of Santa Maria (UFSM), Santa Maria, RS, Brazil
{rwfazul,pitthan}@inf.ufsm.br

Abstract. The Hadoop Distributed File System (HDFS) is a robust and flexible file system designed for reliably storing large volumes of data in distributed environments. Its storage model relies upon data replication and one of its central features is to optimize the placement of the replicas across the cluster for fault tolerance, availability, and performance. To this end, the Replica Placement Policy selects which nodes will store the data blocks. This work presents an experimental investigation of the different placement strategies available in HDFS. For a broader analysis, we consider different stages where the placement of the replicas is necessary, such as writing files in the system, re-replicating blocks among the nodes, and balancing the replica distribution in the cluster. The evaluation results allowed a deeper understanding of the behavior of the policies, in addition to highlighting the advantages and drawbacks of the replica placement concerning optimizations in data availability, data locality, write and read throughput, and in the overall performance of the HDFS.

Keywords: Data replication · Block distribution · Replica placement policies · Distributed file systems

1 Introduction

In the current days, it is common to come across scenarios that deal with large volumes of data, of the most varied types, being generated at high speed. In this context, there are demands for scalability, reliability, availability, and data distribution, which can not always be satisfactorily addressed by traditional tools, so specialized solutions become necessary. One of these solutions is the Apache Hadoop framework [3]: an open-source platform dedicated to the efficient storage and processing of big data in distributed environments.

The Hadoop Distributed File System (HDFS), Hadoop's storage engine, is a reliable and scalable file system, which is incorporated as a persistence layer by several technologies, such as Apache Spark, Storm, and HBase [12]. HDFS follows a master-worker architecture composed of a *NameNode* (NN) and multiple *DataNodes* (DNs). The NN is the master server, responsible for maintaining the

© IFIP International Federation for Information Processing 2022
Published by Springer Nature Switzerland AG 2022
D. Eyers and S. Voulgaris (Eds.): DAIS 2022, LNCS 13272, pp. 151–166, 2022.
https://doi.org/10.1007/978-3-031-16092-9_10

system namespace and controlling the access and distribution of the files, while the DNs are the workers that effectively store and retrieve the data.

In order to handle large files, HDFS uses a storage strategy based on blocks, where the files are split into a sequence of data blocks of fixed size (128MB by default). The HDFS was designed to run on commodity hardware and reliably store the data across machines in large clusters [2]. So, the blocks of a file are replicated and maintained by different DNs. During replication, the selection of the DNs to maintain the replicas is a critical factor for the proper functioning of the HDFS. To select the DNs, the NN follows a Replica Placement Policy (RPP). There are five different RPPs integrated into the Hadoop distribution, and one of them is applied by default in the file system. A good replica placement optimizes data availability and reliability, in addition to reducing write bandwidth consumption and increasing read performance [12]. The current RPP implementation is the first effort in this direction, and it is one of Hadoop's goals to validate the policy on production systems, learn more about its behavior, and build a foundation to test and research more sophisticated RPPs [3].

This work presents a practical investigation of the RPPs available on HDFS. To this end, we consider different stages in which the policies for replica placement are necessary in the file system, such as writing files across the cluster, re-replicating blocks after failures, and redistributing blocks during replica balancing. At each stage, we analyze the behavior of the RPPs and measure the optimizations in availability and performance achieved by their placement strategies. The experimental analysis was conducted in a real, distributed, and heterogeneous environment running HDFS.

The paper is organized as follows. Section 2 is dedicated to data replication and balancing on HDFS. Section 3 presents the official policies for replica placement. Section 4 outlines the main related work. Section 5 exhibits and discusses the evaluation results. Finally, Sect. 6 concludes the paper and points out further research directions.

2   Data Replication in HDFS

Data replication is the primary fault tolerance mechanism and the core of the HDFS storage model. It consists of creating redundant copies of the data blocks so that, in the event of a failure, there are still replicas available in the system [12]. The replicated data are stored in different nodes of the cluster in such a way that the blocks can be accessed from any DN that maintains their replicas. The number of replicas is determined by the Replication Factor (RF), which is configured per file at the time of its creation and can be modified later through system utilities. An RF of n avoids data loss even if $n - 1$ DNs fail at the same time. The default RF is three.

The NN controls and makes all decisions regarding the replication of the blocks, which involves selecting the DNs for storing the replicas based on an RPP. This choice is initially performed when writing files in the cluster, and it is also necessary during the re-replication and redistribution of the data already stored in the file system. In all these moments, the selection of the DNs must be done in order to maintain data availability in the event of failures and improve the system's performance in serving I/O operations over the data. Next, Sect. 2.1 introduces block re-replication, Sect. 2.2 details the redistribution process, and Sect. 3 presents the official RPPs that guide the NN decisions.

2.1   Block Re-replication

Active monitoring is a vital requirement for assuring resilience and fault tolerance in the HDFS. In addition to the initial placement of the blocks performed when writing files, it is necessary that NN constantly monitor the state of the replicas and which data blocks need to be re-replicated. The necessity for data re-replication may arise due to different reasons, such as [3]: (i) the corruption of one or more replicas; (ii) a failure in one or more of the DN storage disks; (iii) the increase of the RF of a file; or (iv) DNs becoming unavailable, either due to network partition that causes some subset of DNs to lose connectivity or due to crash-failures.

Even when running on clusters of commodity hardware, HDFS is designed to maintain reliability and data availability in scenarios with consecutive failures. Therefore, the NN must control the number of existing replicas of each block, ensuring compliance with the RF [11]. To this end, the DNs processes communicate periodically with the NN through heartbeat messages: a fault tolerance mechanism that allows detecting operational failures in DNs [2]. If the NN does not receive heartbeats from a DN within a predefined period[1], it marks the DN as dead and does not forward any new requests to that node. The data in a dead DN is not available to HDFS, which can cause the RF of the blocks previously stored in its node to fall below the specified value.

Since the NN determines the mapping of blocks to DNs and constantly tracks which blocks need to be replicated, it can trigger the re-replication of the under-replicated blocks whenever necessary. To re-replicate a data block, the NN selects a source DN that contains one of its remaining replicas and a target DN that will receive the new copy of the replica stored in the source. As with the initial replication, this selection is performed transparently by HDFS and must be in accordance with the defined RPP.

2.2   Replica Rearrangement

HDFS is built around the idea that the most efficient data processing pattern for files is the write once, read many (WORM) access model. In this sense, a principle of Hadoop – and the reason for its good performance – is to move the computational tasks to where the data are stored and, if it is not possible, to

---

[1] The timeout to set a DN dead is relatively long (over 10 min by default) to avoid replication storms caused by state flapping of DNs [3]. To better suit performance-sensitive workloads, it is possible to configure a shorter interval to mark DNs as stale and exclude their nodes in I/O operations.

the nodes that have a faster network path for the DNs that maintain the blocks needed for the operation. This feature, known as data locality optimization [12], increases the overall throughput when processing large datasets and minimizes read latency and network congestion.

An unbalanced replica distribution tends to affect the locality of the data, resulting in an increased number of intra-rack and off-rack transfers, since tasks assigned to nodes that do not maintain many replicas will possibly not access local data. In addition to increasing the consumption of network bandwidth, the imbalance may cause some nodes to become full and prevent them from receiving new blocks, reducing their read parallelism and leading to performance degradation [3]. Therefore, HDFS works best when the blocks are evenly spread across the cluster. Over time, however, the cluster may become unbalanced, with a large discrepancy in the data volume stored in the nodes.

The main causes of replica imbalance are [5]: (i) the replica placement strategy that, in general, does not consider the node utilization; (ii) the re-replication procedure, which follows the RPP; (iii) the behavior of the client application that, if executed directly on a DN, stores one of the replicas in its node to preserve data locality; (iv) the addition of new DNs to the system, since they will be candidates for replica placement alongside all other DNs [11].

To maintain maximum cluster health and avoid performance bottlenecks, it is necessary to redistribute the data. For this purpose, there is a tool, integrated into the Hadoop distribution, designed for replica balancing: the HDFS *Balancer* [9]. By analyzing the positioning of the blocks, the *Balancer* makes decisions about the redistribution of data between the storage devices in the cluster. The *Balancer* daemon – which should be triggered by the administrator – operates until the utilization of each DN differs from the average utilization of the cluster by no more than a given threshold percentage, which default value is 10% [12]. To this end, it will move replicas from over-utilized to under-utilized DNs, while adhering to the configured RPP.

3   Replica Placement Policies

HDFS instances are commonly spread across multiple racks. In this sense, the placement of replicas on HDFS uses rack awareness[2], both for fault tolerance and performance. The former is achieved by placing replicas of the same block in at least two different racks, assuring data reliability and availability even if an entire rack fails (this could happen, for instance, due to network switch failure or partition within the cluster). The latter is optimized since it is possible to reduce network bandwidth utilization when writing files and to use the bandwidth of multiple racks when reading the data.

There are different RPP implementations available in the Hadoop distribution. They all follow the same interface to select the desired number of targets for

---

[2] HDFS tries to satisfy a read request from a block that is closer to the reader so that local replicas are preferred over remote data. This reduces global bandwidth consumption and read latency [3].

placing block replicas. Next, the five RPPs currently being supported in HDFS are presented.

- **BlockPlacementPolicyDefault**: this is the standard replica placement policy used in HDFS. Considering an RF of three replicas per block, if the writer (client) is running on a DN, it puts the first replica of a block on the local machine, otherwise, an arbitrary DN of the cluster is selected. The second and third replicas are placed in the same remote rack – different from the rack of the first replica – on two distinct nodes. In the case of a higher RF, the next nodes are randomly chosen, while avoiding placing too many replicas in DNs on the same rack by keeping the number of replicas per rack below the upper limit given by (replicas − 1) / racks + 2. The other four RPPs extend this default policy by adding a variety of behaviors to meet specific usage demands.
- **BlockPlacementPolicyRackFaultTolerant**: this policy focuses on placing replicas in as many racks as possible. Considering the standard RF, the local rack is always preferred to store the first replica. In contrast, the second and third replicas are stored in separate remote racks. For this, the cluster must have enough racks (i.e., racks ≥ RF). In the end, the difference in the number of replicas for every two racks is no more than one. This allows data operations to take advantage of the bandwidth of multiple racks, in addition to providing greater availability in the event of a rack failure.
- **AvailableSpaceBlockPlacementPolicy**: this policy aims at a balanced placement of the blocks according to the storage space available in the nodes. In this sense, an effort is made to prioritize DNs to receive replicas based on the used space in their storage devices. This prioritization is controlled by a parameter that represents a fraction of balancing preference, which can have values between 0 and 1. If a value below 0.5 is used, DNs with more space in use will receive more block allocations. By default, this fraction is set to 0.6, which prioritizes DNs with a lower occupation and promotes a balance in terms of the volume of data stored between the nodes.
- **BlockPlacementPolicyWithNodeGroup**: this policy was designed for environments with a node-group layer, that is, an extra layer of locality/failure groups (contained by racks), which maintains logical nodes. This is particularly useful to represent a cluster with a 4-layers hierarchical network topology, where the leaves represent DNs (computers) and inner nodes represent switches/routers that manage traffic in/out of data centers, racks, or physical host (with virtual switch). With this RPP, the placement strategy is adjusted to put the first replica on the local node (or if it is not possible, on the local node-group or the local rack). If the writer is not on a DN, a random DN is selected. The second replica is placed on a DN that is on a different rack. The third replica is placed on a DN which is on a different node-group but the same rack as the second replica node.
- **BlockPlacementPolicyWithUpgradeDomain**: this policy selects nodes for placing block replicas that honor the upgrade domain policy. Upgrade domains allow grouping cluster hosts for optimal performance during restarts.

This RPP follows the same placement strategy as the default one while assuring that all replicas have unique upgrade domains. To this end, it distributes data across a set of hosts in the system (potentially larger than a single rack) that can be updated or restarted at once without compromising service and data availability. This feature is useful for very large clusters, or for clusters where rolling restarts may happen frequently.

Regarding the overhead in the writing process, which involves storing multiple replicas of the same block, HDFS applies a replication pipeline technique. Figure 1 illustrates a possible block distribution of a file based on the *BlockPlacementPolicyDefault*, considering a cluster formed by two racks with, respectively, two and three DNs and using the standard RF of three. As can be seen, for each block (*b1* to *b4*), the same DN maintains a maximum of one of its replicas and, in the same rack, a maximum of two of the three replicas of the block is contained.

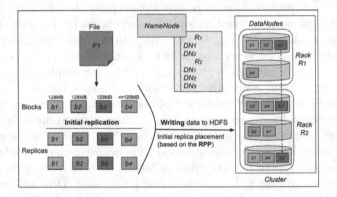

Fig. 1. Standard strategy for block distribution on an HDFS cluster.

In the pipeline of block *b3* represented in Fig. 1, the NN retrieves the list of the three DNs that will store the data block based on the replication target choosing algorithm implemented by the RPP. Then, the first DN in the pipeline (first DN of rack 1) starts receiving the data in portions, writes each portion to its local repository, and transfers the portion to the second DN in the pipeline (first DN of rack 2). This DN, in turn, writes the received portion to its repository and flushes that portion to the next DN (third DN of rack 2). Therefore, the established writing pipeline allows nodes to simultaneously receive and forward data. Besides improving the write operation, it allows the entire replication process to be transparent to the client, who only needs to interact with a single node when writing data in the file system, regardless of the configured Replica Placement Policy.

The cluster administrator must select which RPP to apply in the file system[3] according to the environment composition and the needs of applications and clients. It is important to mention that the mapping of the cluster topology, which involves racks, node-groups, and upgrade domain groups, is specific to the cluster layout and must also be assigned to each host DN by the administrator (this mapping may or may not reflect the physical network topology of the cluster [5]). The NN uses these definitions to distribute blocks when writing the files and to orchestrate necessary actions, such as rolling restarts and upgrades, block re-replication, and replica rearrangement.

4   Related Work

Several studies have been conducted to investigate the data replication mechanism and the replica distribution strategy of HDFS. The work of [1], for example, provided a theoretical analysis of different approaches for writing data blocks across the DNs, namely: default pipeline, parallel broadcast, and parallel server-worker. The study describes the technical specification, features, and specialization for each approach along with its applications. The authors in [6], on the other hand, presented an improved replica placement policy, which is specifically designed for heterogeneous clusters. The proposed policy satisfies all the selection requirements imposed by the standard RPP while striving to ensure a balanced replica distribution.

A study of the replication factor was presented in [4] to determine if changes in its default value allow for performance enhancements in HDFS. Through an adaptive replication system, which increases the RF of the most accessed data, it was possible to optimize the overall availability of data and reduce job execution times. The work of [10], in turn, proposed a re-replication scheme that takes into account performance and reliability perspectives. The scheme aims to balance the workload among the nodes during re-replication and reduce the impact and execution time of the re-replication procedure. To this end, the data blocks are divided into priority groups to balance the system and the DNs for storing the replicas are selected based on the utilization of the storage devices in the cluster.

Regarding data redistribution, in previous work [8], we automated the decision-making process for configuring and triggering the HDFS *Balancer*. Besides that, we modified the balancing policy to take into account reliability and availability attributes. The solution maintains the balance of replicas in the system while redistributing the replicas according to the propensity of node failures in the cluster racks.

In [7], on the other hand, we proposed a customized balancing policy for the HDFS *Balancer*, which focuses on improving data availability through replica balancing. To this end, the balancer starts to prioritize block movements that increase the number of racks in which the blocks are placed. This improves

---

[3] The definition of the RPP to be used in the file system is made in a configuration file (*hdfs-site.xml*), setting the parameter *dfs.block.replicator.classname* with the corresponding classpath for the desired policy.

reliability since placing block replicas in different racks reduces the chances of data loss due to rack failures. Besides that, the additional availability can be used as a way to take better advantage of data locality, thus improving the overall I/O performance of the cluster. The customized policy behaves similarly to the *BlockPlacementPolicyRackFaultTolerant*, however, it is specifically designed for the HDFS *Balancer*. Therefore, it is exclusive to the balancing process and does not interfere with the global RPP used in the file system.

5   Experimentation

The experiments were carried out on the GRID'5000[4] platform, with Apache Hadoop (version 2.9.2) in a fully-distributed operation over 10 nodes of the *site Rennes*. In order to provide a heterogeneous environment, the HDFS instance was set up in two clusters, with 5 nodes in cluster *paravance* (represented by C_1) and 5 nodes in *parapluie* (C_2).

The clusters were configured with two racks each. The racks in C_1, namely R_1 and R_2, kept, respectively, 3 (DN_{01}, DN_{02}, and DN_{03}) and 2 (DN_{04} and DN_{05}) nodes, each one with the following configurations: 2 Intel Xeon E5-2630 v3 CPUs (2.40 GHz, 8 cores/CPU), 128 GB of RAM, 558 GB of storage capacity (HDD), and 2 Ethernet connections of 10 Gbps each. The racks in C_2, namely R_3 and R_4, also maintained 3 (DN_{06}, DN_{07}, and DN_{08}) and 2 (DN_{09} and DN_{10}) nodes, with: 2 AMD Opteron 6164 HE CPUs (1.7 GHz, 12 cores/CPU), 48 GB of RAM, 232 GB of HDD, 1 Ethernet connection of 1 Gbps, and 1 InfiniBand connection of 20 Gbps. The nodes in both clusters were running a Debian GNU/Linux 10 (*buster*) distribution.

To deeply understand the behavior of the RPPs, the test scenario we built considered different situations in which the data distribution in HDFS is affected. To this end, the scenario is divided into 3 stages executed in sequence. In the first stage, detailed in Sect. 5.1, we analyze the placement of replicas during the initial replication resulting from writing files. In the second stage, discussed in Sect. 5.2, we look into the re-replication procedure. In the third stage, presented in Sect. 5.3, we explore the redistribution of data through replica balancing in HDFS.

5.1   First Stage: Data Load

In the first stage, the distribution of the blocks based on the RPPs is done by writing files in HDFS during the initial data load. For this, we used *TestDFSIO* [12] (version 1.8): a distributed I/O bound benchmark that measures HDFS performance through the execution of parallel tasks. An individual experiment was conducted for each RPP and, in every experiment, 20 files of 15 GB each and with an RF of 3 replicas per block were written through a node in R_1 (local rack), totaling a data volume of approximately 900 GB (2400 blocks of 128MB

---

[4] https://www.grid5000.fr.

each and 7200 replicas in total). The average utilization of the cluster after the data load was 28.01%.

Table 1 shows the HDFS status using the RPPs in the first stage. The amount of data distributed among the nodes is displayed through the occupation in GB (O_{GB}) and the utilization percentage ($U_\%$) of each DN. After the initial data distribution with all RPPs, there is a high discrepancy in the volume of data stored in the nodes. This can be seen by the elevated *Standard deviation (σ)* of the occupation and utilization of the DNs. In relation to the *Default* and *NodeGroup* policies, this is explained by their choosing strategy of placing one-third of the block replicas in one rack and two-thirds in a second rack, which can promote inter-rack imbalance in the cluster.

Table 1. HDFS status after loading data with all Replica Placement Policies.

Rack	DataNode	Default		RackFaultTolerant		AvailableSpace		NodeGroup		UpgradeDomain	
		O_{GB}	$U_\%$	O_{GB}	$U_\%$	O_{GB}	$U_\%$	O_{GB}	$U_\%$	O_{GB}	$U_\%$
R_1	DN_{01}	105.93	21.01	89.19	17.69	112.65	22.34	96.96	19.23	63.37	12.57
	DN_{02}	74.16	14.71	71.87	14.25	115.39	22.89	82.88	16.44	76.16	15.10
	DN_{03}	75.55	14.98	100.75	19.98	134.03	26.70	80.03	15.87	104.31	20.69
R_2	DN_{04}	108.39	21.50	129.51	25.68	78.17	15.50	95.96	19.03	155.84	30.91
	DN_{05}	107.87	21.39	83.27	16.51	59.97	11.89	111.16	22.05	57.20	11.34
R_3	DN_{06}	66.90	36.56	68.26	37.24	94.10	51.33	65.79	35.89	76.44	41.70
	DN_{07}	105.27	57.43	74.58	40.69	95.79	52.26	97.12	52.98	68.23	37.22
	DN_{08}	80.38	43.85	87.56	47.76	69.23	37.77	94.14	51.36	77.86	42.47
R_4	DN_{09}	74.25	40.50	125.74	68.59	96.36	52.57	93.97	51.26	126.79	69.17
	DN_{10}	113.60	61.97	77.75	42.42	52.00	28.37	93.69	51.11	101.67	55.46
Standard deviation (σ)		18.32GB	17.29%	21.57GB	17.42%	26.14GB	15.40%	12.25GB	16.59%	31.28GB	19.31%

The *RackFaultTolerant* and *UpgradeDomain* policies, on the other hand, place the replicas in unique racks, however, as the RF is less than the number of racks in the cluster, the distribution of the blocks is also not fully balanced. The highest level of balance considering node utilization was achieved by the *AvailableSpace* policy, which ensures that the replicas are positioned in DNs with less used percent based on their storage capacity. Regarding the data volume maintained by each DN (occupation), the *NodeGroup* policy allowed for a better balance since the configured capacity of the nodes in $C1$ is greater than that of the nodes in $C2$.

To better visualize the occupation status of the cluster at a rack level, Fig. 2 illustrates the data stored in each rack. The *AvailableSpace* policy demonstrates its distinguished behavior by storing the largest volume of data in the rack that maintains the nodes with the greatest storage capacity. It is also noted that its choosing algorithm prioritized the local rack R_1, instead of the remote rack R_2, which also belongs to cluster $C1$. The other four RPPs showed similar results between them, with a slight divergence in the volume maintained in each rack.

Table 2 presents key metrics of I/O operations performed in HDFS with the data distribution based on the RPPs. The performance of the write operation is represented by the *Write time* and the *Write throughput*. The *Default* RPP

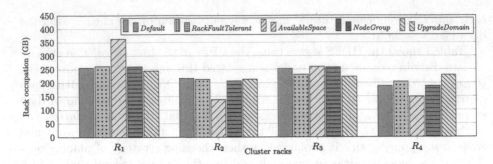

Fig. 2. Data volume stored in each rack after writing the files.

reduces the aggregate network bandwidth used when reading data since most blocks are placed in only two racks rather than three. This improves write performance, however, it does not ensure the block placement with the highest resilience and data availability. The *RackFaultTolerant* and *UpgradeDomain* (each rack was configured in a different domain) policies, in turn, allow for a higher data availability but increase the cost of writing operations since they transfer blocks to more racks.

Table 2. HDFS performance with all Replica Placement Policies in the first stage.

Metric	Default	RackFaultTolerant	AvailableSpace	NodeGroup	UpgradeDomain
Write time	1907.99s	2235.48s	2485.32s	2272.73s	2354.21s
Write throughput	14.76MB/s	20.33MB/s	18.20MB/s	12.48MB/s	16.17MB/s
Blocks in unique racks	0.00%	100.00%	12.79%	0.00%	100.00%
Read time	877.18s	715.54s	843.74s	870.77s	791.21s
Read throughput	46.01MB/s	87.53MB/s	44.34MB/s	57.21MB/s	71.27MB/s
Read avg. I/O rate	397.71MB/s	384.74MB/s	298.39MB/s	345.90MB/s	231.85MB/s

To further analyze the placement of the replicas considering an availability perspective, we used the HDFS utility *fsck* (*filesystem check*) [12] to retrieve the locations of the blocks stored in each rack. The *Blocks in unique racks* row in Table 2 displays the percentage of blocks that were placed in the largest possible number of racks (i.e., three, given the RF) after writing the files with each RPP. The *RackFaultTolerant* and *UpgradeDomain* policies are the only ones that have this concern, thus ensuring that 100% of the blocks achieve maximum availability. This is especially useful in scenarios with two or more racks going down at the same time, as placing replicas on only two racks will cause data loss. However, as the chance of rack failure is far less than node failures, placing replicas in only two racks tends not to impact data reliability and availability so the other RPPs prioritize writing performance. It is worth mentioning that the *AvailableSpace* policy, which placed 12.79% of the blocks in three racks, focuses on a space balanced distribution, and thus it may place the replicas in unique racks when suitable.

In order to investigate possible performance improvements and optimizations in data locality promoted by the RPPs, we considered 10 executions of *TestDF-SIO* – with its default configuration – to read the data stored in the HDFS with each policy. At the bottom of Table 2, we can see the performance of the read operations regarding the arithmetic means of the *Read time* (i.e., the total execution time of the benchmark), *Read throughput*, and *Read average I/O rate*. In general, the *RackFaultTolerant* and *UpgradeDomain* policies performed best, since they enable the applications running on the cluster to use the network bandwidth of one additional rack when operating over the data. In contrast, the other policies stored the replicas in only two racks and resulted in a longer execution time for the benchmark to read the data replicas in the file system.

5.2   Second Stage: Block Re-replication

At this stage, the RPPs are evaluated based on their placement strategies during block re-replication. To emulate a faulty behavior, we insert crash failures in the DNs through the Linux *kill* command. We selected one arbitrary node for racks R_1 and R_3, so that all racks, after the induction of failures, keep exactly two active DNs. When noticing the failure of the faulty nodes (DN_{03} and DN_{08}) for not receiving heartbeats, the NN creates new copies of the under-replicated blocks.

Table 3 shows the state of the cluster after the failures and how the distribution of the new replicas affected the file system. The occupation and utilization of the DNs demonstrate that the imbalance of replicas was further aggravated in the cluster (there was an increase in *Standard deviation* of all RPPs when compared to the first stage), which indicates an unbalanced placement of the re-replicated blocks. It should be noted that the dead DNs are omitted from the table, as they are decommissioned from the cluster. The average utilization of the cluster after the re-replication was 34.87%.

Table 3. HDFS status after re-replication with all Replica Placement Policies.

Rack	DataNode	Default		RackFaultTolerant		AvailableSpace		NodeGroup		UpgradeDomain	
		O_{GB}	$U_\%$	O_{GB}	$U_\%$	O_{GB}	$U_\%$	O_{GB}	$U_\%$	O_{GB}	$U_\%$
R_1	DN_{01}	127.21	25.23	118.53	23.51	137.07	27.18	125.71	24.93	96.37	19.11
	DN_{02}	107.84	21.39	104.59	20.74	139.08	27.58	118.41	23.48	109.72	21.76
R_2	DN_{04}	129.67	25.72	146.99	29.15	110.36	21.89	118.68	23.54	172.72	34.26
	DN_{05}	128.88	25.56	97.64	19.36	96.76	19.19	129.76	25.74	74.28	14.73
R_3	DN_{06}	82.52	45.02	96.50	52.64	116.54	63.57	83.55	45.58	102.61	55.97
	DN_{07}	119.50	65.19	104.34	56.92	116.91	63.78	114.77	62.61	98.14	53.54
R_4	DN_{09}	89.81	48.99	145.91	79.60	119.31	65.08	106.96	58.35	140.31	76.54
	DN_{10}	122.71	66.94	93.73	51.13	71.06	38.76	109.86	59.93	113.64	61.99
Standard deviation (σ)		18.36GB	18.67%	21.69GB	21.72%	21.89GB	20.09%	14.24GB	17.92%	30.30GB	22.86%

The amount of data kept in each rack after the re-replication can be seen in Fig. 3. We note an interesting feature of the *AvailableSpace* policy. In the first stage, this policy had prioritized the nodes in rack R_1 to maintain the replicas. After the failure of DN_{03}, however, the policy chose to store the new replicas in another rack (note the significant decrease in the volume of data stored in R_1 in Fig. 3 compared to Fig. 2). This occurred because the remaining nodes in R_1 (DN_{01} and DN_{02}) were no longer the nodes with the largest available storage space in the cluster and, therefore, it was possible to find more suitable nodes to store the replicas in other racks.

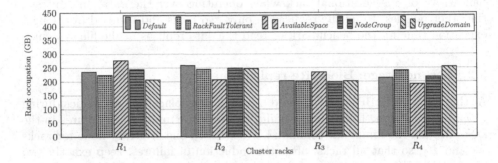

Fig. 3. Data volume stored in each rack after the re-replication of the blocks.

Metrics of the re-replication and subsequent read operations are presented in Table 4. The *Re-replication time* row is equivalent to the elapsed time from the beginning to the end of the re-replication process. We noted that the *Default* policy achieved the highest speed for re-replicating the blocks on component failure, although the performance of the RPPs for storing the new replicas of the under-replicated blocks was not very different from each other. Based on the block mapping, we see that the percentage of *Blocks in unique racks* after the failures has not changed from the first stage, with the exception of the *AvailableSpace* policy, which re-replicated the blocks originally stored in the failed DNs to nodes in a new rack.

Table 4. HDFS performance with all Replica Placement Policies in the second stage.

Metric	Default	RackFaultTolerant	AvailableSpace	NodeGroup	UpgradeDomain
Re-replication time	585.00s	740.00s	607.00s	819.00s	774.00s
Blocks in unique racks	0.00%	100.00%	48.84%	0.00%	100.00%
Read time	1333.76s	1106.51s	1575.18s	1320.06s	1304.59s
Read throughput	23.36MB/s	42.25MB/s	21.97MB/s	35.16MB/s	34.36MB/s
Read avg. I/O rate	127.89MB/s	148.15MB/s	82.71MB/s	134.66MB/s	95.51MB/s

Regarding the performance of the read operations, we execute *TestDFSIO* 10 more times in reading mode. The increase in the overall *Read time* in relation to the values obtained in the first stage is due to the reduced number of active

DNs (less parallelism and available bandwidth). Again, the higher availability provided by the *RackFaultTolerant* and *UpgradeDomain* policies enables the applications running on the cluster to utilize the bandwidth of one additional rack when operating over the data. However, the *AvailableSpace* RPP, even with 48.84% of the blocks with maximum availability, had the longest reading time and the lowest throughput, which can be justified by the elevated data imbalance after the failures.

5.3   Third Stage: Replica Rearrangement

The third stage evaluates the behavior of the RPPs during the redistribution of the blocks already stored in the system achieved by balancing the replica placement on the cluster. For this purpose, the HDFS *Balancer* daemon was triggered with a default balancing threshold of 10%. Table 5 displays the state of the cluster after running the HDFS *Balancer*. The level of balance achieved in the cluster is evidenced by the reduction of the *Standard deviation* of the utilization of the nodes in relation to their respective values before the replica balancing in the first and second stages.

Table 5. HDFS status after replica balancing with all Replica Placement Policies.

Rack	DataNode	Default		RackFaultTolerant		AvailableSpace		NodeGroup		UpgradeDomain	
		O_{GB}	$U_\%$	O_{GB}	$U_\%$	O_{GB}	$U_\%$	O_{GB}	$U_\%$	O_{GB}	$U_\%$
R_1	DN_{01}	168.93	33.50	156.22	30.98	152.69	30.28	154.13	30.57	142.49	28.26
	DN_{02}	131.03	25.99	137.07	27.19	163.65	32.46	145.51	28.86	152.70	30.28
R_2	DN_{04}	153.83	30.51	166.58	33.04	151.92	30.13	141.10	27.98	166.68	33.06
	DN_{05}	155.97	30.93	124.98	24.79	143.31	28.42	167.79	33.28	130.27	25.84
R_3	DN_{06}	76.47	41.72	77.99	42.54	77.36	42.20	77.48	42.27	76.60	41.79
	DN_{07}	71.31	38.90	73.07	39.86	78.99	43.09	73.83	40.28	78.49	42.82
R_4	DN_{09}	78.62	42.89	93.23	50.86	76.35	41.65	75.34	41.10	81.39	44.40
	DN_{10}	75.47	41.17	78.37	42.75	71.06	38.76	77.73	42.41	78.62	42.89
Standard deviation (σ)		42.46GB	6.29%	37.55GB	8.94%	41.55GB	6.16%	41.38GB	6.29%	38.40GB	7.58%

The occupation of the racks after the balancing is exhibited in Fig. 4. It is noticed that the rearrangement of the replicas executed by the HDFS *Balancer* does not aim at inter-rack balance. The tool operates to take the utilization of the nodes to an interval controlled by a lower limit (average utilization of the cluster minus the balancing threshold) and an upper limit (average utilization of the cluster plus the threshold). Thus, as we are running the HDFS instance on a heterogeneous environment, the racks of the nodes with less storage capacity maintain a proportionally smaller volume of data.

Table 6 shows the metrics of the replica balancing process and read operations after running the HDFS *Balancer*. Based on the *Balancing time* we can see that the *UpgradeDomain* and *RackFaultTolerant* policies were the most costly in respect of the execution time of the HDFS *Balancer* in the file system. This is caused by the high number of *Balancing iterations* needed to transfer the

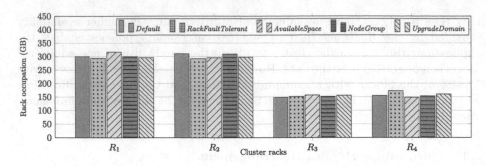

Fig. 4. Data volume stored in each rack after cluster balancing.

replicas between the nodes across the cluster (the amount of data redistributed is represented by the *Data volume moved* row). The *NodeGroup* RPP, on the other hand, had the best performance in the balancing operation, followed by the *AvailableSpace* and *Default* policies. Similarly, these three RPPs do not guarantee that redistribution will store the replicas in three separate racks.

Table 6. HDFS performance with all Replica Placement Policies in the third stage.

Metric	Default	RackFaultTolerant	AvailableSpace	NodeGroup	UpgradeDomain
Balancing time	6263.17s	6740.23s	5490.20s	4524.93s	8982.66s
Data volume moved	111.25GB	116.38GB	119.13GB	116.00GB	144.63GB
Balancing iterations	9	46	8	7	54
Blocks in unique racks	16.42%	100.00%	62.09%	18.59%	100.00%
Read time	824.39s	879.77s	739.66s	946.54s	770.20s
Read throughput	68.86MB/s	74.19MB/s	85.89MB/s	53.88MB/s	70.84MB/s
Read avg. I/O rate	154.17MB/s	176.25MB/s	186.15MB/s	162.59MB/s	176.64MB/s

The percentage of *Blocks in unique racks* after the balancing shows that, apart from respecting the strategies of the *RackFaultTolerant* and *UpgradeDomain* policies, the requirement of placing blocks in exactly two racks of the other policies is relaxed during the HDFS *Balancer* operation. Therefore, with the balancing, all RPPs maintained some replicas in the largest number of racks allowed by the RF. As mentioned in Sect. 2.2, a balanced cluster can take better advantage of the data locality. To investigate this, we run 10 new executions with *TestDFSIO* aimed at reading the data stored in the file system.

Considering the percentage change given by $((T_b - T_a) / T_a \times 100)$, where T_a and T_b represent, respectively, the arithmetic means of the metric under analysis in the 10 runs of the benchmark before (i.e., second stage) and after the balancing, the change in the *Read time* with the *Default*, *RackFaultTolerant*, *AvailableSpace*, *NodeGroup*, and *UpgradeDomain* policies was -38.19%, -20.49%, -53.04%, -28.30%, and -40.96%. These values represent the reduction in the execution time of *TestDFSIO* in the third stage in reference to the times obtained without the balance in the second stage.

In addition, there was an increase in the *Read throughput* of 194.78%, 75.60%, 290.94%, 53.24%, and 106.17%, respectively for each RPP. In the *Read average I/O rate*, the increase was 20.55%, 18.97%, 125.06%, 20.74%, and 84.94% after replica balancing with all RPPs. These results reinforce that replica balancing is beneficial for HDFS health regardless of the replica placement strategy used in the file system.

6   Conclusions and Future Work

In HDFS, the blocks are replicated and distributed among different nodes in the cluster. The choice of the *DataNodes* to maintain the block replicas is essential to data reliability, availability, and overall system performance. Optimizing block placement distinguishes HDFS from other distributed file systems. In this sense, HDFS supports the configuration of five pluggable Replica Placement Policies (RPPs). The system administrator can choose the policy based on the cluster infrastructure and the usage requirements of the clients and their applications.

This work presents an experimental and comparative analysis of the strategies used by the official policies for placing replicas in HDFS. Based on the evaluation results we could understand, in-depth, different characteristics of the behavior of the RPPs. To the best of our knowledge – except for the default policy – no work in the literature has investigated the behavior and performance of the specialized block placement strategies of HDFS. In highlighting the trade-off between fault tolerance, write and read bandwidth of each placement strategy, we hope to support the decision-making process of HDFS cluster administrators in choosing the ideal RPP.

We reinforce that, although the experimentation presented in this work is based on a native Hadoop instance, it applies to other processing frameworks that use HDFS as a persistence layer. In this regard, the *BlockPlacementPolicy-Default*, the standard choice in all HDFS distributions, cuts the inter-rack write traffic, which generally improves write performance, without compromising data reliability or read performance. With the *BlockPlacementPolicyRackFaultToler-ant*, on the other hand, we can place replicas to more than two racks. This ensures the block placement with the best data reliability and availability even in case of racks failing simultaneously.

The *AvailableSpaceBlockPlacementPolicy*, in turn, extends the default policy so that the selection of DNs starts to be made based on the used space in the storage devices of the nodes, which allows interesting results in heterogeneous clusters. *BlockPlacementPolicyWithNodeGroup* introduces a node group level that fits well with infrastructures running on virtualized environments since it guarantees that, in case of node group failure, only one replica will be lost at the maximum as it will never place more than one replica on the same physical host mapped to a node group. In contrast, the *BlockPlacementPolicyWithUp-gradeDomain* addresses the limitation of the default policy on rolling upgrade by adding the concept of upgrade domains into HDFS in which we can group nodes in a new dimension based on the cluster layout in addition to the existing rack-based grouping.

Future research work comprehends an analysis of the behavior and performance of the replica placement policies considering different classes of applications running in the cluster. Besides that, motivated by the achieved results in this work, we plan to validate an alternative for the current RPPs in order to incorporate a temporal perspective of the state of the nodes and the cluster into the data distribution process on the HDFS.

Acknowledgment. This work was developed with the support of CNPq - National Council for Scientific and Technological Development – Brazil. Experiments presented in this paper were carried out using the Grid'5000 testbed, supported by a scientific interest group hosted by Inria and including CNRS, RENATER and several Universities as well as other organizations.

References

1. Abead, E.S., et al.: A comparative study of HDFS replication approaches. Int. J. IT Eng. **3**, 5–11 (2015)
2. Achari, S.: Hadoop Essentials. 1st edn. Packt Publishing Ltd, Birmingham (2015)
3. Apache software foundation: apache hadoop. https://hadoop.apache.org/docs/r3. 3.1/ (2021) Accessed 27 Sep 2021
4. Ciritoglu, H.E., et al.: Investigation of replication factor for performance enhancement in the hadoop distributed file system. In: Companion of the 2018 ACM/SPEC International Conference on Performance Engineering, pp. 135–140 (2018)
5. Cloudera Inc: Scaling namespaces and optimizing data storage. https://docs. cloudera.com/runtime/7.2.6/scaling-namespaces/topics/hdfs-balancing-data-across-hdfs-cluster.html (2020). Accessed 3 Sep 2021
6. Dai, W., Ibrahim, I., Bassiouni, M.: An improved replica placement policy for hadoop distributed file system running on cloud platforms. In: 2017 IEEE 4th International Conference on Cyber Security and Cloud Computing (CSCloud), pp. 270–275. IEEE (2017)
7. Fazul, R., Cardoso, P.V., Barcelos, P.P.: Improving data availability in HDFS through replica balancing. In: 2019 9th Latin-American Symposium on Dependable Computing (LADC), pp. 1–6. IEEE (2019)
8. Fazul, R.W.A., Barcelos, P.P.: Automation and prioritization of replica balancing in HDFS. In: Proceedings of the 36th Annual ACM Symposium on Applied Computing, pp. 35–38 (2021)
9. Shvachko, K., Kuang, H., Radia, S., Chansler, R.: The hadoop distributed file system. In: 2010 IEEE 26th Symposium on Mass Storage Systems and Technologies (MSST), pp. 1–10. IEEE (2010)
10. Shwe, T., Aritsugi, M.: A data re-replication scheme and its improvement toward proactive approach. ASEAN Eng. J. **8**(1), 36–52 (2018)
11. Turkington, G.: Hadoop Beginner's Guide, 1st edn. Packt Publishing Ltd, Birmingham (2013)
12. White, T.: Hadoop: The Definitive Guide, 4th edn. O'Reilly Media Inc, Sebastopol (2015)

An Elastic and Scalable Topic-Based Pub/Sub System Using Deep Reinforcement Learning

Thanos Giannakopoulos and Vana Kalogeraki[(✉)] [ID]

Department of Informatics, Athens University of Economics and Business Athens,
Athens, Greece
{thanos,vana}@aueb.gr

Abstract. The ability to handle large volumes of event data and react to unexpected spikes, in real-time, remains an important challenge in stream processing systems, such as Apache Kafka, due to the amount of custom coding and technical expertise required to configure these systems. In this paper we investigate the use of reinforcement learning as a promising approach to address these issues. By feeding the machine learning technique with system performance metrics under a wide variety of configurations, we can effectively address any changes in the pub/sub system or overload situations while maintaining the desired performance goals. We implement our methodology on the Kafka pub/sub system without any changes in the application logic. Our experimental results illustrate the performance and benefits of our approach.

Keywords: elasticity · pub/sub · deep reinforcement learning

1 Introduction

Pub/sub systems have been increasingly popular communication architectures in recent years to achieve information dissemination between a set of loosely coupled producers (also known as publishers) and consumers (also known as subscribers). Publishers forward their publications to a set of brokers which are then responsible to deliver the publications to subscribers based on the registered subscriptions. They have found application in a wide variety of domains from online games [1] to stock trading [2]. Examples of popular pub/sub systems include Facebook's Wormhole [3], Google's Cloud Pub/Sub [4], Apache's Kafka [5] and Apache's Pulsar [6].

While pub/sub systems present desirable features including scalability, persistency and availability, several challenges emerge as they typically entail a large number of configuration parameters, which makes their tuning a significant issue that overwhelms users to achieve the desirable performance. Identifying a deployment configuration that satisfies user-defined objectives (e.g.,

© IFIP International Federation for Information Processing 2022
Published by Springer Nature Switzerland AG 2022
D. Eyers and S. Voulgaris (Eds.): DAIS 2022, LNCS 13272, pp. 167–183, 2022.
https://doi.org/10.1007/978-3-031-16092-9_11

on execution time), while avoiding unnecessary over-provisioning, is a significant challenge especially when these are deployed in cloud environments. On the other side, under-provisioning, i.e., allocating fewer resources than required, may lead to services that cannot meet the service level requirements set by the client, and thus must be avoided. Furthermore, pub/sub systems are often deployed in diverse and often dynamic environments, and mechanisms used to ensure robust operation and performance for one environment configuration may not be appropriate for another configuration. While tunable policies provide fine-grained control, configuring a large number of parameters can be overwhelming for users. As a result, users often accept the default settings. Finally, manually tuning requires in-depth knowledge of both the applications and the environment. Nevertheless, it is labor-intensive, time-consuming, and often leads to suboptimal decisions.

The popularity of Machine Learning has grown significantly in recent years as it provides systems with the ability to learn and enhance their operation automatically. In particular, Reinforcement learning (RL) is a type of machine learning algorithm that enables software agents and machines to automatically evaluate the optimal behavior in a particular environment to learn what to do or how to map situations to actions, so as to maximize a numerical reward signal and improve its efficiency. The learner is not told which actions to take, but instead must discover which actions yield the highest reward by trying them. In the most interesting and challenging cases, actions may affect not only the immediate reward but also the next situation and, through that, all subsequent rewards. These two characteristics, *i.e.*, trial-and-error search and delayed reward, are the two most distinguishing features of reinforcement learning. Reinforcement learning has important benefits over supervised learning as it does not need labeled input/output pairs to be presented and over unsupervised learning which is typically about finding hidden structure and correlations between a set of unlabeled data. State-of-the-art learning approaches can rely on either online or offline schemes to find a (near) optimal configuration. In our work we focus on *online approaches* that can work efficiently even when no a priori knowledge of the execution environment or the deployed application is available.

In this paper we present our approach for building a robust, scalable and elastic pub/sub system utilizing Deep Reinforcement Learning techniques. Our solution addresses the challenges outlined above by combining the following novel features: We investigate Deep Reinforcement Learning as a promising approach to addressing these issues in environments where the dynamics of the environment and the rewards at each state may change and are not necessarily known in advance. By feeding the machine learning technique with system performance metrics under a wide variety of configurations and conditions, we can efficiently address any workload changes or overload situations in the pub/sub system and maintain the desired performance goals. We investigate two different algorithms, namely Deep Q Networks and Double Deep Q Networks where the goal is to learn a policy to tell the Deep Learning Reinforcement agent what action to take under what circumstances. We implement our approach on top of Apache Kafka, a general-purpose pub/sub system, without the need to modify its architecture or change the producer and consumer application logic. Our approach implements elasticity by dynamically determining whether brokers need to be added or removed from the Kafka cluster based on user demands (*i.e.*, on execution time). We collect a set of performance metrics via the Prometheus monitoring tool, the collected statistics are sent to the Deep Reinforcement Learning Agent to decide the appropriate scaling action. Our experimental evaluation illustrate the performance, scalability and elasticity of our approach.

2   System Architecture and Model

In this section we first present a brief introduction to the Kafka pub/sub messaging system and then we describe our system architecture and model.

2.1   Apache Kafka

We chose Kafka [23], a popular, state-of-the-art, topic-based pub/sub system as our messaging system. In Kafka each published message corresponds to a specific topic and topics are further divided into partitions. The partitions are distributed across the brokers that comprise the Kafka cluster. Each partition can be hosted on a different broker, which denotes that a single topic can scale horizontally across multiple servers for redundancy and scalability.

A Kafka producer is an application that acts as a source of data in a Kafka cluster. A producer can publish messages to one or more Kafka topics; the message is directed to the appropriate partition. Incoming messages are assigned to *partitions* using a *consistent-hashing* mechanism on the message key [17] while partitions are assigned to the cluster's brokers using a round-robin policy. Each partition has exactly one partition leader which handles all the read/writes requests to that partition. If the replication factor is greater than one, the additional replica partitions act as followers. This synchronization is achieved through the ZooKeeper service. Kafka Consumers are subscribers wishing to read records from one or more topics and one or more partitions of a topic. Consumers can work together as part of a consumer group. Consumer groups act as a level of parallelism on a Kafka cluster as consumers that are part of the same group would be assigned with different partitions.

Despite the wide adoption of topic-based pub/sub systems, the problem of how to dynamically adjust the number of brokers in the cluster when overloads, load imbalances or skewness occurs due to the volume of messages in the pub/sub system, to maintain the service required by the users, still remains a significant challenge.

2.2   System Architecture and Model

Figure 1 presents our system architecture comprising a Kafka cluster running in a Docker Container where the containers communicate via an overlay network. The benefit of the Docker Container is that it simplifies and automates the deployment process and seamlessly scale our system to use multiple machines. For a machine to be part of the system it needs to have a Docker daemon installed.

During operation, each Broker in the Kafka Cluster is configured to run with a JMX exporter where these metrics are exposed to a form that can be collected by the Prometheus monitoring tool (http://prometheus.io), an open source, metrics-based monitoring system. The collected statistics are sent to the Deep Reinforcement Learning Agent, which in turn makes the appropriate Scaling action. Three scaling actions are supported: *Scale Up*: a Broker needs to be added to the Kafka Cluster, *Scale Down*: a Broker must be removed from the Kafka Cluster, and *No Scaling*: no change in the number of Brokers in the Cluster.

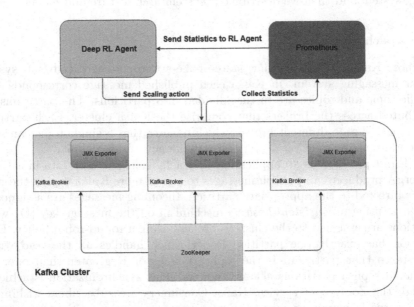

Fig. 1: System architecture

Our system collects a set of metrics from each Kafka broker via the use of Prometheus. Each Kafka Broker is configured to run with a JMX exporter where these metrics are exposed to a form Prometheus can retrieve. More specifically, our system keeps track of the following metrics: (i) *CPU utilization* (mean rate, 95th%), (ii) *number of bytes in/out per second* (mean rate, 95th%), (iii) *number of messages in/out per second* (mean rate, 95th%), (iv) *response queue time* (mean rate, 95th%) which denotes the time it takes to send the response to the Requestor, (v) *number of produce requests* (mean rate, 95th%) (vi) *requests per second* (mean rate, 95th%) (vii) *requests waiting in the purgatory* (mean rate, 95th%).

We denote as *total time* (mean rate, 95th%), the amount of time taken to service a request (Produce, Fetch Consumer and Fetch Follower), computed as the sum of the following three types of requests: (a) *request queue time* (mean rate, 95th%): the time the request spends in the queue once it has been received but before processing starts, (b) *local time*: the time spent being processed by the partition leader, (c) *remote time*: The time spent waiting for the follower response before processing completes, We denote as *response queue time*, the time it takes to send the response to the requestor. The total time is utilized when we compute the reward that our agents collect.

Requests Waiting in the Purgatory. The purgatory holds requests waiting to be satisfied. It is only used for Produce and Fetch requests. Each type of request has different parameters that determine if it will be added to purgatory:

- Produce requests will be added to purgatory until the partition leader receives an acknowledgment from in-sync replicas. The number of acknowledgments the partition leader requires is determined by the **acks** parameter. When acks=all, means that the leader will wait all in-sync replicas to acknowledge the record and then send the next one.
- Fetch requests are added in the purgatory if there is not enough data to fulfill the request. So wait until enough data is available or the max waiting time for the request has passed.

Monitoring the size of purgatory is useful in order to determine the underlying causes of latency.

3   Proposed Methodology

3.1   Deep Reinforcement Learning

The goal of Reinforcement Learning (RL) is to discover which actions yield the highest numerical reward by trying them, not only for the immediate reward but also for all subsequent rewards. Reinforcement learning has important benefits compared to supervised learning in that it does not need labeled input/output pairs to be presented, and over unsupervised learning which is typically about finding hidden structure and correlations between a set of unlabeled data. One of the most popular RL algorithms is Q-learning. The goal is to learn a policy, which tells an agent what action to take under what circumstances. Q-Learning is a model-free algorithm as it does not require a model of the environment and the goal is to learn the value of an action in a particular state.

The core of the Reinforcement Learning algorithms is to estimate the action-value function, using the Bellman equation as an iterative update,

$$Q_{i+1} = E[r + \gamma \max_{a'} Q_i(s', a')|s, a]. \tag{1}$$

where r is the reward, γ is the discount factor and a is the learning rate. This kind of value iteration algorithms converge to the optimal action-value function as the number of iteration goes to infinity, $Q_i \to Q*$ as $i \to \infty$. These methods are impractical, because the action-value function is estimated separately for each sequence, so we do not get any generalization. Also standard Reinforcement Learning is mostly limited to domains which are fully observed or to domains where features can be handcrafted e.g. with the bucket method. It works best when the number of possible states and actions are finite.

In our approach we use a non-linear function approximator i.e. a Neural Network. We refer to a Neural Network function approximator with weights θ as a Q-network. We train a Q-network by minimizing the loss function $L_i(\theta_i)$ at each iteration i,

$$L_i(\theta_i) = E_{s,a\sim\rho(.)}[(y_i - Q(s,a;\theta_i)^2] \tag{2}$$

where $y_i = E_{s'\sim Environment}[r + \gamma max_{a'} Q(s',a';\theta_{i-1})|s,a]$ is the target for iteration i and (s,a) is the probability distribution over states s and actions α. We refer to $\rho(.)$ as the behaviour distribution. Note that the parameters from the previous iteration θ_{i-1} are fixed when minimizing the loss function $L_i(\theta_i)$ and depend solely on the network weights, compared to targets used for supervised learning which are fixed before training.

If we differentiate the loss function with respect to the weights we have the following gradient:

$$\nabla_{\theta_i} = E_{s,a\sim\rho(.);s'\sim Environment}[(r + \gamma max_{a'} Q(s',a';\theta_{i-1}) \\ -Q(s,a;\theta_i))\nabla_{\theta_i} Q(s,a;\theta_i)]. \tag{3}$$

A closed-form solution to obtain directly the weights that minimize the loss function exists but may be time-consuming if we have a very large number of examples and features. So in our approach we use Stochastic gradient descent. If we update the Q-network at each time step we have the familiar Q-learning algorithm.

Deep Q Network Algorithm. Our first approach is based on a Deep Q Network. First we utilize a technique known as Experience Replay. We store the tuple (s,a,r,s') at each time step in a dataset D with maximum capacity N, known as replay memory. During the inner loop of the algorithm, we sample a mini-batch of experiences from the replay memory and train the Q-network. The sample is drawn uniformly from the replay memory i.e. every tuple has the save probability to be chosen. In our approach we sample experiences regardless of their significance. Alternatively, one could use the Prioritized Experience Replay method in order to replay important transitions more frequently, and therefore learn more efficiently. With the use of Experience Replay, we break the correlation of data, and because each experience is potentially used in many updates we have greater data efficiency. Overall, the use of the replay memory smooths the learning process and helps the Q-network to avoid to fall into local minimums and that we will eventually find the optimal policy of every state-action pair.

Deep learning requires a large amount of hand-labeled training data which are later used as the target values when minimizing the loss function. In our case the target value, for iteration i, has the following form:

$$y_i = E_{s'\sim Environment}[r + \gamma max_{a'} Q'(s',a';\theta_i)|s,a] \tag{4}$$

where Q' is a different Neural Network, called Target Network. The Target Network has the same architecture as the initial Q-network but with frozen parameters. Then, every C-steps we update the Weights of the Target Network to match the Weights of the initial Q-network. This leads to a more stable training because it keeps the target function fixed for C time steps.

Another benefit of the Deep Q Network algorithm is that it is able to find which input data play an important role on the behaviour of the Q-network and which are not. Given the above, we feed the Q-network with a 37 vector as input (this is the total number of metrics we collect from the Monitoring component), and it decides which inputs are important. So the best action to take here is to feed the network with all information available. Those inputs that are not significant will have weights approaching to zero.

Double Deep Q Network Algorithm. The Deep Q Network Algorithm is known to overestimate action values, which can impact training especially early on. If the DQN takes action 1 for example and learns a high Q value for that specific action, that means that action 1 is going to be selected more, compared to the other possible actions. This further overestimates the Q value for that state action which leads to training instability and poor performance.

The idea in the **Double Deep Q Network** to reduce overestimations is to decouple the selection and the evaluation of an action. As above, we use the Q-network to select and evaluate actions using the ϵ-greedy strategy. But when it comes to computing the target y_i, we first find which action to take using the Q-network Q and evaluate that action based on the target Q-network Q'. The formula for that is:

$$y_i = E_{s' \sim Environment}[r + \gamma Q'(s', argmax_{a'} Q(s', a'; \theta_i); \theta_i^-)|s, a] \qquad (5)$$

As earlier, the weights of the target Q-network θ^- are replaced with the weights of the Q-network θ every C-steps.

3.2 Scaling Decisions

In this section we describe our process for adding and removing brokers from the Kafka cluster. When a broker is added, it will not automatically be assigned any partitions, so we have to come up with a reassignment plan to move already existing partitions to the newly added broker, in order to fully operate and be part of the Kafka cluster. For this purpose, we utilize a simple round robin partition technique. First, we calculate how many partitions must be moved to the new broker, the total number of partitions divided by the number of active brokers, including the new one. Then we start constructing our custom reassignment plan by simply beginning from a random broker, picking one partition from the broker and adding it to the reassignment plan which is in JSON format, and then sequentially perform the same operation on each broker we encounter, until we reach the appropriate amount of partitions. Using this scheme we can achieve a fair redistribution of the partitions among the available brokers in the Kafka cluster. So we are evenly spreading the load. When removing a broker from the

Kafka cluster, we follow the same procedure. First, we get the partitions which are located on the broker marked for removal. Then, we again construct a custom reassignment plan by allocating each partition to a broker following the round robin technique, starting from a random broker and sequentially going to the next one until all partitions are matched to a broker. We utilize the Kafka partition reassignment tool to move the partitions across the brokers.

This tool supports three modes:

- *generate*: In this mode, given a list of topics and a list of brokers, the tool generates a reassignment plan to move the topics to the brokers specified in the list.
- *execute*: In this mode, the user provides a reassignment plan and the tool executes it. It can be either the reassignment plan from the generate mode or a handcrafted one.
- *verify*: In this mode, the tool verifies if the partitions in the reassignment plan moved successfully to their specified broker.

We make use of the above modes provided by the partition reassignment tool. The generate mode outputs the current partition assignment, so we have a complete view of where each partition is located in the cluster. We use this information to construct our custom assignment. Note that we do not use the proposed assignment of the tool as it outputs random movements between the active brokers in the cluster and as a result incurs a large overhead. In our approach we tried to minimize the number of movements as much as possible. In the execute mode, we provide our custom reassignment plan as a json file. This is the step where the actual movement of the partitions takes place. Finally, the verify mode is important when we remove one of the brokers. We remove the broker from the cluster only when the reassignment plan finishes execution.

The operation of the Reassign Partitions Tool are summarized below.

1. First the tool updates the Zookeeper path "/admin/reassign_partitions" with the partition assignments we specified in the JSON file we created.
2. The Kafka Controller listens to the above path for changes. It gets notified from a ZooKeeper Watch.
3. For each specified partition, the following procedure is executed:
   (a) Start new replica partitions in RAR-AR (RAR = Reassigned Replicas, AR = original list of Assigned Replicas)
   (b) Wait until the new replica partitions are in sync with the leader partitions.
   (c) Check if the leader partitions are in RAR, if not elect a leader from RAR.
   (d) Stop replicas from AR-RAR.
   (e) Clear the Zookeeper path "/admin/reassign_partitions".

Note that the tool only updates the path. The Kafka Controller is responsible to execute the reassignment. To make sure that records are not lost during the cluster expansion, we utilize the acks setting in the Kafka producer configuration. It denotes the number of brokers that must receive the record before we consider the sending of a message successful. In our case we used the option, $acks = all$.

This way we ensure that we will not loose any records during cluster scaling, even if producers and consumer perform write and/or read operation on the partitions marked for movement.

4 Evaluation

We evaluated our approach in our local cluster comprising physical machines Intel Core i7-8700k and Intel Core i7-9750H, each with 16 GB DDR4 RAM, running Ubuntu 20.04 and with the Docker daemons installed. The training of the Deep Q Network and Double Deep Q Network was performed on an Nvidia RTX 2070 with 8 GB GDDR6 memory. The RTX features 2,304 CUDA cores which makes it ideal for performing multiple computations simultaneously compared to a single CPU, which in our case comprises 12 logical cores.

Our Deep Learning model is a 3-layer fully connected network. The first layer consists of 64 neurons, the second layer 128 neurons and the third one of 256 neurons. We initialize the weights of our network using Xavier uniform initializer, to address the problem of vanishing and exploding gradients [18]. One key point of our implementation is that we perform layer normalization on the input sample to improve the training speed. In our case, our input sample is a 37th dimensional vector with each column comprising a different feature. Each feature has its own range of values, e.g. one feature is the active number of brokers, at a given time point, ranging from 3 to 11 brokers, and another feature is the average producer latency, again at the same time point, ranging from 0 to 500 in milliseconds. So normalizing the input sample will help us reduce the training time.

Machine learning algorithms that use a variation of Gradient descent, as an optimization technique, require data to scale as it helps the model to converge quickly towards the global minimum. In standard Deep Learning, the most used normalization technique is batch normalization [19], but it cannot be applied on online tasks such as our Deep Q Network and Double Deep Q Network implementations. Thus, we used layer normalization [20], that was designed to overcome the drawbacks of batch normalization. Layer normalization can be applied on a single training sample compared to batch normalization, and that is the main reason we chose it for our network.

We utilize the following hyper-parameters: mini-batch size (number of training cases over which SGD update is computed) was set to 10, the replay memory size (SGD updates are sampled from the replay memory buffer) was set to 42, the target network update frequency was set to 5, the discount factor (gamma used in the Q-learning update) was set to 0.99, and the update frequency was set to 1 (selecting value 1 results in updating after every scaling action). The optimization method we used was RMSprop, a stochastic gradient descent method that maintains a moving (discounted) average of the square of gradients and divide the gradient by the root of this average. The learning rate used by the Adam optimizer was set to 0.00025, the initial value of the ϵ exploration was 1 and the final exploration was 0.1 and we perform 10 random action at the start of the first two episodes. Some important aspects to note: (a) We do not clear out the replay memory after each episode, this enables us to recall and build batches of experiences from across episodes. (b) We used RMSprop as our optimization algorithm with zero momentum value(as in [21,22]).

Each experiment runs a total time of 30 min. At time-step 0 we create the required topics and initialize the producers and the consumers. We perform one scaling action every 40 sec. A scaling up or scaling down action takes roughly 20 sec. We performed experiments with 3 different reward functions, keeping the same network architecture and hyperparameters, and comparing the results of the two different learning algorithms, DQN and Double DQN. For the experiments we used a total of $1.8M$ records per producer, each record had a size of 124 bytes. We used 4 Producers, 4 Consumers. We varied the number of Brokers between 3 and 11 and each topic had 16 partitions. The DQN and Double DQN agents were trained for 10 episodes.

In our experiments we evaluated our approach with the following reward functions:

Reward Function as a Function of the Number of Active Brokers. In our first reward function we defined the immediate reward r as a function of the number of active brokers, as:

$$r_t = -NumberOfActiveBrokers_t \qquad (6)$$

where we give a negative reward at each time step. This way we incentivize our DQN and Double DQN agents to reduce the number of brokers to the minimum.

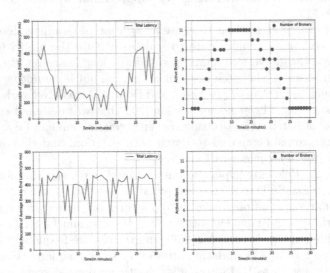

Fig. 2: DQN in early (top row) and later (bottom row) stages of training (reward as a function of brokers).

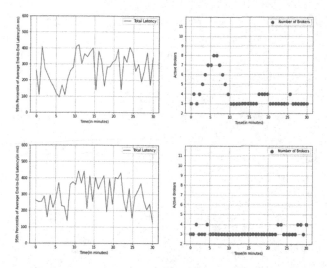

Fig. 3: Double DQN in early (top row) and later (bottom row) training (reward as a function of brokers).

Reward Function as a Service Level Objective (SLO). A service-level agreement (SLA) is a commitment between a service provider and a client. SLA defines the metrics by which the service is measured, and the penalties, in case the agreed-on service levels not be achieved. For our purposes we want the 95th% of the Average End-to End Latency to be under 200 milliseconds. Choosing the appropriate SLO was complex, but we set this value of 200 ms as it was reasonable for our setting with 11 active brokers. The reward in this case is a piecewise function and depends on the percentage difference of the actual value with the SLO.

Summarizing, our second reward function has the following form:

$$
r_t = \begin{cases}
-2C & \text{if Total Latency is 200\% over SLO} \\
-3/2C & \text{if Total Latency is 150\% over SLO} \\
-C & \text{if Total Latency is 100\% over SLO} \\
-1/4\,C & \text{if Total Latency is 50\% over SLO} \\
-1/10\,C & \text{if Total Latency is over 10\% SLO} \\
0 & \text{Otherwise}
\end{cases}
$$

Reward Function as a Weighted Sum of Active Brokers and SLO. Our third reward function was defined with respect to both the number of active brokers and the SLO and had the following form:

$$
NormalizedBrokerCost_t = -\frac{ABr - MinBr}{MaxBr - MinBr} \tag{7}
$$

where AB is the number of Active Brokers at timestep t, MinBr is the minimum number of Brokers and MaxBr is the maximum number of Brokers. For our

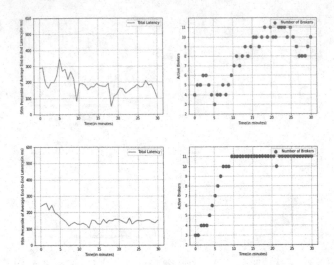

Fig. 4: DQN in early (top row) and later (bottom row) stages of training (reward as a function of SLO).

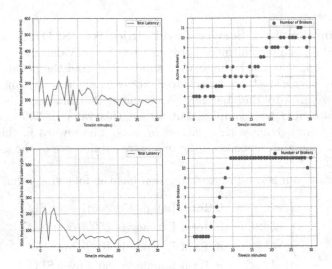

Fig. 5: Double DQN in early (top row) and later (bottom row) stages of training (reward as a function of SLO).

setup MinBr has a value of 3 while MaxBr a value of 11. The SLA cost has the following form:

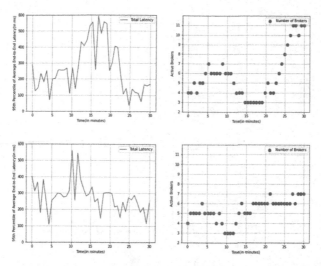

Fig. 6: DQN in early (top row) and later (bottom row) stages of training (reward as function of both active brokers and the SLO).

$$SLACost_t = \begin{cases} C & \text{TotalLatency is 200\% over SLO} \\ (80/100)C & \text{TotalLatency is 150\% over SLO} \\ (60/100)C & \text{TotalLatency is 100\% over SLO} \\ (40/100)C & \text{TotalLatency is 50\% over SLO} \\ (20/100)C & \text{TotalLatency is over SLO} \\ 0 & \text{Otherwise} \end{cases}$$

where $C = -1$. Note that SLAClost ranges between -1 and 0. We combine the different costs into a single cost function using a Simple Additive Weighting (SAW) technique. According to SAW, we define the reward function as follows:

$$r_t = W_{brokers} * NormalizedBrokerCost_t + W_{sla} * SlaCost_t \qquad (8)$$

where $W_{brokers}$, W_{sla} satisfy the restriction $W_{brokers} + W_{sla} = 1$. In the experiments we used $W_{brokers} = W_{sla} = 50\%$ and the SLO was set to 300ms.

As we observe from the results presented above (Figs. 2, 3, 4, 5, 6 and 7), for the three different reward functions, both DQN and Double DQN agents performed well and quickly achieved the expected behavior, at each a scaling action. Our evaluation results illustrate that, independently of the reward function, each agent was able to achieve the goal i.e. to maximize the expected value of the cumulative sum of a received scalar signal (reward), with no adjustment of the Deep Learning Model or hyperparameters across each learning algorithm. Both agents performed equally well, with respect to the total number of rewards accumulated across each episode. The third reward function, Double DQN achieved higher performance on almost each training episode. Regarding the first reward

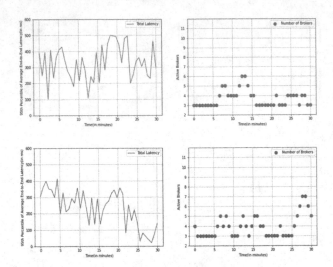

Fig. 7: Double DQN in (top row) and later (bottom row) stages of training (reward as function of active brokers and the SLO).

function, both agents learned that the optimal behavior was to keep the number of active brokers to the bare minimum. While on the second reward function, in order to keep the latency below the predefined threshold, both agents learned that in order to achieve that they must keep the number of active brokers to the maximum. When using the third reward function, there is a trade off between the number of active brokers and the SLO. As our experiments indicate, both agents managed to learn the optimal policy, satisfying the SLO most of the time while keeping the number of active brokers to the least required.

5   Related Work

There has been work on adaptation and load balancing techniques in pub/sub systems. The main difference between topic-based and content-based pub/sub systems is the fact that the latter organize brokers in an overlay network so the load balancing problem is solved by either dynamically changing the network topology [7] or by updating the routing paths [8]. The authors in [8] propose a new publication routing algorithm that takes into account broker resources and publication popularity among subscribers for content-based pub/sub systems. In [7] the authors propose a dynamic load balancing technique for content-based publish/subscribe systems. Their algorithm distributes the incoming load by offloading subscribers from heavily loaded brokers to less loaded brokers. However, they use simple threshold based techniques for determining when a node is overloaded and try to balance the load in the set of nodes that reside to the same overlay as they examine the problem in a content-based pub/sub system. In [9] the authors proposed an approach to address the problem of hot topics in pub/sub systems by exchanging load related information about the brokers. The authors in [10] examined the load balancing problem in topic-based pub/sub systems where the goal is to automatically construct an overlay network and then establish the appropriate publication routing. Similarly, authors in [11] proposed a distributed algorithm to build and maintain a routing structure that can be used by topic-based pub/sub systems that exploit overlay networks. Furthermore, in [12] they deal with the problem of congestion avoidance in content-based pub/sub systems. They consider the congestion invoked due to unsubscriptions. In a topic based system like Kafka this would not create problems as there is no hierarchy (*i.e.*, similar to the routing tables) of the brokers. Similarly, Pietzuch et al. [13] presented a pub/sub congestion control scheme that adjusts the rate of publishing new messages, allowing brokers under recovery to eventually catch up, and other brokers to keep up. In our problem we assume that we cannot control the rate at which publishers send their messages to the brokers. In our work our aim is to use machine learning techniques with system performance metrics in order to build the appropriate robustness and drive the decisions that will enable us to develop elastic and scalable pub/sub systems.

Machine learning techniques provide a promising adaptation approach to maintaining QoS properties of QoS-enabled pub/sub middleware in dynamic environments. The problem of autonomic adaption has also been studied in the context of service level agreements. For example, Herssens et al [14] study the problem of autonomically adapting service level agreements (SLAs) when the context of the specified service changes, to offer QoS for Web services. Their goal is to negotiate the QoS agreement to fit the needs of the dynamic environment. [15] et al. and [16] et al. apply machine learning techniques to deal with parameters uncertainty or simplify the configuration of QoS-enabled middleware and adaptive transport protocols to maintain specified QoS as systems change dynamically. The results of their work show that decision trees and neural networks can effectively classify the best protocols to use in adaptive environments.

6   Conclusions

In this paper we propose our approach for building a robust, scalable and elastic pub/sub system utilizing Deep Reinforcement Learning techniques. We evaluated our approach on Apache Kafka, with two algorithms, Deep Q Networks and Double Deep Q Networks, with three different reward functions. Our performance evaluation illustrated that, each agent was able to achieve the goal and thus can be efficiently utilized to address system changes or overload situations.

Acknowledgment. This research has been supported by the H2020 LAMBDA Project 734242, the EU ICT-48 2020 project TAILOR (No. 952215), the H2020 Auto-Fair project (No. 101070568).

References

1. César, C., Zhang, K., Kemme, B., Kienzle, J., Jacobsen, H.A.: Publish/subscribe network designs for multiplayer games. In: Proceedings of the 15th International Middleware Conference, pp. 241–252 (2014)
2. Yoav, T., Naaman, N., Harpaz, A., Gershinsky, G.: Hierarchical clustering of message flows in a multicast data dissemination system. In: IASTED PDCS, Phoenix, AZ, USA, vol. 5 (2005)
3. Sharma, Y., et al.: Wormhole: reliable pub-sub to support geo-replicated internet services. In: 12th USENIX Symposium on Networked Systems Design and Implementation, NSDI 2015, vol. 15, Oakland, CA, USA, pp. 351–366 (2015)
4. Google Cloud Pub/Sub. https://cloud.google.com/pubsub/
5. Kreps, J., Narkhede, N., Rao, J., et al.: Kafka: a distributed messaging system for log processing. In: Proceedings of the NetDB, Athens, Greece, pp. 1–7, June 2011
6. Apache Pulsar. https://pulsar.apache.org/
7. Cheung, A.K.Y., Jacobsen, H.-A.: Dynamic load balancing in distributed content-based publish/subscribe. In: van Steen, M., Henning, M. (eds.) Middleware 2006. LNCS, vol. 4290, pp. 141–161. Springer, Heidelberg (2006). https://doi.org/10.1007/11925071_8
8. Salehi, P., Zhang, K., Jacobsen, H.A.: PopSub: improving resource utilization in distributed content-based publish/subscribe systems. In: Proceedings of the 11th ACM International Conference on Distributed and Event-based Systems, DEBS 2017, Barcelona, Spain, pp. 88–99 (2017)
9. Dedousis, D., Zacheilas, N., Kalogeraki, V.: On the fly load balancing to address hot topics in topic-based pub/sub systems. In: 2018 IEEE 38th International Conference on Distributed Computing Systems (ICDCS), ICDCS 2018, Vienna, Austria (2018)
10. Chen, C., Jacobsen, H.-A., Vitenberg, R.: Algorithms based on divide and conquer for topic-based publish/subscribe overlay design. IEEE/ACM Trans. Networking **24**(1), 422–436 (2016)
11. Turau, V., Siegemund, G.: Scalable routing for topic-based publish/subscribe systems under fluctuations. In: 2017 IEEE 37th International Conference on Distributed Computing Systems (ICDCS), ICDCS 2017, Atlanta, GA, USA, pp. 1608–1617. IEEE (2017)
12. Chen, M., Hu, S., Muthusamy, V., Jacobsen, H.A.: Congestion avoidance with incremental filter aggregation in content-based routing networks. In: 2015 IEEE 35th International Conference on Distributed Computing Systems, ICDCS 2015, Columbus, OH, USA, pp. 557–568 (2015)
13. Pietzuch, P.R., Bhola, S.: Congestion control in a reliable scalable message-oriented middleware. In: Endler, M., Schmidt, D. (eds.) Middleware 2003. LNCS, vol. 2672, pp. 202–221. Springer, Heidelberg (2003). https://doi.org/10.1007/3-540-44892-6_11
14. Herssens, C., Faulkner, S., Jureta, I.J.: Context-driven autonomic adaptation of SLA. In: Bouguettaya, A., Krueger, I., Margaria, T. (eds.) ICSOC 2008. LNCS, vol. 5364, pp. 362–377. Springer, Heidelberg (2008). https://doi.org/10.1007/978-3-540-89652-4_28
15. Hoffert, J., Mack, D., Schmidt, D.: Using machine learning to maintain pub/sub system GOS in dynamic environments. In: Proceedings of the 8th International Workshop on Adaptive and Reflective Middleware, ARM 2009, Urbana, IL, USA, pp. 1–6 (2009)

16. Russo, G.R., Cardellini, V., Presti, F.L.: Reinforcement learning based policies for elastic stream processing on heterogeneous resources. In: 13th ACM International Conference on Distributed and Event-based Systems (DEBS 2019), pp. 31–42, Darmstadt, Germany, June 2019
17. Karger, D., et al.: Web caching with consistent hashing. Comput. Netw. **31**(11), 1203–1213 (1999)
18. Glorot, X., Bengio, Y.: Understanding the difficulty of training deep feedforward neural networks. In: Proceedings of the Thirteenth International Conference on Artificial Intelligence and Statistics, vol. 9, pp. 249–256, Chia Laguna Resort, Sardinia, Italy, 13–15 May 2010
19. Ioffe, S., Szegedy, C.: Batch normalization: accelerating deep network training by reducing internal covariate shift (2015)
20. Ba, J.L., Kiros, J.R., Hinton, G.E.: Layer normalization (2016)
21. Mnih, V.: Playing Atari with deep reinforcement learning, NIPS deep learning workshop (2013)
22. Mnih, V., et al.: Human-level control through deep reinforcement learning nature, vol. 518, pp. 529–33, February 2015
23. Kafka streams API. https://kafka.apache.org/documentation/streams/

... Russell, S.J., Norvig, P., et al. (20..). Reinforcement learning: a brief review for ... an... appropriate processes of ... Proc. ... for ... International ...

Zhang, W., et al. (2019).

Sedgel, D., et al. Well-posting with deep ... Training ... and Mach. ... (2018) 1501-1516. (2018).

Tassa, Y., et al. ... Deep reinforcement learning of manipulation ... tasks ... and an efficient ... inverse ... Proc. IEEE Int. Conf. on ... (2019) ... Deep learning ... Machine ... Int... (2019).

Wolski, ... Schneider, ... Deep reinforcement learning ... and analysis in ... computer vision ... deep learning ... (2018).

Wu, Y., et al. ... Int. ... Conf. on Computer Vision (2018).

Xu, Jun, J., Plenert, M. ... ... deep ... Int. Conf. ... deep learning ... (2019).

Zhu, Y. ... ... and ... deep reinforcement ... and ... ... 1517-1524 (2019).

... ...

Invited Paper

Challenges in Automated Measurement
of Pedestrian Dynamics

Maarten van Steen[1(✉)], Valeriu-Daniel Stanciu[2], Nadia Shafaeipour[3],
Cristian Chilipirea[4], Ciprian Dobre[5], Andreas Peter[6], and Mingshu Wang[7]

[1] Digital Society Institute, University of Twente, Enschede, The Netherlands
m.r.vansteen@utwente.nl
[2] Faculty of Electrical Engineering, Mathematics and Computer Science, University of Twente,
Enschede, The Netherlands
[3] Faculty of Geo-information Science and Earth Observation, University of Twente, Enschede,
The Netherlands
[4] Azure Cloud, Microsoft, Bucharest, Romania
[5] Faculty of Automatic Control and Computer Science, Politehnica University of Bucharest,
Bucharest, Romania
[6] Department of Computer Science, University of Oldenburg, Oldenburg, Germany
[7] School of Geographical & Earth Sciences, University of Glasgow, Glasgow, UK

Abstract. Analyzing pedestrian dynamics has since long been an active and
practical field of interest. Since the introduction of, in particular, smartphones,
various organizations saw a simple means for automatically measuring pedestrian dynamics. The basic idea is simple: network packets sent by WiFi-enabled
devices can be collected by sensors and by extracting the unique MAC address
from each packet, it should be possible to count how many devices are detected
by a single sensor, as well as how devices move between sensors. Although this
approach has been commercially deployed for many years, it is now largely forbidden (at least in the EU) due to obvious privacy infringements. In this paper,
we address challenges and some potential solutions to automated measurement of
pedestrian movements while protecting privacy. The results come from learning
the hard way: having run experiments extensively over the past years, we have
gradually gained considerable insight in what is possible and what may lie ahead.

1 Introduction

Understanding pedestrian dynamics is a long-standing scientific field motivated by
questions from very different domains (e.g., tourism [11], urban planning [14], safety
and security [12]). Automating the measurement of pedestrian dynamics allows for
collecting more accurate data than what is possible by manual means. In the past
decade, much attention has been spent on using the fact that people carry network-
connected devices such as smartphones (see, e.g., the extensive surveys conducted by

---

This is an internally reviewed accompanying paper to a keynote delivered by Maarten van Steen
at DAIS 2022, and is to be considered as background information for that talk.

© IFIP International Federation for Information Processing 2022
Published by Springer Nature Switzerland AG 2022
D. Eyers and S. Voulgaris (Eds.): DAIS 2022, LNCS 13272, pp. 187–199, 2022.
https://doi.org/10.1007/978-3-031-16092-9_12

our team [7,23]). Such devices regularly transmit network packets, and many of those packets contain information that uniquely identifies the transmitter, such as its MAC address in WiFi or Bluetooth communications. The basic idea is that such identifiers can be used as a proxy for the person carrying the associated device. In this way, it becomes possible to, in principle, gather statistics on the whereabouts of a pedestrian by simply capturing his or her movements through identification of the device that is being carried.

There are several problems with this approach. For one, such schemes infringe upon a person's privacy and are largely forbidden, as formulated in the European General Data Protection Regulation (GDPR). However, the strict regulation on the automated collection of data transmitted by devices is being alleviated in the case data is used for **statistical counting**, and under the condition that pedestrians are informed, as well as that the data is discarded after the statistics have been computed [6]. Although these measures allow for some automated gathering of data, the question of how to do so in a privacy-preserving manner remains open.

Next to privacy infringements, there are other problems pertaining to the data gathered by collecting network packets. Many modern devices use randomized MAC addresses whenever possible, effectively making it impossible to check whether a device has been detected for a long time at a specific location, or has moved between two locations. MAC address randomization is offered by device manufacturers in light of privacy considerations, but it is not a technique that can be applied to all packets. Likewise, detecting packets in outdoor environments is by itself already difficult, certainly if packets can be captured by multiple sensors at the same time as it makes it much harder to determine the location of a device.

In this paper, written for a nonexpert, we address several of these problems, with an emphasis on privacy protection. We discuss potential solutions based on our own experience with experiments we conducted in the past five years, as well as some solutions that are currently being explored by others.

2   Automated Measurement of Pedestrian Behavior

Key to automated measurement of pedestrian dynamics is capturing network traffic from a device carried by a person and extracting an identifier of that device. Capturing network traffic and extracting an identifier is done by means of a **sensor** that knows the communication protocol (WiFi, Bluetooth). A WiFi access point can be re-purposed to record the MAC network address transmitted by a device and use these as device identifiers. However, such a **raw device identifier** is considered to be personal information and recording it can be considered intrusive. Common practice has therefore been to transform a raw device identifier RID to a **pseudonym** PID using a secure one-way encryption function F (e.g., a collision-resistant cryptographic hash function). The pseudonym is unique for a given raw device identifier, but the function makes it computationally infeasible to derive the raw identifier from the pseudonym. In other words, the inverse function F^{-1} is infeasible to compute. In this way, one can use the pseudonym $PID = F(RID)$ as a device identifier. Given a sufficiently strong hash function (several of which are known to exist, such as SHA256), it is impractical to determine the RID from the PID alone.

Schemes are also being deployed in which a provably secure **parameterized** one-way encryption function is used to generate the pseudonym. To illustrate, consider such a function $F_{T,S}$ with two parameters, a parameter T related to a **time span**, and a parameter S associated with a group of one or more specific **sensing locations**. The values of the parameters determine which pseudonym is generated, given an identifier as input. In other words, if we take RID as the raw device identifier, we can recognize that device through the pseudonym $PID = F_{T,S}(RID)$ (here T and S can be considered what are known as salts for the hash function). If we change either T or S, $F_{T,S}(RID)$ will change as well. Note that F is collision resistant: when changing the value for T or S, a pseudonym is generated that makes it practically impossible to associate it with any other pseudonym based on RID [9].

To illustrate, if T spans only a single day, yet S is the same for a number of sensing locations, it becomes computationally impossible to identify the same physical device over periods lasting more than one day. It will be possible to identify the same device as being at different sensing locations during a single day. If we change S per location (i.e., different sensors use different encryption functions), identifying the movement of a device across multiple sensing locations is computationally infeasible.

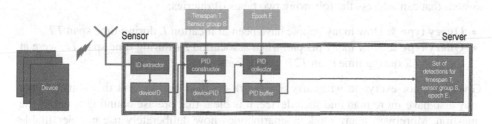

Fig. 1. The general organization of many current sensors for measuring pedestrian dynamics.

Current approaches are summarized in Fig. 1. Devices transmit signals that are captured by a sensor σ, which subsequently extracts a *device identifier*, typically the aforementioned RID. This identifier is then (securely) transmitted to a server where it is converted to a *device pseudonym*, and handed over to a *PID collector*. The latter generally collects *PIDs* for a relatively small detection period, or time window, referred to as an **epoch**, and places detected *PIDs* in a buffer, ignoring *PIDs* that had already been encountered during that epoch. An epoch typically lasts 5 min and effectively identifies the time of a detection (e.g., as the tuple $\langle year, month, day, hour, timeslot \rangle$). In this way, the collector registers the unique devices it has seen during that epoch and avoids any double counting. At the end of the epoch, each collected device is added to the set of detections as a tuple $\langle PID, E, \sigma \rangle$, which tells when ($E$) and where ($\sigma$) a device with identifier PID was detected.

In practical situations, we see that commercial companies use so-called WiFi probe messages to identify devices, let T span a single day, and often use a different value for S per sensor. A probe message is broadcast by a WiFi-enabled device in search of a WiFi access point to set up a connection. Such schemes allow for footfall counting on a per-daily basis. We also see cases where T spans much longer intervals and where S is the same for all sensors, which effectively allows for tracking. Recently, this led to a fine of 600k € in The Netherlands for violation of the GDPR.[1]

In the following, we assume sensor nodes to be trusted and to follow a single fundamental design principle:

> **FDP1**: Any data produced by a collection of (trusted) sensors cannot be traced back to a physical device.

This principle states that no matter how we combine the data coming from sensors, it should be impossible to identify an actual physical device, and thus its owner. As a consequence, any system processing this data, data generated by any collection of trusted sensors, is secure by design. Ideally, no extra security measures need to be implemented for the processing system. Note that stating the principle does not mean that it can be easily established. For example, when only very few devices are detected, it may become difficult to protect the privacy of their owners. Also, as we shall see, we do need to rely on a noncolluding server.

Given the GDPR and its alleviation for measuring pedestrian dynamics, we focus our work on **secure and privacy-aware statistical counting**. In particular, we want a system that can address the following two types of queries:

- **Query type 1**: How many people have been at location L during time span T?
- **Query type 2**: How many people, when at location $L1$ during time span $T1$, were at location $L2$ during time span $T2$?

Given that not everyone will carry a network-enabled device, and that some people may also have more than one such device, it is clear that precise counting is out of the question. Moreover, many modern smartphones now deliberately use nonidentifiable information when transmitting specific network packets (namely for the WiFi probe requests which are used for automated measurements), typically in the form of randomized MAC addresses. In addition, it is well known that radio signals as used in wireless communication systems often exhibit highly unpredictable behavior [4]. This means that we need to deal with missing network packets, but also packets which are received at a much larger distance than would normally be possible considering the specifications of the wireless medium.

In addition, simply assuming that sensors can be trusted is easier said than done. We therefore also require the following:

> **FDP2**: A sensor may not store any information that may be traced back to a physical device any longer than strictly necessary for statistical counting,

> **FDP3**: A sensor may not share information that may be traced back to a physical device.

In other words, even storing pseudonyms needs to be limited to a minimal amount of time and those pseudonyms need to be confined to the sensor. This leads to the design sketched in Fig. 2.

---

[1] https://autoriteitpersoonsgegevens.nl/en/news/dutch-dpa-fines-municipality-wi-fi-tracking.

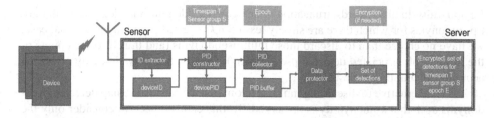

Fig. 2. The design of a privacy-protecting sensor.

There are a number of important differences from current approaches. First and foremost, we introduce a separate **data protector**. A data protector takes a collection of *PIDs* as input and produces a set of detections from which it is computationally infeasible to extract any original *PID*. We explain below how this can be achieved. Second, the whole path from ID extraction to an anonymized set of detections takes place at the (trusted) sensor. We do not trust the server collecting data from many sensors or the communication medium between the sensor and the server. If we need to store data external to the sensor, we do so only after the sensor has taken sufficient privacy-protecting measures. Thirdly, all data that we stored until handed over to the protector is deleted after the elapse of an epoch. Only the protected set of detections is kept.

3 Protecting Privacy Through Detection k-anonymity

3.1 Approach

In a first attempt to protect privacy, we developed a method based on achieving k-anonymity [15]. To explain, let **PID** denote the set of all possible *PIDs*. We devise a mapping m to a new set of pseudonyms **MPID**, such that for each detected $pid \in$ **PID** there are at least $k - 1$ other detected pseudonyms $\{pid_1, \ldots, pid_{k-1}\} \subset$ **MPID** with $m(pid) = m(pid_i)$. To rephrase this, assuming that each sensor stores mapped pseudonyms, then for each such stored pseudonym associated with some epoch, we are guaranteed that the sensor actually detected at least k different devices during that epoch. We denote such a mapped pseudonym as a **multipseudonym**. It is important that combining multipseudonyms preserves this k-anonymity.

A straightforward mapping is the one that simply truncates detected pseudonyms. This works fine, in particular if we can assume that pseudonyms are effectively drawn uniformly at random (which can be achieved by using a secure hashing function that generates a pseudonym from a detected MAC address). A uniform distribution guarantees that no biases are introduced when removing bits, and thus no systematic error when trying to map multiple *PIDs* to the same multipseudonym. For each epoch, a sensor then stores truncated pseudonyms as multipseudonyms and records how many different pseudonyms it detected for each stored multipseudonym. A problem, however, is that we need to determine *a priori*, i.e., at design time, how many bits to keep without knowing if that choice will lead to having detected enough pseudonyms to guarantee

k-anonymity. In other words, truncation of detected pseudonyms may leave us with multipseudonyms for which there are simply less than k detected pseudonyms. In that case, we have no choice than to discard those multipseudonyms (and thus also the counts of the number of associated detected pseudonyms). Clearly, this may seriously affect the accuracy of counting pedestrians.

As an alternative to discarding multipseudonyms, we can also remap detected pseudonyms such that k-anonymity is preserved. To this end, we need to consider only the multipseudonyms and their associated detected pseudonyms that violate k-anonymity. A naive approach is to generate an unused multipseudonym and assign that to the first k detected pseudonyms (for which k-anonymity was violated); generate another unused multipseudonym for the next k detected pseudonyms, and so on. This solution works fine for a single location, but not if we want to count how many pedestrians moved from location A to B. The problem is that any relation with what was detected at A is lost when generating multipseudonyms at B (at least for those detected pseudonyms that violated k-anonymity). We then might have just as well discarded them.

We thus need a *systematic* way of mapping k-anonymity-violating detected pseudonyms (we refer to them simply as violating pseudonyms), and apply that method to all sensors. We proceed as follows with what we denote as a **correction method**. Assume a sensor has n violating pseudonyms for a specific epoch. It then sorts those n pseudonyms and subsequently keeps only the top $\lfloor n/k \rfloor$ ones. Using the remaining $n - \lfloor n/k \rfloor$ violating pseudonyms, it then systematically increases the counts for every one of the remaining top of violating pseudonyms. In this way, in principle, almost none of the counts for the other violating pseudonyms are lost. Moreover, if this procedure is used at location A as well as B, we see that both locations will be assigning the same multipseudonym to the same detected pseudonym, just as we wanted. The details can be found in [15], along with a proof that when results from different sensors are combined, k-anonymity is preserved.

3.2 Evaluation

We have evaluated this setup using simulations as well as real-world data. For the latter, we used data on subway trips from Beijing [22, 24]. That data set can be used to mimic WiFi-based detections. The set consists of check-in and check-out records, each record containing a unique card identifier, the identifier of the station where the card is being checked, as well as a timestamp. For our purposes, namely counting the number of devices that were detected at location A during some epoch e_1 and later at location B during epoch e_2, the data is just fine: each check-in or check-out corresponds to a WiFi-based detection of a device; the card identifier is analogous to a MAC address. (Note that although we also have real-world measurements on WiFi data, those measurements do not provide us with ground truth: they do not tell us which device actually moved from one location to another. In contrast, the Beijing data set gives us an accurate account of movements, making it, in principle, ideal for mimicking WiFi-based measurements.)

We apply the k-anonymity algorithm as explained above, for different values of the epoch length, the size of truncated pseudonyms (i.e., the number of bits to keep), as well as for different values of k. A check-in or check-out counter is treated as a sensor. The idea is that each counter applies the algorithm and sends the k-anonymized data to a central server. If we consider an isolated trajectory, i.e., only those trips that have been made between two specific locations, we attain high accuracy of counting the number of trips between two locations. Results are generally better for lower values of k, yet this is partly explained by the sometimes limited number of actual detections during an epoch. We also see that there is a trade-off between the length of an epoch and accuracy: the smaller an epoch is, the fewer detections we will have, in turn affecting the accuracy (depending on k). The length of an epoch becomes less important once enough detections can be guaranteed.

However, matters may easily deteriorate when combining trips, as also examined in [15]. Let us return to the situation of counting pedestrians moving from A to B. Assume that the sensor at A collected a set of pseudonyms $\mathbf{PID_A}$, which were then mapped to the multiset $\mathbf{MPID_A}$. Likewise, at location B we have sets $\mathbf{PID_B}$ and $\mathbf{MPID_B}$. If there are no intermediate junctions, the multiset $\mathbf{MPID_A} \cap \mathbf{MPID_B}$ represents the devices that had moved from A to B.

Now consider the situation that we have two intermediate junctions $Z1$ and $Z2$ on the path from A to B. At $Z1$ the sensor detects $\mathbf{PID_{Z1}}$ devices entering the flow of pedestrians moving from A to B, which are mapped to the multiset $\mathbf{MPID_{Z1}}$. Assume that $\mathbf{MPID_A} \cap \mathbf{MPID_{Z1}}$ is nonempty. At junction $Z2$, the sensor detects $\mathbf{PID_{Z2}}$ devices (mapped to $\mathbf{MPID_{Z2}}$) *leaving* the flow again. If $\mathbf{PID_{Z2}} \subseteq \mathbf{PID_A}$ then, clearly, the final count at B will be false: it will have been contaminated by devices entering at $Z1$ that were mapped to the same multipseudonyms as those at A, which then for counting purposes go unnoticed by the devices that left at $Z2$. This situation is sketched in Fig. 3.

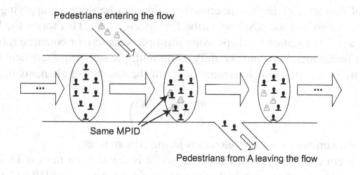

Fig. 3. The effect of devices entering and leaving a flow.

3.3 Reflection

Although the described approach toward k-anonymity is highly efficient, it turns out that it is fairly sensitive to perturbations in flows of pedestrians between two locations. Moreover, when considering practical situations such as subway networks, we have found that setting correct values for epoch length and truncation sizes may be tricky. It is yet unclear whether the approach is practically feasible.

4   Protecting Privacy Through Homomorphically Encrypted Bloom Filters

4.1   Approach

An alternative to k-anonymity is to have sets of pseudonyms represented by **Bloom filters** [2]. A Bloom filter is a constant-space probabilistic storage mechanism. Being probabilistic, a Bloom filter can indicate that an item that was not included in the set is actually present. The opposite is not true, if the Bloom filter indicates that an item is not in the set it is guaranteed that this is true. The Bloom filter is represented using a vector of m bits, initially all set to 0. Using a collection of k hash functions, an element x is added to a Bloom filter by setting the position $h_i(x)$ to 1 for each of the k hash functions. Each element can thus be represented as an m-bit vector consisting of exactly k bits set to 1. A bitwise OR operation is performed each time an element is added.

A Bloom filter has the important property that one cannot retrieve the elements of the set it represents other than by exhaustively testing for all possible elements. In other words, a Bloom filter supports *only* membership tests. To check if x is in a set A, one needs to check if every position $h_i(x)$ for the Bloom filter BF representing A has been set to 1:

$$x \in A \text{ only if } \prod_{i=i}^{k} BF[h_i(x)] = 1$$

(In the following, we will use the same notation for a set A and its representation by means of a Bloom filter.) A Bloom filter allows for testing whether an element is in the union of two sets, or in their intersection (this can be done by applying the OR operation for union and the AND operation for intersection). This forms the basis for counting at a single location (perhaps using multiple sensors), or counting movements (between different locations, and certainly using multiple sensors). Statistical counting is possible by means of a simple estimation n^* of the number of elements in a Bloom filter [17].

$$n^* = -\frac{m}{k} \ln \left(1 - \frac{X}{m} \right)$$

where X is the number of nonzero elements in the Bloom filter.

One problem with the approach sketched so far is that the sensors would, in principle, need to share Bloom filters, which violates our design principle *FDP3*. Considering that testing for membership entails a bitwise AND operation, which is equivalent to a multiplication of 0's and 1's, we can test for such membership using **multiplicative homomorphic encryption**. Such an encryption scheme enables the multiplication of two encrypted numbers without the need to first decrypt those numbers. To clarify, let $[p]$ denote the homomorphically encrypted version of the number p. Then, with multiplicative homomorphic encryption, we have

$$[p] * [q] = [p * q]$$

The basic idea is that a third party (e.g., a crowd expert) who needs the value of a statistical count provides a **public key** by which each sensor homomorphically encrypts the entries of its Bloom filter. Note also that if a value p is encrypted, leading to $[p]_1$, and that same value is encrypted a next time, leading to $[p]_2$, the two encrypted values will be different: $[p]_1 \neq [p]_2$ and an observer will not be able to distinguish the two underlying values to be the same. Such an encrypted filter can be handed out to another sensor without disclosing any detections. This latter sensor can still compute an intersection $[A]$ using its own Bloom filter (which has been homomorphically encrypted with the same public key). Then, by simply shuffling the elements of that (encrypted) intersection, the result will be an encrypted Bloom filter $[A^*]$, in principle representing a *different* set of devices (which have nothing to do with the actual detected devices) yet of the same estimated size: $A \neq A^*, |A| = |A^*|$. This encrypted Bloom filter $[A^*]$ is handed out to the entity having the private key, who can then compute $|A^*|$. Obviously, no sensor would ever hand out its (encrypted) Bloom filter to the third party, as this would violate *FDP3*.

4.2 Evaluation

Our initial motivation for developing an anonymization technique based on k-anonymity was our assumption that using Bloom filters was simply too expensive in terms of computational and storage resources. At that time, we were considering that sensors would need to do handle all possible queries and also store results for those queries. We were wrong. For many practical situations, using a Raspberry Pi4 as the basis for a sensor, in combination with offloading the encrypted Bloom filters to a centralized server, is enough. In our experiments, assuming that a sensor needs to detect at most 10,000 *PIDs* during a single epoch (again, meaning to be able to detect at most 10,000 different devices during, say, 5 min), it takes just over 2 min for a sensor to process a complete pipeline of collecting data, constructing a Bloom filter, and subsequently encrypting the filter. The implementation is optimized in the sense that it makes optimal use of multiple cores. A serial implementation takes close to 8 min. When we can assume that at most 1000 devices need to be detected per epoch, these numbers drop to tens of seconds. Not surprisingly, the server, even lightweight versions, can easily handle the generated workloads. Our conclusion is that there are no serious problems when it comes to performance.

We have also tested our setup against real data, gathered during a multi-day outdoor festival. In this case, we evaluated how our method of privacy protection would lead to the same results as the ones coming from the dataset as collected by the sensors that were using the original pseudonyms. Because Bloom filters are probabilistic in nature, deviations are to be expected in comparison to processing raw data. Again, we see that we attain high accuracies in the 90–98% ranges for both footfall counting as well as measuring the size of crowd flows. Some of these results have been reported in [16].

4.3 Reflection

There are reasons to believe that the described Bloom-filter approach is the way to go for automatically measuring pedestrian dynamics. Yet, there are several challenges that need to be addressed before drawing final conclusions.

The setup described so far implicitly relies on the assumption that devices are detected by only one sensor at a time (this is why we can state that a flow moved from one location to another). In practice, avoiding simultaneous detections of the same device by multiple sensors may not be possible, or even desirable. For example, for purposes of reliability, we may wish to install multiple sensors at a single location and combine their detections as if they came from one, more powerful, sensor. In principle, this is possible by constructing the union of (encrypted) Bloom filters over the same epoch but from different sensors. Such a construction can be efficiently done by a server, as described above. To what extent unions affect the design of Bloom filters remains to be seen: there is a trade-off between the length m, the number of hash functions k, and the accurate representation of sets of a given size, although unions of Bloom filters are known to be lossless. More important is that constructing unions requires **additive homomorphic encryption**, implying that we may need a more advanced encryption scheme, or use two partial homomorphic schemes side-by-side. It is yet unclear what this would mean for the design and implementation of the monitoring system as a whole. Homomorphic encryption schemes are known to be generally computationally hungry [1].

A final remark is in place. We essentially looked at combining only two Bloom filters, and relied on the closed formula for estimating the size of the intersection [17], as well as an improvement for that formula [13]. However, Bloom filters are probabilistic data structures, meaning that when more than two filters are combined it is seen that the estimated size becomes increasingly less accurate. No closed formula is known for combining more than two Bloom filters. This implies that for practical implementations, we need to look much closer into the accuracy of the final result after having combined, in whatever way, several Bloom filters.

5   Other Challenges

Although protecting privacy has been a major issue in automated measuring pedestrian dynamics, there are many other issues that need to be taken into account. Let us consider a number of those that we encountered in the past years, of which some have also been reported in [4].

5.1   Behavior of Carry-On Devices and (non)overlapping Sensor Ranges

The whole idea of automated measurements assumes that carry-on devices send out packets at some minimal frequency. We have found that this may be a flawed assumption. In fact, the behavior of different devices, especially from different manufacturers, may vary widely, as also reported by others [10]. Together with the fact that wireless communication is inherently difficult, making many transmitted packets impossible to detect, even when in advertised range, means that automated measurements have an unexpectedly low number of detections. One possible solution is to increase the length of an epoch, as it simply increases the chance of capturing packets from a device that is within range of a sensor. On the other hand, long epochs can easily complicate deciding where a device actually is: just imagine that within a single epoch a device is detected at two locations (which may easily happen when a device moves from one location to another within that epoch). Effectively, increasing epochs means that devices may more easily be detected by multiple sensors during the same epoch. Yet, even if epochs are small enough, we still need to handle the case in which sensor ranges overlap. Determining a location of a detected device may turn out to be difficult, in turn, hindering the process of determining the size of crowd flows.

After running real-world experiments trying to distinguish bystanders looking at a marching crowd and the marching crowd itself, Groba [10] draws the conclusion that the behavior of carry-on devices may be so unpredictable that it may be close to impossible to answer this type of questions or to accurately measure pedestrian dynamics.

5.2 MAC-Address Randomization

The statistical counting techniques described above are independent of the actual technique for detecting a device. So far, we have gained considerable experience with WiFi-based detections, which have shown to be prone to many unreliable measurements, notably in outdoor environments [3,5]. Making things more difficult is the generalization of the use of MAC-address randomization. When devices are associated to an access point, such as, for example, when roaming within a public network or within international networks such as Eduroam, they will always use their uniquely assigned MAC address. In other cases, when a device is actively seeking for a network, we see that increasingly often MAC-address randomization is deployed. This randomization makes it much more difficult to identify devices. Attempts have been made to automatically fingerprint devices by considering other fields in the transmitted signals (see, e.g., [20], which follows a machine-learning approach). We are investigating to what extent the negative effects of MAC-address randomization can be mitigated to increase the accuracy of device identification, along with other techniques. Others are also developing techniques that may prove to be useful [18]. In addition, it remains unclear to what extent MAC randomization is effective [8,21], and to what extent it actually affects accurately counting pedestrian dynamics. For example, if the used random MAC address remains the same during an epoch, footfall counting may still be possible.

5.3 Stationary Versus Nonstationary Devices

As a final challenge, detections are hindered by the fact that many stationary WiFi-based devices mingle with nonstationary devices. When counting pedestrian (flows), the two need to be separated. For flows, this may be simple if we can assume that stationary devices at one location do not show up at another. For footfall counting, which takes place at a single location, ensuring that only nonstationary devices are counted is important.

A simple solution to this problem is to filter out pseudonyms that have been seen for a long time. Unfortunately, such an approach may easily violate *FDP2*, which boils down to keeping information on a detected device too long. Fortunately, we can use our Bloom-filter approach for distinguishing stationary devices. The basic idea is to still register detected pseudonyms in a Bloom filter, but now to count how often a specific entry is set, leading to a counting Bloom filter. Assuming that over time a stationary device is more often detected than a nonstationary one, we can set a watermark on all entries of the counting Bloom filter to separate what we see as entries belonging to stationary devices and those that do not. We then extract two new Bloom filters: one of which the counts per entry were less than the chosen threshold, and one with entries that counted equal or more than the threshold. Again, all operations can be done on homomorphically encrypted Bloom filters. Eventually, only the encrypted Bloom filter with detections from nonstationary devices is returned, after having shuffled its entries so that only counting can be done.

6   Conclusions

Automatically measuring the dynamics of pedestrians continues to be a difficult problem. It is somewhat surprising to see the optimism that various groups report on attained accuracies, but above all that so few groups have been paying attention to the protection of privacy. We have come to the conclusion that privacy can be successfully protected using a combination of Bloom filters for storing detected pseudonyms, together with homomorphic encryption techniques for combining filters under encryption. At the same time, more work needs to be done, notably when it comes to settings in which sensors have overlapping ranges, or when many Bloom filters need to be combined.

Regardless of our means to protect privacy, we need to be aware of the difficulty of gathering accurate detections. MAC-address randomization is one hindrance, but there are many more, as we have discussed. We speculate that once privacy protection is indeed considered to be safe, we may be able to open paths to smartphone apps that assist in measuring crowd dynamics, operating completely unobtrusively, in the background. This approach is very similar to the apps used for warning a user that he or she was in close range to a COVID-infected person, which used the privacy-protecting protocol Decentralized Privacy-Preserving Proximity Tracing (DP-3T) [19].

References

1. Acar, A., Aksu, H., Uluagac, A.S., Conti, M.: A survey on homomorphic encryption schemes: theory and implementation. ACM Comput. Surv. **51**(4), 1–35 (2018)
2. Bloom, B.H.: Space/time trade-offs in hash coding with allowable errors. Commun. ACM **13**(7), 422–426 (1970)
3. Chilipirea, C., Dobre, C., Baratchi, M., van Steen, M.: Identifying movements in noisy crowd analytics data. In: 19th International Conference Mobile Data Management (MDM 2018), pp. 161–166. IEEE Computer Society Press, Los Alamitos, CA, June 2018
4. Chilipirea, C., Petre, A., Dobre, C., van Steen, M.: Presumably simple: monitoring crowds using WiFi. In: 17th International Conference on Mobile Data Management, pp. 220–225. IEEE, IEEE Computer Society Press, Los Alamitos, CA, June 2016
5. Chilipirea, C., Baratchi, M., Dobre, C., van Steen, M.: Identifying stops and moves in WiFi tracking data. Sensors (Switserland) **18**(11) (2018)
6. Council of the European union: proposal for a regulation of the european parliament and of the council concerning the respect for private life and the protection of personal data in electronic communications and repealing directive 2002/58/EC (Regulation on Privacy and Electronic Communications). ST 5008 2021 (2021)

7. Draghici, A., van Steen, M.: A survey of techniques for automatically sensing the behavior of a crowd. ACM Comput. Surv. **51**(1), 1–40 (2018)
8. Fenske, E., Brown, D., Martin, J., Mayberry, T., Ryan, P., Rye, E.: Three years later: a study of MAC address randomization in mobile devices and when it succeeds. Proc. Priv. Enhancing Technol. **2021**(3), 164–181 (2021)
9. Ferguson, N., Schneier, B., Kohno, T.: Cryptography Engineering: Design Principles and Practical Applications. John Wiley, New York (2010)
10. Groba, C.: Demonstrations and people-counting based on Wifi probe requests. In: 2019 IEEE 5th World Forum on Internet of Things (WF-IoT), pp. 596–600 (2019)
11. Lai, Y., Kontokosta, C.: Quantifying place: analyzing the drivers of pedestrian activity in dense urban environments. Landscape Urban Plan. **180**, 166–178 (2018)
12. Martella, C., Li, J., Conrado, C., Vermeeren, A.: On current crowd management practices and the need for increased situation awareness, prediction, and intervention. Saf. Sci. **91**, 381–393 (2017)
13. Papapetrou, O., Siberski, W., Nejdl, W.: Cardinality estimation and dynamic length adaptation for bloom filters. Distrib. Parall. Databases **28**(2), 119–156 (2010)
14. Southworth, M.: Designing the walkable city. J. Urban Plan. Dev. **131**(4), 246–257 (2005)
15. Stanciu, V.D., van Steen, M., Dobre, C., Peter, A.: k-anonymous crowd flow analytics. In: MobiQuitous 2020–17th EAI International Conference on Mobile and Ubiquitous Systems: Computing, Networking and Services, pp. 376–385, December 2020
16. Stanciu, V.D., van Steen, M., Dobre, C., Peter, A.: Privacy-preserving crowd-monitoring using bloom filters and homomorphic encryption. In: Proceedings of the 4th International Workshop on Edge Systems, Analytics and Networking, pp. 37–42. ACM Press, New York, NY, April 2021
17. Swamidass, S.J., Baldi, P.: Mathematical correction for fingerprint similarity measures to improve chemical retrieval. J. Chem. Inf. Model. **47**(3), 952–964 (2007)
18. Torkamandi, P., Kärkkäinen, L., Ott, J.: An online method for estimating the wireless device count via privacy-preserving Wi-Fi fingerprinting. In: Hohlfeld, O., Lutu, A., Levin, D. (eds.) PAM 2021. LNCS, vol. 12671, pp. 406–423. Springer, Cham (2021). https://doi.org/10.1007/978-3-030-72582-2_24
19. Troncosa, C., et al.: Decentralized privacy-preserving proximity tracing. CoRR abs/2005.12273 (2020)
20. Uras, M., Cossu, R., Ferrara, E., Bagdasar, O., Liotta, A., Atzori, L.: Wi-Fi probes sniffing: an artificial intelligence based approach for MAC addresses derandomization. In: 25th International Workshop on Computer Aided Modeling and Design of Communication Links and Networks (CAMAD), pp. 1–6. IEEE (2020)
21. Vasilevski, I., Blazhevski, D., Pachovski, V., Stojmenovska, I.: Five years later: how effective is the MAC randomization in practice? The no-at-all attack. In: Gievska, S., Madjarov, G. (eds.) ICT Innovations 2019. CCIS, vol. 1110, pp. 52–64. Springer, Cham (2019). https://doi.org/10.1007/978-3-030-33110-8_5
22. Wang, M., Zhou, J., Long, Y., Chen, F.: Outside the ivory tower: visualizing university students' top transit-trip destinations and popular corridors. Reg. Stud. Reg. Sci. **3**(1), 202–206 (2016)
23. Wijermans, N., Conrado, C., van Steen, M., Li, J., Martella, C.: A landscape of crowd-management support: an integrative approach. Saf. Sci. **86**(7), 142–164 (2016)
24. Zhou, J., Wang, M., Long, Y.: Big data for intra-metropolitan human movement studies: a case study of bus commuters based on smart card data. Int. Rev. Spat. Plan. Sustain. Dev. **5**(3), 100–115 (2017)

Author Index

Printed in the United States
by Baker & Taylor Publisher Services